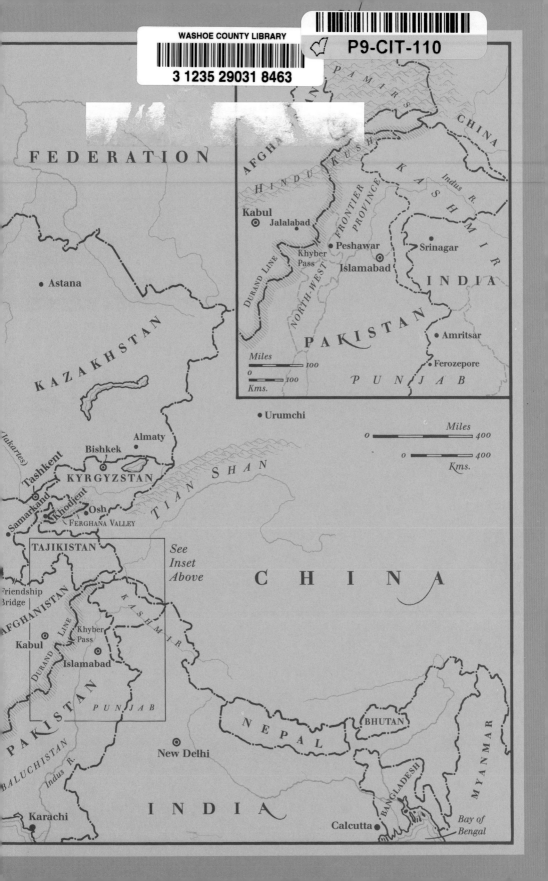

FEDERATION

• Astana

KAZAKHSTAN

(Jakartes)

• Urumchi

Bishkek
• Almaty

Tashkent

KYRGYZSTAN

TIAN SHAN

Samarkand

•Khodjent
• Osh

FERGHANA VALLEY

TAJIKISTAN

See
Inset
Above

Miles
0 ─────── 400

0 ─────── 400
Kms.

C H I N A

Friendship
Bridge

AFGHANISTAN

KASHMIR

Khyber
Pass

Kabul ◉

DURAND LINE

Islamabad ◉

P A K I S T A N

P U N J A B

N E P A L

BHUTAN

BALUCHISTAN

Indus R.

New Delhi ◉

MYANMAR

BANGLADESH

• Karachi

I N D I A

Calcutta •

Bay of
Bengal

Inset

PAMIRS

CHINA

AFGHAN

HINDU KUSH

FRONTIER PROVINCE

KASHMIR

Kabul
◉ Jalalabad

Indus R.

Khyber
Pass

• Peshawar

• Srinagar

DURAND LINE

NORTH-WEST

Islamabad

I N D I A

P A K I S T A N

• Amritsar

Miles

0 ─────── 100

0

100
Kms.

• Ferozepore

P U N J A B

THE DUST
of EMPIRE

THE DUST
of EMPIRE

THE RACE FOR MASTERY
IN
THE ASIAN HEARTLAND

KARL E. MEYER

A Century Foundation Book

PublicAffairs
NEW YORK

Portions of this book appeared in different form in World Policy Journal, published by the World Policy Institute at New School University, and in the Los Angeles Times Book Review.

BOOK DESIGN AND COMPOSITION BY JENNY DOSSIN. SET IN BEMBO MT.

Library of Congress Cataloging-in-Publication data
Meyer, Karl Ernest.
The dust of empire : the race for mastery in the Asian heartland / by Karl Meyer.— 1st ed.
p. cm.
Includes bibliographical references and index.
ISBN 1–58648–048–0
1. Asia, Central—Politics and government. 2. Asia, Central—Foreign relations—Great Britain. 3. Great Britain—Foreign relations—Asia, Central. 4. Asia, Central—Foreign relations—United States. 5. United States—Foreign relations—Asia, Central. 6. Asia, Central—Foreign relations.
I. Title.
DS329.4.M46 2003
958—dc21
2002037186

FIRST EDITION
10 9 8 7 6 5 4 3 2 1

For Shareen

CONTENTS

They are the dust of empire.

Whoever travels without a guide
Needs two hundred years for a two-day journey.

RUMI

They cannot scare me with their empty spaces
Between stars—on stars where no human race is.
I have it in me so much nearer home
To scare myself with my own desert places.

ROBERT FROST, "Desert Places"

FOREWORD

EXOTIC, ROMANTIC, strategic, complicated, dangerous; there is no shortage of vivid adjectives that describe the nations of Central Asia. But for most Americans, "obscure" has been the term that seemed most appropriate when talking about countries such as Kazakhstan, Uzbekistan, and many of their neighbors. For decades, the region, when discussed at all, was treated as a land of romance entangled in the fact and fiction of tales of the "great game for empire" played out during the nineteenth century between imperial Russia and imperial Britain. To be sure, the United States became involved in the region during the 1970s and 1980s, albeit on an officially covert basis, aiding the revolt in Afghanistan against a Soviet-supported puppet regime. (At the time, of course, few anticipated that America might be arming and financing some of the very forces that are today most hostile to it.) This engagement was one of a few exceptions to the reality that the broad swath of territory extending from Iran to China was mostly the subject of governmental and popular indifference—an attitude based on the seemingly reasonable assumption that what happened there had little to do with Americans or American interests.

More recently the United States, like other great powers before it, has discovered that, no matter how preponderant its military strength, it does not always have the ability to choose either its adversaries and entanglements or the place and timing of its conflicts. This paradox was brought home forcefully and terribly by the events of September 11, 2001, and their aftermath. The sources of potential threats now appear to extend well beyond what were once considered the major post–Cold War areas of concern, such as North Korea and Iraq. Intelligence officials have made clear that they believe terrorists intent on doing great harm to the United States are operating in dozens of countries, including many of those in

Central Asia, as well as here at home. Indeed, the first major foray for U.S. forces after September 11 was the military action in Afghanistan. Going forward, it is clear that containing and preempting multiple sources of potential danger, as well as retaliating after a terrorist act has taken place, will require exceptionally good judgment about where and when America should commit its forces and focus its energies. Thus it has become a national priority to learn more about potential adversaries and the locales that nurture or hide them.

Few research projects, therefore, could be as timely as this study by Karl Meyer, noted journalist and editor of the *World Policy Journal*, on the history and contemporary politics of Central Asia. Meyer is one of the rare authors who has so mastered his topic that he can write about it from commanding heights, fashioning a work that is at once analytical and journalistic. The lessons here, and there are many, are illuminated by vivid anecdotes drawn from the history of Western involvement in Central Asia. Meyer's recent book, *Tournament of Shadows: The Great Game and the Race for Empire in Central Asia*, cowritten with his wife, Shareen Blair Brysac, provided a foundation of research and travel for this more policy-oriented work.

Meyer succeeds in giving us a feel for the antecedents of the current governments and major influences in important countries in the region. He is at once a reliable reporter and a sure-footed guide to policy issues. He gives us the geography, the political economy, and the idiosyncratic histories of the "invented nations" and ancient tribal and religious groupings that constitute the keys to understanding the region. He effectively traces the tale of modern Western involvement in Central Asia, including the decades of Soviet domination of a large fraction of the area. There are high policy stakes here for the United States, and Meyer understands and emphasizes them, but he neither preaches nor lectures, instead conveying information in a way that makes a reader with virtually no background on the subject feel significantly informed and even entertained. He concludes the work with advice that is both realistic and hopeful, advice that should be heeded by those who will make decisions about these matters in the years to come.

This book is part of a broad Century Foundation program examining American foreign policy in the post–Cold War era. It complements works we have supported on specific areas such as Turkey, by Morton Abramowitz, and Russia, by a joint task force set up in collaboration with

the Stanley Foundation; on explorations of broad issues involved in foreign policymaking, by Henry Nau, Walter Russell Mead, and Robert Art;
and on American intelligence policy in a book exploring national security by Gregory Treverton and our major, ongoing examination of the issues involved in homeland security. Through these and many more
projects, we have been attempting to contribute to the debates raised by
the sweeping reorientation of American interests since the end of the Soviet regime.

In this context, the optimal conditions for decisionmaking at the
highest levels of American government involve a sharp increase in knowledge about many new issues related to terrorism, including more understanding of those parts of the world in which fundamentalist Muslims
hold sway. Today, when both policymakers and large segments of the public have a keen curiosity about organizations and nations that previously
were on the periphery of our interest and attention, it makes good sense
to reinforce any available expertise on both the new architecture of terrorism and the new realities of geopolitics. For example, it is time to go
beyond the current official focus on past intelligence failures and pay
more attention to (and increase resources for) conventional sources of information about the world, including the routine work by State Department officials and academics. This important work about Central Asia
should help stimulate that redirection of emphasis, even as it enriches a
reader's understanding of the region.

On behalf of the trustees of The Century Foundation, I commend
Karl Meyer for this remarkable study of a critical area of concern for
American foreign policy. He has been an exceptional author, one who is
both a pleasure to work with and, more important, to read.

Richard C. Leone, PRESIDENT
The Century Foundation

January 2003

PAX BRITANNICA, SQUARED

THREE IMPULSES animate the pages that follow, the author's hope to inform, to interpret, and to provoke. Each requires elaboration. My subject is an area of the world little known to most Americans: the great swath from the Caucasus to the borders of China that forms the Asian heartland. Bounded on the south by the Indus River in Pakistan and on the north by the Kazakh steppe, it is a region with comparatively few inhabitants but surprisingly many cultures, creeds and languages. It encompasses forbidding mountains, inland seas and monotonous deserts. And until September 11, 2001, most Americans had little reason to care about this strand of Asia and its contentious states, most of them once imperial bagatelle, formerly ruled by Russia, Britain, Persia or Ottoman Turkey.

Post–9/11, as the American and allied military presence swelled in the region, so did curiosity about its peoples and their past. This book is meant to feed and sharpen that appetite by providing basic information in a readable manner for an audience of educated nonexperts. I have not hesitated to inject my own judgments and generalizations to advance the discussion and provoke debate. For me, it has been a fascinating sojourn, building on the travel and researches that led to an earlier book written with my wife, Shareen Blair Brysac, *Tournament of Shadows: The Great Game and Race for Empire in Central Asia*. The chapters that follow bring the narrative forward to the issues confronting the United States and its allies today.

Clearly limned on the post–9/11 screen is a reality that many Americans are reluctant to face or acknowledge. Like it or not, Washington is the seat of an empire whose awesome economic power has given it an unparalleled global reach. True enough, America is not an empire in a formal sense; our official creed is republican and our schoolbooks celebrate our anticolonial origins—which to many non-Americans is additional evidence that those wielding this power are either knaves or fools or both. America's military expenditures exceed those of all other NATO members put together. The United States can afford this expense because its economy surged during the 1990s. Thus the Bush administration in 2002 could allocate $329 billion for defense, or about 3.2 percent of America's gross domestic product, whereas the Reagan administration's arms buildup in 1985 consumed twice that share of GDP. As a result, after September 11 Washington needed negligible help from its coalition partners to mount an effective air and ground assault on Afghanistan's terror-sheltering Taliban regime. Nobody has more shrewdly examined this mind-boggling imbalance than Yale University's Paul Kennedy, author of *The Rise and Fall of Great Powers*. "Everyone knew that, with the Soviet Union's forces in a state of decrepitude, the U.S. was in a class of its own," Kennedy observed in a widely read essay in the *Financial Times* in February 2002. "But it is simply staggering to learn that this single country—a democratic republic that claims to despise large government—now spends more each year on the military than the nine next largest national defence budgets combined. Only a few Americans realize that fact, and many have denounced former President Bill Clinton for allegedly underfunding the U.S. military. Had this really been the case—and there have been many comparisons to Baldwin and Chamberlain in the 1930's—then it is difficult to see how the U.S. armed forces could have produced such an impressive and overwhelming display of power in recent months. . . .To put this another way, a couple of years ago the U.S. was responsible for about 36 per cent of total world defence spending; its share now is probably closer to 40 per cent, if not more."

The resulting asymmetry is overwhelming when compared to the Taliban or other so-called rogue regimes, and equally impressive when compared to America's allies. But as this book shall argue, the asymmetry is also cultural and psychological in a hundred less obvious ways. More than a billion people around the world speak some form of English, and more than 400 million speak it as their mother tongue. It is the language of the Internet and Silicon Valley, of air travel and more than half the world's scientific periodicals; three-fourths of the world's mail is in English, and as the lingua franca it helps account for American primacy in global broadcasting and banking, in higher education and popular culture. Emerson's observation in the nineteenth century is more valid than ever in the twenty-first: "The English language is the sea which receives tributaries from every region under heaven."

Yet by instructive paradox, the universality of English was made possible by the empire against which Americans rebelled. Not only did the British assemble the largest overseas empire known to history, consisting of a fourth of the world's landmass and a fourth of its population, but they joined their far-flung possessions by trade and telegraphy. Areas that the British did not colonize or directly govern were controlled when necessary by artifice (e.g., Egypt) or surreptitious wire pulling (e.g., Persia). At its Victorian meridian, the makers of this empire saw themselves not only as top dogs but also as the best of all breeds. Although Victoria's remote subjects, especially if they were people of color, could not become facsimiles of a proper Britisher, they were welcome to copy Britain's benign institutions: Parliament, common law, free press and free trade. And no imperial bond was stronger than that of sports. Whatever else divides the empire's former subjects, they remain united to this day by their passion for soccer, cricket and rugby, as well as tennis, golf and boxing, all British innovations. Not surprisingly, the modern Olympics were born in the brain of Baron de Coubertin, a French Anglophile infatuated with *Tom Brown's School Days,* a romantic evocation of the playing fields at Rugby when Thomas Arnold was its headmaster. When the summer games were revived in Athens in 1896, among the few disapproving spectators was the French proto-fascist Charles Maurras, who was offended by the Americans chattering in their wretched "patois" and worried that the jargon of Anglo-Saxon games would do "too much to promote a language with which the planet was already infested."

Maurras was right to worry. Having first rebelled against Britain, the United States twice in the last century came to the old country's rescue; it did much to undermine the empire by promoting self-determination and then, step by step, took up Britannia's burdens in the Balkans, the Middle East, the Far East and not least along the legendary North-West Frontier as the strategic ally of Pakistan. The new and dependent relationship was already apparent in 1943 during the North African campaign, when the future Conservative prime minister Harold Macmillan murmured these remarks to the Laborite Richard Crossman, who fortunately recorded them: "We, my dear Crossman, are Greeks in this American Empire. You will find the Americans much as the Greeks found the Romans—great big, vulgar, bustling people, more vigorous than we are and also more idle, with more unspoiled virtues but also more corrupt. We must run Allied Force Headquarters as the Greek slaves ran the operations of the Emperor Claudius." (It should be noted that Macmillan's mother, like Winston Churchill's, was an American.)

In a real sense, America now sits where Britain did in the 1890s, only the old empire is squared. Even at her apogee, Britannia had nothing like America's economic and military preponderance, and her rulers were nervously aware of the Germans, Russians, French and the upstart Yanks all snapping at their heels. The thesis of this book is that the moral and diplomatic dilemmas confronting Washington today differ in degree but not in kind from those that confronted Britain before World War I. In truth, Americans are if anything more certain that their institutions are the envy and exemplar of less fortunate breeds, and that most of the world's people would gladly change places with them. Hence the special shock of September 11. Hence what may seem like digressions in the chapters that follow are in fact essential tiles in a mosaic. It is my belief, for example, that it is impossible to make sense of the struggle over Kashmir without some knowledge of how India's partition came about. This is particularly worth stressing for American readers, some of whom regrettably tend to dismiss anything that occurred even a year ago as ancient and irrelevant history.

Two final matters. On spelling, at risk of consistency, I have hewed to most familiar forms, for example, Bokhara, not Bukhara, Boghar or Bocara, except in quoted texts, where the author's spelling is respected. I have tried to avoid jargon terms like "hegemony" and "paradigm." Having coauthored a book on the Great Game, I now find the term so hackneyed and inaccurately overused that it does not appear in the pages that follow. My hope is that the book will not only kindle interest in the Asian heartland but also help restore to memory the unfairly neglected attainments of these friends of Asia and/or champions of human rights: Abdul Ghaffar Khan, W. Morgan Shuster, Mohammad Mossadeq, Edmund Morel and the elder George Kennan. Finally, nothing in this work could have emerged from my brain and computer without the essential and patient assistance of my wife, Shareen Blair Brysac, to whom this book is dedicated.

KARL E. MEYER

New York, January 2003

I
PATTERNS OF MASTERY, BRITISH AND AMERICAN

Winston Churchill as second lieutenant, Queen's Own Hussar's, en route to 1895 to survey the rebellion in Cuba, where he saw action on his 21st birthday. Two years later, he joined the Malakind Field Force, seeing grislier action on India's North-West Frontier.   *Photo courtesy Corbis.*

Forty-year-old Theodore Roosevelt left his desk job in Washington for Cuba to lead 490 Rough Riders up San Juan Hill in 1898, a victory that vaulted him into the Vice Presidency, then into the White House.

Photo courtesy Theodore Roosevelt Collection, Harvard University.

I S THERE AN American empire? Are Americans imperialists? When a superpower exercises global influence, what means are legitimate, effective and comparatively benign? And if a superpower gets the answers wrong, what are the penalties? These are scarcely new questions, but in the months following September 11, 2001, they were asked more generally and, in America, more anxiously. The focus of this book is the vast region of mountain and steppe that geopolitical analysts like Sir Halford Mackinder once grandly dubbed the Heartland or World Island, now an area of belated security concern to Washington. It is my belief that a fair understanding of this distant region, and its inhabitants' discontents, requires a prior examination of the broad questions.

My own response, briefly stated, is that while Americans may not see themselves as an imperial people, they are so perceived across the globe. For reasons just or unjust, rational or otherwise, there is widespread unease about American methods and motives, even among the educated foreign elites whose children attend American universities. These doubts derive in part from the profound imbalance, or asymmetry, between American power and that of every ally or potential adversary. In these circumstances, American influence is most effective when exercised jointly, when Washington's purposes are clearly articulated and consistently pursued, and when security arrangements do not compromise the claims of decency and transparency that are America's most valued assets. A go-it-alone arrogance, it seems to me, is the surest means of sparking conflicts that can threaten American predominance. An obvious parallel is the unraveling of Great Britain's supremacy, which began with the outbreak of the morally disabling Boer War at the end of the nineteenth century.

A consideration of imperialism, past and present, serves as the frame for what follows. Examined within is the theme of asymmetry, and its consequences. It is my hope that even readers familiar with the subject may discover new material in these pages. My claim to authority is not that of a specialist, but of a generalist who has spent much of his career as a writer mediating between experts and the public, seeking to convey (in

Walter Lippmann's phrase) a picture of reality on which citizens can act. This is not the picture viewers find on the television screen, the main source of foreign news for most Americans. For all its merits of speed and enterprise, television journalism almost always lacks context. What we normally receive is a hailstorm of filmed snippets and breathless commentary. Television's effect on viewers was graphically anticipated by John Henry Newman in *The Idea of the University* (1873): "They see visions of great cities and wild regions; they are in the marts of commerce, or amid the islands of the South; they gaze on Pompey's pillar or on the Andes, and nothing which meets them carries them forward or backward, to any idea beyond itself. Nothing has a drift or relation; nothing has a history or a promise. Everything stands by itself, and comes and goes in its turn, like the shifting scenes of a show, which leaves the spectator where he was."

L ET US BEGIN with maps. I have on my desk a globe, circa 1938, on which the world's overseas colonies and dominions are tinted in different colors: red for Britain's empire, green for France's and orange for other European holdings (Italian, Dutch, Belgian, Portuguese and Spanish). Most of Africa and South Asia is thus colored, although the cautious cartographers failed to indicate Japan's conquests of Korea, Manchuria and great swaths of China. Scrolling halfway around the northern latitudes, tinted pale pink, is the former Soviet Union with its fifteen national republics: a contiguous imperium stretching from the Baltic Sea to the Bering Strait. Yet as the twentieth century ended, so did these empires, becoming one with Nineveh and Tyre, their existence terminated by global war, rebellion, voluntary decolonization and the collapse of Communism. A statistic suggests the scale of change. At its founding in 1945, the United Nations had 51 charter members; as of 2002, the number had more than tripled, to 189.

On its face, this seems cause for celebration. No country has promoted the principle of self-determination more robustly than the United States, the first new nation to inscribe consent of the governed on its founding document. Woodrow Wilson's Fourteen Points and Franklin Roosevelt's Four Freedoms helped fan resistance among the world's colonial peoples. Indeed, taking the long view, Wilson was in a real sense a more successful revolutionary than Lenin. In 1918, he informed a joint session of Congress that "self-determination is not a mere phrase. It is an imperative principle of action. . . ." So it proved after the dissolution in 1991 of Lenin's Soviet empire, when, from the Baltic to the Adriatic, from the Balkans to Central Asia, nineteen new nations sprang into existence.

Yet from the outset, prescient Americans sensed the dangers implicit in Wilson's imperative. Secretary of State Robert Lansing feared the phrase was "simply loaded with dynamite." In his private diaries, Lansing worriedly wondered what unit Wilson had in mind. Did he mean a race, a territorial area or a community? For without a definite unit, the principle would be "dangerous to peace and stability." In his entry for December 30, 1918, Lansing elaborated: "It [the promise of self-determination] will raise hopes that can never be realized. It will, I fear, cost thousands of lives. In the end, it is bound to be discredited, to be called the dream of an idealist who failed to realize the danger until too late to check those who attempt to put the principle into force. What a calamity that the phrase was ever uttered! What misery it will cause! Think of the feelings of the author when he counts the dead who died because he coined a phrase! A man who is leader of public thought should beware of intemperate or undigested declarations."

It needs adding that Secretary Lansing (1864–1928) was not a reactionary or an isolationist, but a moderate Democrat and New York attorney who helped found the American Society of International Law and edited its *Journal* for twenty years. Moreover, in one of those instances of synchronicity that makes research a pleasure, Lansing's nephews happened to be Allen and John Foster Dulles. In their youth, the Dulles brothers joined "Uncle Bert" during the summer to fish for smallmouth bass on Lake Ontario, where they listened wide-eyed to tales told by yet another kinsman and fly fisherman, John Watson Foster, a Civil War veteran who was also a onetime secretary of state, a former U.S. envoy to Russia and author of *A Century of American Diplomacy: 1776–1876*. On that catboat, one may surmise, was nurtured the air of invincible entitlement that the Dulles brothers brought to their Cold War actions during the Eisenhower years.

Lansing's fears were cruelly realized in the post-Soviet 1990s by "ethnic cleansing" in former Yugoslavia; by unremitting brawls in the Caucasus between Russians and Chechens, between Armenians and Azeris, between Georgians and Abkhazians, between South Ossetians and Georgians; by the internecine toll in disputed Kashmir; by a dozen intertwined civil wars in sub-Saharan Africa; by the separatist risings in Indonesia, the

Philippines and Sri Lanka; by the never ending Arab-Israeli conflict; and by the convoluted disorders of Afghanistan. In fact, at the Paris Peace Conference, Wilson himself acknowledged the perplexities of self-determination. He was visited by a delegation of Irish Americans protesting British efforts to prevent Irish nationalists from making their case. One of the delegates, Francis Patrick Walsh, a prominent lawyer and wartime head of the U.S. Commission on Industrial Relations, later related to the Senate Committee on Foreign Relations what he said were the president's words:

> You have touched on the great metaphysical tragedy of today. . . . When I gave utterance to those words I said them without the knowledge that nationalities existed which are coming to us day after day. Of course Ireland's case, from the point of view of population, from the point of view of the struggle it has made, from the point of interest it has excited in the world, especially among our own people, whom I am anxious to serve, is the outstanding case of a small nationality. You do not know and cannot appreciate the anxieties that I have experienced as the result of these many millions of people having their hopes raised by what I said.

Wilson's second thoughts do him credit. Extending statehood to a hundred-odd entities has not brought the world appreciably closer to peace and prosperity. Even the smallest of the new states, enclaves or "autonomous republics" seems to harbor still smaller minorities whose rights may be threatened, as in Kosovo, East Timor, Moldova, Macedonia, Kuwait, the Baltic States and Fiji. In a wider perspective, we thus perceive an implicit paradox. In an era obsessed with globalization, the world's state system is fragmented as never before, with the concomitant reality that the United Nations and its affiliated agencies lack the resources, the mandate and most of all the will to address effectively the human and material catastrophes in what used to be called the Third World.

NONE OF THE ABOVE constitutes an argument in favor of imperialism. To allow frustration or nostalgia to incline us to the old-style imperial system is to disregard its racism, brutality and rapacity, as well as the self-delusion of its rulers. A compendium of Anglo-Saxon vainglory can be found in William L. Langer, *The Diplomacy of Imperialism, 1890–1902*. With unerring eye, Langer exhumed specimen British estimates of their right to rule as their empire reached its apogee. The empire, averred Lord Rosebery, Gladstone's successor in 1894 as Liberal prime minister, was "the noblest example yet known to mankind of free adaptable just government. . . . When a community is in distress or under oppression, it always looks first to Great Britain." By 1900, Rosebery was all but lost in adoration. As he rhapsodized in a speech at Glasgow, "How marvelous it all is! Built not by saints and angels, but the work of men's hands; cemented with men's honest blood and with a world of tears; welded by the best brains of centuries past; not without taint and reproach incidental in all human work, but constructed on the whole with pure and splendid purpose. Human and yet not wholly human—for the most heedless and the most cynical must see the finger of the Divine. . . . Do we not hail in this less the energy and fortune of a race than the supreme direction of the Almighty?"

And so agreed Lord Curzon, the celebrated viceroy to India, for whom (in 1894) the empire was "under Providence, the greatest instrument for good the world has seen." Ditto Joseph Chamberlain, the most robust of colonial secretaries: "We are a great governing race, predestined by our defects as well as our virtues, to spread over the habitable globe." To doubters who recalled the scores of bloody "little wars" during Queen Victoria's reign, the colonial secretary rejoined, in what became the hackneyed phrase others borrowed to condone every future horror, "You cannot make omelettes without breaking eggs."

It is hard to overstate the euphoria that gripped the British in late Victorian times. Even so resolute a skeptic as Bertrand Russell confessed to being a Liberal imperialist and enthusiastic free trader. Crowded on the same bandwagon were Manchester manufacturers and Fabian Socialists, high-minded preachers and jingo journalists, thoughtful Cambridge dons like J. R. Seeley, author of the best-selling *Expansion of England*, and maverick radicals like Sir Charles Dilke, author of an earlier best-seller, *Greater Britain*. Britain was to them the indispensable nation, standing taller and therefore able to see farther. To be born British, as Cecil Rhodes famously remarked, was to draw a winning ticket in life's lottery.

Yet the decade following Queen Victoria's triumphant diamond jubilee in 1897 shed a new and harsher light on imperialism. A first glimpse came in 1898 near Khartoum on the banks of the Nile. There Major General Horatio Herbert Kitchener arrived by rail and steamboat as commander in chief, or sirdar, of an Anglo-Egyptian force 26,000 strong, armed with eighty cannons and forty-four machine guns. Kitchener's mission was to settle an old account and reassert British dominion over the Sudan, which had become a base for Islamic extremism in a domain extending over a million square miles.

Fourteen years earlier, General Charles ("Chinese") Gordon had been slain at Khartoum by fanatic followers of Mohammed Ahmed, known as the Mahdi, the son of a carpenter rising seemingly from nowhere to challenge the Sudan's Egyptian and British overlords. The Mahdi preached a simple but potent doctrine: return to the basic tenets of Islam and reject everything that resembles the customs of "Turks" and infidels—"Turks" being synonymous with corrupt Egyptians. From the thousands who acclaimed him as the messiah, the Mahdi demanded fidelity to decrees forbidding drinking, smoking, music, dancing, feasts, buying brides, cursing, fine clothing and jewelry. Entranced by the purity of his example, moved by his denunciation of apostate Muslims and impressed by his eloquence and sparkling eyes, his followers multiplied. His legend grew when a powerful sheik presented the Mahdi with a noble bride and a mysterious Crusader sword inscribed in Arabic but bearing the double eagle of the Holy Roman Empire.

The Mahdists sought to achieve their master's goal through a universal jihad, or holy war, that would repel European armies and purify the entire Muslim world. With the death of Gordon, the Sudan was theirs. Six months later, the Mahdi too was dead, but the uprising continued under his designated heir, Abdullah ibn Mohammed, known as the Khalifa. Over and again, the Khalifa's dervish warriors repelled punitive raids, but Kitchener and his new weapons proved their undoing. With a former royal engineer's rigorous planning, Kitchener prepared for battle at Omdurman, the Mahdist capital opposite Khartoum, its river approaches defended by seventeen forts and some sixty guns. In the main engagement, pitting 50,000 defenders against half as many expeditionaries, the Khalifa blundered by ordering a frontal attack in daylight against infantry squares backed by howitzers and machine guns. The outcome was foreordained, its butchery made more terrible by flesh-shredding dum-dum bullets. A British war correspondent wrote: "Our men were perfect, but the Dervishes were superb—beyond perfection. It was the largest, best and bravest army that ever fought against us for Mahdism, and it died worthily of the huge empire Mahdism won and kept so long. Their riflemen, mangled by every kind of death and torment that man can devise, clung round the black and green flag, emptying their poor, rotten, home-made cartridges dauntlessly. Their spearmen charged death at every minute hopelessly. . . . It was not a battle but an execution."

When the smoke and stench abated, it appeared that Anglo-Egyptian fatalities totaled 28 Britons and 20 non-Britons, while 10,800 dervishes lay dead. In *The River War* (1899), Lieutenant Winston Churchill, who accompanied Kitchener's force as a cavalry officer and journalist, put the best face on the engagement in cadences that could have been scored by Elgar: "What enterprise that an enlightened community may attempt is more noble and more profitable than the reclamation from barbarism of a fertile region and large populations? To give peace to warring tribes, to administer justice where all was violence, to strike the chains off the slave, to draw the richness from the soil, to plant the earliest seeds of commerce and learning, to increase in whole peoples their capacities for pleasure and diminish their chances of pain—what more beautiful ideal or more valuable reward can inspire human effort? The act is virtuous, the exercise invigorating, and the result often extremely profitable."

P*ace* Churchill, not everybody was so entranced. Citizens of conscience, conservatives as well as liberals on both sides of the Atlantic, began to contemplate with concern, and then with horror, the fruits of what France called *la mission civilisatrice*. We tend to forget the manic energy and sheer bloody-mindedness that characterized the final spasm of the imperial age. From 1876 until 1915, roughly a fourth of the earth's territory was distributed or redistributed among fewer than a dozen states. Leading the imperial league was Great Britain, which grew by some 4 million square miles, followed by France (3.5 million), Germany (1 million plus), Belgium and Italy (nearly 1 million each) and the United States (100,000 square miles, taken mostly from Spain). Japan roughly matched American gains, with conquests in China, Korea and Russia. There were even crumbs for the sclerotic empires of Portugal (300,000 square miles) and Spain (the hard-to-calculate and still disputed rocky wastelands in Morocco and the Western Sahara). This tally does not take account of the continuous overland expansion of the tsar's empire, discounted for losses suffered during the 1905 Russo-Japanese War.

The rivalry was greatest, and the toll highest, in Africa. So intense was the European competition that Otto von Bismarck invited contenders to Berlin in 1884–1885 to sort out who should own Africa. The chief supplicants were the French, then gripped by expansionist fever, and King Leopold II of the Belgians, who sought the Iron Chancellor's approval for his personal, purportedly philanthropic acquisition of the Congo. With energetic lobbying by the explorer Henry Morton Stanley, Leopold got the support he needed in Berlin, while Bismarck soothed the French and won from Britain unexpected acquiescence for German colonization in Southwest and East Africa. This and other agreements marked the formal beginning of what the *Times* of London accurately dubbed the "scramble for Africa."

If the motives for the scramble remain in dispute, its means were not mysterious. The decisive factor was the fully automatic machine gun developed in 1884 by Britain's Hiram Maxim. In Uganda in 1892, two Maxims enabled the British to prevail over a French-backed monarch, and in southern Africa in 1896 Cecil Rhodes swept away Matabele warriors and created the new colony bearing his name. The message was replicated in Kenya in 1897, underscored a year later at Omdurman, reinforced in punitive expeditions against the Ashanti on the Gold Coast and the Fulani in Nigeria in 1902–1903. As a Fulani fighter vainly protested, "War now be no war. I savvy Maxim-gun kill Fulani five hundred yards, eight hundred yards far away. . . . It be no blackman fight, it be white man oneside war. It no good."

As massacre reports multiplied, so did protests at home. In a poem titled "The Traveller," the Anglo-Catholic poet Hilaire Belloc compressed its essence in a final couplet: "Whatever happens, we have got / The Maxim Gun, and they have not." Equally sardonic was Henry Labouchère, an anti-imperialist dissenter in Parliament who thus parodied "The White Man's Burden," Kipling's paean to imperialism:

Pile on the Brown Man's burden,
And if ye rouse his hate,
Meet his old-fashioned reasons
With Maxims—up to date,
With shells and Dum-Dum bullets

A hundred times make plain
The Brown Man's loss must never
Imply the White Man's gain.

Through the smoke of battle, meanwhile, critics also noted the rise of a new imperial breed: the proconsul, the high-handed quasi-monarch exercising plenary authority in the name of an often inattentive metropolitan government. Arguably the most regal was George Nathaniel Curzon, viceroy to India from 1898 until 1905. Prime Minister Arthur Balfour liked to complain that Curzon behaved as if India were an independent country, and not always a friendly one at that. Stretching a vague authorization to counter Russian designs on Tibet, Curzon in 1903–1904 sent a small army to Lhasa, its victories crucially assisted by two Maxims nicknamed "Bubble" and "Squeak." In Africa, Britain's formidable proconsuls were Frederick Lugard, creator of Nigeria, and Alfred Milner, the architect of the Union of South Africa. France's entries included General Hubert Lyautey, who from 1903 to 1914 completed the conquest of Morocco, leaving his idiosyncratic stamp on North Africa's last surviving independent state, and Jean-Baptiste Marchand, the bold leader of the provocative 1899 march to Fashoda, a dusty Nile settlement seven hundred miles south of Khartoum, in an attempt (thwarted by Kitchener) to make France master of the Nile's headwaters.

A latecomer to imperialism, the United States posted its proconsuls in the newly annexed Philippines, their mission being to extinguish an uprising among those Filipinos who ill-advisedly favored independence. In 1900, the portly William Howard Taft arrived in Manila to end the rebellion and nurture democracy among America's "little brown brothers." His taskmaster was General Arthur MacArthur, a Civil War hero and the father of Douglas MacArthur, who later reigned as the uncrowned monarch of occupied Japan. In two years, the senior MacArthur overwhelmed the insurgents at a cost of 4,234 American fatalities and some 20,000 rebel lives. Their epitaph was supplied by Mr. Dooley, the Chicago Irish saloonkeeper and brainchild of Finley Peter Dunne: "Poor dissolute uncovered wretches, ye miserable childish minded apes, we propose f'r to larn ye th' uses of liberty. We can't give ye anny votes . . . but we'll threat ye th' way a father shud threat his childhern if we have to break iv ry bone in ye'er bodies."

IT IS EVERY generation's vanity to assume that its afflictions—war, poverty, human rights abuses, pollution or whatever—are wholly novel, the unique torments of its own age. More often, what we confront are old trials in new guises, our misperception usually based on lack of knowledge, or curiosity, about the past. The Edwardian era, to cite one example, is commonly associated with liverish self-indulgence and up-stairs-downstairs deference. This is a half-truth; in Britain it was also a pe-riod of chronic labor strife, searing partisanship, feminist rebellion, constitutional crisis and armed mutiny (as elaborated seven decades ago by George Dangerfield in *The Strange Death of Liberal England*). Terrorism proliferated across the world. In the decades before the outbreak of World War I, six heads of state—in Russia, Spain, France, Austro-Hungary, Italy and the United States (McKinley)—were assassinated by anarchists, and on July 30, 1914, as France braced for war with Germany, a demented pa-triot, screaming "pacifist" and "traitor," fatally shot the Socialist leader Jean Jaurès as he sat with friends in a Paris café. Selecting symbolic buildings is not a new terror tactic. London's Greenwich Observatory was the target in 1894 of a failed bomb attack, an incident that inspired Joseph Conrad's *The Secret Agent* (1906). In America, the years before 1914 were a time of unusual violence, marked by industrial war at Homestead (1892) and Coeur d'Alene (1892), the Pullman strike (1894) and the Ludlow strike (1913–1914), the last being (in Richard Hofstadter's judgment) "one of the clearest examples of the use of armed forces by employers to oppose labor organizations"—not to speak of lynchings, race riots, assassinations, bomb attacks and vigilante killings.

Before the Great War the international system, then consisting of an elaborate minuet among emperors and kings, punctuated by spasms of democracy, was as prone to violence as it is today. Though six big em-pires—British, French, German, Austro-Hungarian, Russian and Ot-toman—strove to contain insurrections, they were like keepers of a dike racing back and forth as waters burst through one bung hole after another. In the 1900s, two events presaged the end of European empire: the Boer War and the exposure of slave labor in the Belgian Congo.

On October 11, 1899, Britain initiated a war in southern Africa that was supposed to end by Christmas but lasted nearly three years. Almost half a million imperial soldiers were required to subdue 88,000 whiskered farmers in what was Britain's costliest engagement since Waterloo. Britain found little support elsewhere for a conflict whose stated purpose was to preserve British "paramountcy" in southern Africa. Maxims, dum–dum bullets and barbed wire trenches failed to cow Boer sharpshooters. To punish their guerrilla resistance, Lord Kitchener—now a peer and once again the avenging commander—herded Boer families into the new century's first concentration camps, where more than 20,000 noncombatants perished ("methods of barbarism," protested Sir Henry Campbell-Bannerman, leader of the Liberal opposition). The war finally ended in a compromise that entrenched white rule in a new Union of South Africa, only to be followed by a Liberal outcry when a Conservative government approved the transport of half-starved Chinese workers to work Transvaal's gold mines—whose deposits were inarguably the major reason for Britain's attack on two Boer republics.

Nobody monitored these moral anomalies more closely than Mark Twain. In "To a Man Sitting in Darkness," which appeared in the *North American Review* for February 1901, he noted what quick learners Americans had become in the imperial game. Only the year before the United States had joined a multinational force to end a two-month siege of diplomatic missions in Peking. The besiegers were called Boxers, a mystical, profoundly anti-Western secret society whose followers rose fanatically against missionaries and their foreign patrons, who had carved up China like a carcass. After the rising was crushed, Twain noted, an official of the American Board of Foreign Missions complained that Washington did not exact enough blood money, adding: "*The soft hand of the Americans is not as good as the mailed fist of the Germans*" (Twain's italics). In the Philippines, the United States had expeditiously borrowed Kitchener's methods for humbling those who imprudently fought for their homes and freedom. Should we continue, he wondered, conferring civilization on distant strangers who sit in darkness? Or would it not be better "to get our Civilization-tools together and see how much stock is left on hand in the way of Glass Beads and Theology, and Maxim Guns and Hymn Books, and Trade-Gin and Torches of Progress and Enlightenment (patent adjustable ones, good to fire villages with, on occasion)."

He reserved his deadliest darts for the British colonial secretary, Joseph Chamberlain, "Imperial Joe," the begetter of the Boer War, "this strange and over-showy onslaught of an elephant upon a nest of field-mice, on the pretext that the mice had squeaked an insolence at him." In Twain's judgment, "Mr. Chamberlain manufactures a war out of materials so inadequate and so fanciful that they make the boxes grieve and the galleries laugh, and he tries hard to persuade himself that it isn't purely a private raid for cash, but has a sort of dim, vague respectability about it somewhere, if he could only find the spot; and that, by and by, he can scour the flag clean again after he has finished dragging it through the mud."

For imperialists, a fresh debacle followed in 1904 with the publication in London of *King Leopold's Rule in Africa,* by Edmund Morel. Until then, Leopold had been able to bribe or bar inquisitive journalists, and the impression prevailed that the monarch was somehow the benign white father of a colony eighty times bigger than Belgium itself. Whatever Leopold's original purposes, the misnamed Congo Free State had proved unexpectedly lucrative with the advent of the automobile and the resulting voracious demand for rubber, then found mostly in the wild forests of the Congo and the Amazon basin. As prices soared, Leopold's agents treated African gatherers of rubber as virtual slaves, severing hands and limbs to discipline the recalcitrant. This was the inspiration for Conrad's *Heart of Darkness,* a prototype for Mr. Kurtz being Captain Léon Rom of the Force Publique, with his collection of twenty-one African heads. Shockingly, through murder, starvation, exhaustion and exposure, through disease and declining birth rates, the Congo's population shrank from some 20 million in the 1880s to little more than 10 million in the 1920s, a decimation so appalling that Belgians to this day tend to ignore or dispute what can justly be termed ethnocide.

A small host of troublemakers helped expose this atrocity, among them the African American missionary William H. Shepherd and the British consul and Irish patriot Sir Roger Casement (later hanged by the British for his aid to the Easter Rising during World War I). But Edmund Morel, the son of a French father and British mother, was the gifted agitator who became Leopold's nemesis. As a young clerk at a Liverpool shipping firm, Morel had been sent to Antwerp to supervise imports from the Free State. He noticed something odd in the manifests: goods and gold flowed from Africa, with virtually nothing shipped in return. In 1901, having confirmed that forced labor accounted for the imbalance, Morel quit his job. He raised money to publish the *West African Mail,* an illustrated weekly dealing with "the Congo Question," and founded the Congo Reform Association. He captured European attention with a stream of books, articles, speeches, affidavits and graphic photographs. He sailed in 1904 to the United States, where he was received by Theodore Roosevelt (Morel reminded the president that America had been the first nation to recognize the Free State), and met with Booker T. Washington, who took a delegation of black Baptists to the White House in hopes of bringing pressure on Leopold. Morel sought out Mark Twain, who was so affected that he contributed a memorable broadside, *King Leopold's Soliloquy*, which Morel published in 1907. Isolated and rattled, his system censured even by the commission of inquiry he had appointed in hopes of exoneration, the King of the Belgians died unmourned in 1909.

By then, imperialism's British devotees were less euphoric. A bad African war, the Chinese labor scandal, revulsion over Leopold's penal colony, and ongoing little wars contributed to the landslide electoral defeat of Arthur Balfour's Conservatives by the less imperial Liberals in 1905. A bellwether of change was Winston Churchill, who a year before the election had switched from the Tories to the Liberals. After the vote he was given his first important post—undersecretary for the colonies. He immediately faced the moral quandaries of imperial police work. A fresh uprising had broken out, this time in Sokoto, the capital of the Fulani federation in northern Nigeria, where a self-styled Mahdi named Mallam fomented a revolt in which two British Residents, a white officer and seventy mounted infantry had been butchered with hoes, axes and spears. Frederick Lugard, the high commissioner in northern Nigeria and veteran of a half dozen similar campaigns, proposed striking back with Maxims. However, Churchill balked at the "extermination of an almost unarmed rabble," grumbling to colleagues that Lugard imagined himself a tsar with Nigeria as his "sultry Russia." Lugard resigned and was dispatched from vast Nigeria into virtual exile as governor of the tiny crown colony of Hong Kong. Churchill added this minute to the order barring a punitive expedition: "The chronic bloodshed which stains the West African seasons is odious and disquieting. Moreover the whole enterprise is liable to be misrepresented by persons unacquainted with imperial terminology as the murdering of natives and stealing of their lands."

However, if serving as imperial policeman was misrepresented by the ill-informed as "murdering . . . natives," how then was order to be kept or restored? If imperialism was morally reprehensible, what might be put in its place? To these urgent questions, new and interesting responses were already in the air, their relevance the more obvious with the outbreak of the Great War in 1914.

NOTHING DID MORE to undermine imperialism than "the war to end all wars," as H.G. Wells was the first to miscall it. The conflict's human and moral toll was devastating. In its first four months, 300,000 Frenchmen perished and 600,000 were maimed, almost a tenth of the republic's males of military age—and this was but the beginning of a war that persisted until November 1918, claiming some 10 million lives. As to other costs, imagine a country that as a result of the war effectively lost 22 percent of its national territory, incurred debts equivalent to 136 percent of gross national product (a fifth of it owed to foreign bankers), suffered inflation and unemployment rates not seen for a century and experienced an equally unparalleled wave of labor unrest. "This was not Germany—as the reader may forgivably have assumed—but Britain, the supposed victor," craftily writes Oxford University's reigning iconoclast, Niall Ferguson, in *The Pity of War.* Britain's lost territory (he reminds us) comprised twenty-six counties in Ireland, where the wartime Easter Rising brought about civil war and then partition, the prelude to the Troubles that afflict Ireland still.

That the war broke out was no surprise, but the inability of the belligerents to end the hemorrhage was. No egregious ideological differences separated the contenders, whose diplomats knew each other well, most of them speaking a common language (French) while serving kings and queens related by blood and marriage. The late king Edward VII was the uncle of Germany's Kaiser Wilhelm II; his niece Alexandra was the tsarina of Russia, his nephew Nicholas, the tsar. His daughter was queen of Norway, another niece was queen of Spain, his wife's family occupied the Danish throne, still another niece, Marie, was to be queen of Romania, and through his multitude of relatives and in-laws, the avuncular Bertie, and of course his son and successor George V, was linked to virtually all of Europe's courts.

Once the killing began, the crowned heads of Europe found themselves, so to speak, in the same basket. Family ties did not breed comity. The bloodbath mocked Europe's claims of civilized superiority to backward non-Christians elsewhere. The war's casualties included four empires—German, Russian, Austro-Hungarian and Ottoman—and its conduct prepared the way for Communism, Fascism and Nazism. World War I, justly remarks John Keegan in his history of the conflict, left "a legacy of political rancour and racial hatred so intense that no explanation of the causes of the Second World War can stand without reference to those roots. The Second World War, five times more destructive of human life and incalculably more costly in material terms, was the direct outcome of the First."

The First World War and its ambiguous peace bewildered and disheartened even the heartiest imperialists. Lord Curzon, named British foreign secretary in 1919, all but faded away before his death four years later, his high hopes (writes his early biographer Harold Nicolson) "gradually clouded by disillusion, mortification and defeat." The British literary sensation of 1918 was Lytton Strachey's *Eminent Victorians*, a demolition of past pillars of church, empire and public school, signaling the rise of Bloomsbury and the eclipse of Kipling and company. This was followed in two years by *The Economic Consequences of the Peace* by John Maynard Keynes, an assault on the Versailles Treaty with this penultimate sentence: "Never in the lifetime of men now living has the universal element in the soul of man burnt so dimly." Though David Lloyd George survived as prime minister (with Winston Churchill his postwar colonial secretary), he and his cabinet lurched from one imperial crisis to another—Black and Tan killings in Dublin, the massacre of unarmed Indians at Amritsar, the ethnic butchery of Greeks by Turks (and vice versa) in Smyrna, the machine-gunning of nationalist rioters in Cairo, the British armies mired in the Caucasus, the unprovoked RAF bombings of Kabul and the strafing of Kurdish villages in recently invented Iraq. The new mood was crystallized in a 1922 parliamentary contest in the depressed Scottish city of Dundee. There Churchill, standing as a National Liberal, faced as his Labor opponent Edmund Morel, King Leopold's old nemesis. Morel continued to make trouble during wartime by exposing the covert connivance among the imperial powers that had helped to bring on the Great War. Defying censors, he managed to publish *Ten Years of Secret Diplomacy*, for which he was assailed as a German agent and sentenced in 1917 to six months hard labor. After Versailles, his views became commonplace. At Dundee, Morel easily outpolled Churchill and was reelected in 1924. Churchill meantime made his peace with the Conservatives and was returned to Parliament in the same general election from a safe seat in suburban Epping.

Through all these upheavals, it occurred to some of imperialism's defenders that the empire really lacked clothes. Who needed colonies anyway? Merely by asking the question, an otherwise conventional British journalist produced a worldwide best-seller five years before the war, *The*

Great Illusion: The Relation of Military Power to National Advantage (1909). Norman Angell, then Paris correspondent of London's mainstream *Daily Mail*, argued that the global naval race then under way conferred no economic benefits, that armed conquest was a delusion and colonialism a losing game. If the sun began to set on the British empire, would it make any difference to the average Briton? None whatsoever, he contended, because Britain did not "own" her colonies and because the expense of defending them outweighed the benefits. A world without colonies, he continued, would be locked together by the same calculations that gave richer creditor nations a stake in the health and stability of poorer debtors. Annexation did indeed open backward areas to trade, but it also opened them to penetration by rival powers. It was a complete fallacy to believe that the victor in a modern war could make the vanquished pay its costs, he held, because of the modern world's intermeshed monetary systems. Angell accurately predicted that a general European war would yield no winners but only losers; being proved right earned him a knighthood, and in 1934 Sir Norman was awarded the Nobel Peace Prize.

CRITICS POINTED OUT, also accurately, that Angell understated grievously the irrational element in political behavior and that his pacific global system assumed universal acceptance of binding monetary rules. Still, *The Great Illusion* touched a nerve. Was it really necessary to tint the globe to benefit from empire? Why not leave a backward realm's political structure intact and govern indirectly through the traditional shah, emir, khedive, sultan, nawab, maharajah or wali?

The British had extensive experience doing just that in India. Building on a practice pioneered by their Mogul predecessors, the makers of British India evolved what became known as the subsidiary alliance system. Native rulers could keep their thrones so long as they contributed taxes and soldiers to the Raj and discreetly heeded the British Residents posted to their courts. So successful was the system that by 1947, India's year of independence, there remained no fewer than six hundred princely states, composing half the territory and a fourth of India's population. But the system had its defects, as foreseen by a British observer in the 1850s: "The native Prince, being guaranteed in the possession of his dominions but deprived of so many of the attributes of sovereignty, sinks in his own esteem, and loses that stimulus to good government which is supplied by the fear of rebellion and deposition. He becomes a *roi fainéant*, a sensualist, an extortionist miser or a careless and lax ruler. . . . Thus despite the Resident's counsels and attempts to secure good government, the back of the state, so to speak, is broken; the spirit of indigenous political life has departed: the native community tends to dissolution; and annexation is the eventual inevitable remedy."

Defects notwithstanding, the system spread through the empire. Its principal proponent in Africa was Frederick Lugard, the proconsul for Nigeria, who expressly drew on the Raj methodology in establishing indirect rule of the Yoruba, Ibo and Hausa kingdoms. Traditional rulers reigned, but actual authority was wielded backstage by Residents and political officers. During his years as governor-general (1914–1919), Lugard effectively created the Federation of Nigeria, which has held together despite wars and tyranny and remains the largest, most populous African state.

Yet it was in the Middle East that indirect rule found its most significant application and its most percussive results. Its shape was foreshadowed in Egypt, which a contributor to the great eleventh edition of the *Encyclopaedia Britannica* (1910) described with a solemn, straight face as "a tributary state of the Turkish empire, [which] is ruled by an hereditary prince with the style of khedive." Hardly so. From the opening in 1869 of the Suez Canal, mastery of Egypt became a matter of vital concern to Britain. When a nationalist rebellion in 1882 threatened the Egyptian khedive, Britain intervened to save his government and protect the canal, "the imperial lifeline." The troops stayed on, despite repeated assurances that the occupation was "temporary," and remained until 1952. From the outset, Egypt served as a laboratory for indirect rule. A monarch reigned, but Egypt's real ruler was Sir Evelyn Baring, later Lord Cromer, who bore the modest title of British consul from 1883 until his retirement in 1907. Cromer was a member of the Baring banking family (hence his malicious nickname, Overbaring) and came of age in India as personal secretary to the viceroy, Lord Northbrook (who happened to be his cousin). As Jan Morris writes of Cromer in *Pax Britannica* (1968), "His mandate of power was indeterminate. His use of it was masterly. He was in practice the absolute ruler of Egypt, in whose presence nationalist aspirations withered—giving office to any leading nationalist, Cromer thought, would be 'only a little less absurd than the nomination of some savage Red Indian chief to be Governor-General of Canada.'" Doubtless Cromer rescued Egypt from insolvency, and he was credited with promoting significant public works, notably the original Aswan dam, completed in 1900. But for the Egyptians, the cost was the perpetuation of a humiliating sham.

The British went to elaborate lengths to sustain the myth that they were simply Egypt's temporary guests. When Kitchener reconquered the Sudan in 1898, Baring devised the appropriate new term for its changed status: it became the "Anglo-Egyptian Sudan," a condominium, ostensibly meaning a jointly ruled territory. When the redoubtable Kitchener assumed Cromer's role in 1914, the title remained modest and misleading: he was simply the British agent. He filled this post until July, when he was summoned to London to serve as war minister; his mustache and index finger were then immortalized in recruiting posters exhorting, "Your Country Needs You!"

In the weeks after the outbreak of war, the British cabinet under Prime Minister H. H. Asquith favored the annexation of Egypt, thereby ending the fiction that it was still part of the Ottoman empire. In Cairo, however, Kitchener's aides objected, insisting that annexation would violate forty years of British policy, and urged that Egypt be given protectorate status, with a token promise of eventual genuine statehood. The cabinet backtracked, and the lawyer-scholar David Fromkin describes what happened next in his book, *A Peace to End All Peace: Creating the Modern Middle East, 1914–1922:* "The Cabinet, in this instance, allowed Kitchener's Agency to establish the prototype of the form of rule that the field marshal and his staff eventually wanted Britain to exercise throughout the Arabic-speaking world. It was not to be direct rule. . . . In Kitchener's Egypt, a hereditary prince and native Cabinet ministers and governors went through the motions of governing. They promulgated under their own name decisions recommended to them by the British advisers attached to their respective offices; that was the form of protectorate government favored by the Kitchener group. In the artful words of Ronald Storrs [Kitchener's staff specialist in eastern affairs]: 'We deprecated the Imperative, preferring the Subjunctive, even the wistful Operative mode.'"

It thus transpired by war's end that Britain, colluding secretly with France and throwing a crumb here and there to the United States and Italy, dismembered the Ottoman empire and won approval at Versailles for a patchwork of new Arab states, each with flags, thrones and high commissioners, to be protected or administered by, or mandated to, the Allied victors—with the added complication that Britain won assent for its promise to establish a national homeland for the Jews in its mandated territory of Palestine. Oil was an essential element in delineating frontiers. The oil-bearing province of Mosul was added to Basra and Baghdad so that the future state of Iraq would have the necessary revenues to support Faisal I, the Hashemite monarch whom the British had enthroned. As Lloyd George delicately explained to the House of Commons in March 1920, "It is not proposed that we should govern this country as if it were an essential part of the British empire, making its laws. That is not our point of view. Our point of view is that they should govern themselves and that we should be responsible as the mandatory for advising, for counselling, for assisting, but that the government must be Arab. That is the condition of the League of Nations, and we mean to respect it." Observing all of this, Archibald Wavell, later Field Marshal Earl Wavell, who had fought in the Palestine campaign, was moved to remark (giving Fromkin his title), "After 'the war to end war' they seem to have been pretty successful in Paris at making a 'Peace to end Peace.'"

Turn the calendar forward, and the parallels to the current situation in Central Asia and the Caucasus become obvious, with similar pitfalls facing the United States.

A RE AMERICANS imperialists? Do they dominate an empire? Although most Americans would heatedly disallow the term "imperialist," to all the world, Washington is the seat of an empire, if of a special kind. "We are a people," writes Ronald Steel in *Pax Americana* (1967), "on whom the mantle of empire fits uneasily, who are not particularly adept at running colonies. Yet, by any conventional standards for judging such things, we are indeed an imperial power, possessed of an empire on which the sun truly never sets, an empire that embraces the entire western hemisphere, the world's two great oceans, and virtually all of the Eurasian land mass that is not in Communist hands. We are the strongest and most politically active in the world. Our impact reaches everywhere and affects everything it touches. We have the means to destroy whole societies and rebuild them, to impede social change or to stimulate it, to protect our friends and devastate those who oppose us. We have a capacity for action, and a restless, driving compulsion to exercise it, such as the world has never seen."

Thirty-plus years on, no detail in that paragraph needs changing. In the judgment of the historian Arthur M. Schlesinger Jr., Americans are rulers of an "informal empire" that is "richly equipped with imperial paraphernalia: troops, ships, planes, bases, proconsuls, local collaborators, all spread wide around the luckless planet." The problem is that Americans tend to resent these simple truths being uttered and show small talent for empathetic reflection on how others, less favored, may view us. This has been noticeably true of Washington's relations with its neighbors in the Western Hemisphere—which in its political, economic and cultural aspects has provided a kind of dress rehearsal for America's superpower diplomacy.

Save for the acquisition of great chunks of Mexico, the island of Puerto Rico, a base in Cuba and a slice of Panama, the United States has not engaged in territorial aggrandizement at the expense of Latin America. Indeed, Washington honored its word to Panama by withdrawing on December 31, 1999, from the Canal Zone. Yet tellingly, neither the president, vice president nor any member of the U.S. cabinet took part in ceremonies on the isthmus, an occasion deemed a "loser" by the White House. It fell to former President Jimmy Carter to represent the United States. The disrespect implicit in this gesture was the more galling because it wasn't intended; it was merely reflexive. The abiding U.S. attitude toward its Latin neighbors, it is fair to say, is not so much imperial as imperious.

Nobody more bluntly expressed this attitude at its crudest than Grover Cleveland's secretary of state, Richard Olney. The occasion was a boundary dispute in 1895 between Venezuela and British Guiana, with the former insisting that Britain had illicitly expanded its colony's frontier. President Cleveland called for arbitration and amid popular applause invoked the hallowed Monroe Doctrine to check British designs. Secretary Olney followed with this ultimatum: "Today the United States is practically sovereign on this continent, and its fiat is law upon the subjects to which it confines its interposition. Why? . . . It is because in addition to all other grounds, its infinite resources combined with its isolated position render it master of the situation and practically invulnerable as against any or all other powers." In the end, Lord Salisbury, the British prime minister, prudently submitted the dispute to arbitration and agreed in 1899 to divide the contested land with Venezuela.

None of Olney's successors at State have spoken so crudely, but American deeds have conveyed the same message. Over the succeeding decades, whenever Washington has felt its vital interests threatened in the hemisphere, it has resorted unilaterally to invasion and/or outright occupation (Mexico, Haiti, Dominican Republic, Honduras, Nicaragua, Grenada, Panama), to supporting covert or proxy wars (Cuba, El Salvador, Nicaragua, Panama), to promoting coups against elected leaders (Guatemala, Chile), to a naval blockade (Cuba), to mining harbors (Nicaragua) and, at least once, to assassination (Rafael Trujillo, the Dominican dictator). Before the advent in 1934 of President Roosevelt's Good Neighbor policy, U.S. Marines were routinely dispatched to compel repayment of debts or, as President Wilson once said, to teach Latin Americans to elect better men. The old paternal attitude inspired a campaign boast uttered by the young FDR while running for the vice presidency in 1920. Speaking in Butte, Montana, he recalled his feats as Wilson's assistant secretary of the navy: "You know, I have had something to do with running a couple of little republics. The facts are that I wrote Haiti's Constitution myself and, if I do say it, I think it's a pretty good Constitution."

Most of the time, to be sure, Washington did not have to draft constitutions to make its views felt. Even in dealings with its biggest neighbors—Canada, Mexico, Brazil, Argentina, Venezuela—the United States is favored by a lopsided imbalance of power. This is apparent in the advantages enjoyed by the U.S. ambassador in any Western Hemisphere capital: he or she stands heads taller than every other envoy and almost always has direct access to the country's chief of state. By contrast, the region's diplomats in Washington usually fade into the crowd and rarely enter the Oval Office. This disparity persists even for Mexico, despite a much-touted free trade agreement, despite shared border and immigration problems, despite Mexico's oil bonanza and America's concern with narcotics, and despite the recent election of a pro-business, pro-American, English-speaking president, Vicente Fox. As Alan Riding observes in *Distant Neighbors: A Portrait of Mexico*, "The asymmetry of power determines how Mexico and the United States view each other. Differences of history, religion, race and language serve to complicate their relationship. . . . But all these variables are overshadowed by the inescapable and unique fact that a vulnerable developing country shares a 2,000 mile border with the world's richest and strongest power. . . . Intentionally or not, Mexico has been the target of American disdain and neglect, and above all, a victim of the pervasive inequality of the relationship."

Nowhere in the hemisphere has this inequality fused so closely with the classic modes of indirect rule as in Cuba, with implications that bear directly on America's future relations with Central Asia and the Caucasus.

I T IS A LONG-STANDING characteristic of American diplomacy to have it both ways: to pride ourselves on our republican virtue, our devotion to human rights, our belief in self-determination and our anti-colonial heritage—while enjoying the prerogatives of our asymmetrical power, pressing others to open their markets while selectively closing our own, entering into secretive security arrangements that mortgage the sovereignty of our partners and, when deemed necessary, using our leverage, overtly and covertly, to alter another country's policies or even its leadership. This is the essence of the informal empire that Schlesinger described, and the pretense that it does not exist constitutes the kind of humbug that exasperates, and occasionally infuriates, even our friends.

That it is also self-injuring humbug seems to me one of the lessons of America's painful relations with Cuba. From the early days of the republic, Americans looked with covetous eyes at Cuba, "the pearl of the Antilles," just ninety miles from Florida. Yet the decrepit Spanish empire continued to hug its few remaining possessions, including Cuba as well as the Philippines and Puerto Rico. In 1895, Cuban nationalists, armed by a junta in New York and inspired by the exiled poet and journalist José Martí, struck hard in eastern Cuba (where Martí was among the first casualties). Americans applauded the insurrection and excoriated the Spanish commander, General Valeriano Weyler, whose tactics earned him the epithet "Butcher." All this and the crushing of the rising were graphically depicted by American journalists and visiting Britons (including the twenty-one-year-old Winston Churchill). Hence the sensation when the battleship *Maine* blew up in Havana harbor on February 15, 1898, killing 266 U.S. seamen. To American expansionists and their journalistic claque, it was a clear case of state-sponsored terrorism, crying out for vengeance (though recent evidence supports the belief that the explosion was accidental). An initially hesitant President William McKinley soon leaned to war. Then on February 25 Navy Secretary John Long took the afternoon off. His chief deputy, Theodore Roosevelt, acting on his own authority,

[handwritten margin note: OFTEN VICE VERSA]

[handwritten margin note: HE'S VERY GOOD AT "HUMBUG"]

brashly ordered the Pacific Squadron, moored in Hong Kong, to prepare
for battle in the Philippines. So it happened that when hostilities began,
the conflict spread to Manila Bay, where Admiral George Dewey's superior guns sank the entire Spanish squadron, ten vessels in all, on May 1,
1898.

Dewey's victory signified the arrival of the United States as a global
power. After the "splendid little war"—Secretary of State John Hay's
phrase—Americans had confirmed their martial prowess in both Asia and
the Caribbean. The war proved the making of TR. He took time from his
office job in Washington to lead his Rough Riders up San Juan Hill in
Santiago, Cuba, generating the glory that led to his election as governor
of New York and then as vice president in 1900. (Chicago's Mr. Dooley
said that Roosevelt's account of his feats deserved to be titled "Alone in
Cuba.") Yet victory over Spain posed a quandary for the McKinley administration. After prayerful reflection, the president decided that the
United States should annex the Philippines and help Christianize its
inhabitants (most of whom were already Christian). Puerto Rico too became a U.S. possession, and by act of Congress in 1914 its Spanish-speak-
ing inhabitants, willy-nilly, were granted U.S. citizenship.

Yet what of Cuba? The island, with its lucrative sugar plantations and
its strategic offshore location, seemed too big a prize to yield up altogether, even though its people had been promised independence. Washington equivocated by establishing military rule in 1898 under an energetic
proconsul, Dr. Leonard Wood, an army surgeon who had fought with the
Rough Riders. Wood's great achievement was the elimination of yellow
fever, but the island's final status was still uncertain when he presided over
the election of an assembly in 1900 to draft a constitution. While the document was being debated, an ultimatum came from Washington: Cuba
had to agree to a special constitutional amendment concocted mostly by
Secretary of War Elihu Root and sponsored by Senator Orville Platt of
Connecticut. The Platt Amendment limited Cuba's powers to make
treaties with other foreign powers and included the humiliating provision
that "Cuba consents that the United States may exercise the right to in-
tervene for the preservation of Cuban independence, the maintenance of
a government adequate for the protection of life, property, and individual
liberty." As Root was at pains to explain, this did not mean what it seemed
to mean. He wrote to Wood, "I hope you have been able to disabuse the
minds of members of the convention that the intervention described in

the Platt Amendment is synonymous with intermeddling or interference with the affairs of the Cuban government. It of course means only the formal actions of the government of the U.S.A. based upon just grounds of actual failure or imminent danger and is in fact but a declaration of acknowledgment of the right to do what the U.S.A. did in April 1898 as the result of the failure of Spain to govern Cuba."

For thirty-two years, until 1934, the Platt Amendment was in effect. For Cuba, writes Hubert Herring in his history of Latin America, this imposed "a split personality on the presidents of the newborn republic, who were under bond to serve two masters, the Cuban electorate and the government in Washington. In the futile effort to propitiate both masters, they could please neither." Although Franklin Roosevelt finally abrogated the Platt Amendment as part of his Good Neighbor policy, its legacy persisted. It was a byword in Havana that the U.S. ambassador was the second most powerful person in Cuba—a line used by John F. Kennedy to taunt his Republican rival, Richard Nixon, in the 1960 presidential campaign, a year after Fidel Castro took power. Cuba and its sugar industry, its hotels, casinos and brothels became a favored haven for U.S. investment. "It is a striking paradox," concluded the authors of a Foreign Policy Association report in 1934, "that as a consequence of its struggle for political independence, Cuba lost control over its economic resources." Smaller farmers were absorbed into a latifundia system, so that 70 percent of all acreage in the 1940s was concentrated into 8 percent of total holdings. Of 174 sugar mills, only 55 were Cuban owned, and it was reckoned in 1946 that half of the billion-dollar sugar industry was under American control and more than a fourth of cultivated land American owned.

Yet Cuba was richer than other Latin countries and boasted better schools and a growing middle class. What made the system unendurable even to its beneficiaries was the rise of Fulgencio Batista's despotic military dictatorship with the perceived complicity of the United States. The historian Hugh Thomas thus commented on Batista's rigged election, "For all interested in political decency Batista's *golpe* in 1952 was intolerable, an event comparable in the life of an individual to a nervous breakdown after years of chronic illness. . . . It seemed the final insult that *Time* magazine, the dream machine for the north, should in April for the first time feature Cuba on its cover with a specially effulgent representation of the head of Batista, the Cuban flag behind him spread like a halo, accompanied by the bright comment: 'Cuba's Batista: he got past Democracy's sentries.'"

In the end, the most hurtful wound inflicted by indirect rule is psy-chic. Direct foreign control tends to unite a subject people, their resistance forging a sense of nationhood, while indirect rule delegitimizes indige-nous leaders and creates a despised class of collaborators. Experience ar-gues that the more overwhelming the American penetration—economic, political, military and cultural—in a weaker, ostensibly sovereign country, the greater the likelihood of repressive rule and a radical backlash. Cuba is an obvious instance, as was South Vietnam during the 1960s and 1970s, and Iran during the heyday of the shah, from 1953 to 1979. Conversely, where the American presence is minimal—in Eastern Europe during the Cold War or in today's Iran—ordinary people are more liable to view America with sympathetic curiosity or outright admiration. In foreign re-lations, so history suggests, overbearing dominion breeds neither affection nor respect.

The relevance of the preceding discussion will become clear as we consider the future of the five former Soviet republics in Central Asia and the three in the Caucasus, all of them once out of bounds to Western pen-etration and most of them new allies of America in its war against terror-ism. Given their location, and in some cases their possession of oil and natural gas reserves, the temptation will be powerful to forge links with incumbent regimes, to mesh their security services with America's, to bind them by trade agreements to U.S. markets, to post an eager cadre of soldiers and diplomats in their capitals. In my belief, it is a temptation to be resisted.

II

RUSSIA

The Long Talons of Memory

Russian cavalry is here portrayed by the keen-eyed Baron Sigmund von Heberstein, prescient envoy of the Holy Roman Empire, who wrote of Muscovy's Grand Prince in 1519, "He speaks, and it is done. He is unacquainted with contradictions."

From Rerum Moscoviticarum Ceomentarii. *Courtesy New York Public Library.*

A S A GENERALITY, Americans think of the world in terms of sea-
ports and airports, whereas Central Asians and their neighbors
look inwardly to a vast realm tied together by caravan routes,
rails, mountain passes, rivers and nowadays by oil pipelines. Americans
commonly dwell in a perpetual present, while inhabitants of the Asian
heartland and their imperial former masters inhabit a gallery where whis-
pering voices never cease recalling past triumphs or prior humiliations.
From the beginning of America's war in Afghanistan, "military asymmetry" became a fashionable cliché to characterize a conflict pitting a high-
tech superpower against bearded holy warriors and cave-dwelling
terrorists. But examined more closely, all other aspects of the conflict—
psychological, cultural, geographic and economic—appear asymmetrical
as well. One cannot think sensibly about Washington's interests and policies in the Asian heartland without first appraising the gulf, or more precisely the chasm, that looms between the United States and the peoples of
the entire region, together with their difficult neighbors, Russia and Iran.

Geography and psychology come first. That they are closely linked
was recognized long ago by Sir Halford Mackinder (1861–1947), the Oxford geographer and influential begetter of geopolitics. Our mental maps,
he maintained, derive from preconceptions rooted in our upbringing, as
illustrated by the different ways seafarers and landsmen view the world's
physical features. Americans of an older generation, especially easterners,
tended to the mariner's view when they looked abroad, picturing seas,
coastlines and ports with far more clarity than a continent's interior parts.
A commitment to freedom of the seas, and to maintaining a big navy to
ensure that right, long ago became bedrock American policy, reinforced
by Captain Alfred Thayer Mahan's *The Influence of Sea Power upon History*,
the influential book that was read by everybody in Washington who mattered after its publication in 1890. With the advent of air power, pioneered
by the Wright brothers at Kitty Hawk in 1903, succeeding generations
projected the maritime attitude skyward. The word "airport," with its nau-
tical associations, made its debut in print in Atlanta in 1921, according to

the compilers of the Oxford English Dictionary. Extending the analogy, the terms *captain, crew, steward, flight deck, hatch, cabin,* and so forth, were used to designate the personnel and layout of the new aircraft (not *airships,* a term reserved for lighter-than-air craft).

How different is the mental map prevalent among Eurasian nomads and their settled neighbors in Russia and on the Iranian plateau. The horse and the camel were to them what the caravels were to Europeans in the age of exploration and conquest. It was here, on the steppe, that horses were first domesticated, and here that cavalry first provided the sinews of power for enormous overland empires. Rapid movement over immense distances on horseback became feasible over the level grasslands forming an unbroken highway from Manchuria to Ukraine, a span of thirty-five hundred miles. So it was that Europe and China repeatedly suffered invasions by horse-borne raiders from the steppe, beginning in the first millennium B.C. with the marauding Scythians, of whom Herodotus wrote, "Their country is the back of a horse." From this equine culture, the world acquired first the saddle and then the stirrup.

"Even more interesting," writes the American scholar-explorer William Montgomery McGovern in *The Early Empires of Central Asia,* "is the effect Central Asia has had upon clothing, especially the masculine costume. By reason of their domestication of the horse, and their adoption of horseback riding, the early inhabitants of Central Asia were forced to discard their skirt-like costume which had been well-nigh universal among early peoples, and to develop that ingenious piece of clothing we call trousers." And later came boots, harness plates, sword-belt buckles, superb gold jewelry and the wealth of tomb treasures that are among the prizes of art museums in St. Petersburg, Moscow and Kiev. Little of this is commonly known or remembered in the United States.

We forget as well, save in the dimmest outlines, the military and political prowess of these nomads. A notable example is Jenghiz Khan (c. 1155–1227), the Mongol conqueror who in the West remains a byword for barbarous ferocity. Edward Gibbon thought otherwise, remarking of him: "The Catholic inquisitors of Europe, who defended nonsense by cruelty, might have been confounded by the example of a barbarian, who anticipated the lessons of philosophy and established by his laws a system of pure theism and perfect toleration." Contemporary chronicles noted the Great Khan's pragmatic respect for other religions (like most Mongols, he was a Shamanist), though the hard price for tolerance was submission. Concerning ferocity, scholars differ about the credibility of the appalling numbers his Golden Horde was said to have slaughtered to punish resistance or perfidy, since the figures are implausibly high and the toll was reported by non-Mongols. (Like his own people, the Great Khan was illiterate.) A fair-minded modern judgment is struck by the British historian David Morgan, that the Mongol invasions were a "truly awful, frequently final experience" for those in their immediate path but that the impact was patchy, with some areas escaping lightly or completely. All accounts agree that a superb communications network enabled Jenghiz to govern a huge sprawling empire that extended from Korea to Poland, the largest contiguous realm known to history. His express couriers, riding in relays, galloped upwards of two hundred miles a day. In his broad-gauged *Empire of the Steppes*, France's René Grousset writes of the Great Khan: "By unifying all the Turko-Mongol nations into a single empire, by imposing an iron discipline from China to the Caspian, Jenghiz Khan suppressed the endless intertribal wars and afforded the caravans a security they had never known. . . . In this respect Jenghiz Khan was a sort of barbarian Alexander, a pathfinder who opened up new roads to civilization."

If a pragmatic toleration held together the empire of the first Great Khan, its expansion reflected his strategic genius. Jenghiz's mounted archers could accurately fell targets seven hundred feet distant, using powerful composite bows. His cavalry moved in disciplined unison, lofting flares and flagged arrows to signal lightning swerves and massed assaults, employing repeatedly the feigned retreat to lure gullible adversaries. He was a master of deception: his spare horses carried dummy warriors, and he played like a virtuoso on divisions in the enemy camp. The mounts themselves were a hardy marvel, distinguished by their pale golden coats, narrow chests, long necks and sturdy legs, capable of moving a hundred miles a day on meager forage. These were "the good Turcoman horses" that Marco Polo praised, the "heavenly horses" coveted by the Chinese, the descendants of which, the long-necked Akhal-Teke, are still bred in Turkmenistan. (Nikita Khrushchev once presented a pair to Queen Elizabeth II.)

Yet the steeds were but the instruments of a supple intelligence whose caliber was appraised by the American scholar-explorer Owen Lattimore: "As a military genius, able to take over new techniques, Chinggis stands above Alexander the Great, Hannibal, Caesar, Attila and Napoleon." Lattimore wrote as a friendly interpreter of Mongolia, but no such bias can be ascribed to Captain B. H. Liddell Hart, deemed the foremost British military thinker between the two world wars. Liddell Hart put the Mongols and their chief at the top: "In scale and in quality, in surprise and in mobility, in the strategic and in tactical indirect approach, their campaigns rival or surpass any in history." In *Great Captains Unveiled*, Liddell Hart examined in detail the Great Khan's mobile strategies, and the author later noted with pride that his work became the textbook in 1927 for Britain's first mechanized force. (Liddell Hart's theories were also applied, regrettably to more purpose, by the Wehrmacht General Heinz Guderian.)

No less fascinated by the empires of the steppe was Halford Mackinder, the doyen of geopolitics. Writing in the wake of the Great War, drawing on his own experiences as British commissioner for South Russia in 1919–1920, Mackinder identified the Eurasian heartland as the key to global dominion. This was a region, he stressed, to which sea power could be refused access. Its northern approaches were protected by a vast white shield and its southern edges hemmed by formidable mountain ranges. Within the heartland, there was no impediment to cavalry moving from steppe to forest. In winter, ice-covered rivers doubled as highways for invaders. Given modern technology, he feared, the heartland's potential was still more ominous. No scraps of paper, "even though they be the written constitution of the League of Nations," offered any guarantee against a hostile power (e.g., Germany or Russia) dominating the impregnable heartland. Armies now had at their disposal not only railways but also motor cars and aircraft: "In short, a great military power in possession of the Heartland and of Arabia could take easy possession of the crossways of the world at Suez." That disaster, so he warned in 1919, was averted during World War I but only just, and the realities of geography remained, offering more tempting opportunities to land power as against sea power. As he summed it up (his italics):

> *Who rules East Europe commands the Heartland:*
> *Who rules the Heartland commands the World Island:*
> *Who rules the World Island commands the World.*

So it seemed from the outside. But looking more closely at Russia, the most powerful of the heartland's neighbors, one can see the same landscape from a different perspective.

A N ABIDING asymmetry in historical memory has long haunted Russia's relations with the United States. Before 9/11, Americans assumed almost as a birthright their relative immunity from overseas attack. No hostile power had invaded the continental United States since the War of 1812, when British redcoats sacked Washington. Pearl Harbor was a profound shock, but Hawaii was offshore. After World War II, an atomic America was able to check even the threat of hostile nuclear deployment, as confirmed by the Soviet Union's withdrawal of its stealthily installed missile bases from Cuba in 1962. Few great powers have been so favored for so long. This helps account for the disbelieving alarm following the terror attacks on New York and Washington—and for the renewed allure of a foolproof missile shield that could extend invincibility to the very heavens.

Russia's experience is the obverse. No vast oceans protect it from likely enemies. The main physical features of its homeland are forest and steppe, so that Russia, in Sir Bernard Pares's phrase, is "the land of vast horizons, distant dreams, active life, and constant danger." As Pares elaborates in his *History of Russia*, "With few natural barriers, the great hosts from the East moved wholesale, bag and baggage, men, women and children, horses and cattle, and even habitations. Every such invading people was a vast army, torn from its bearings, holding land by no title but war, and bound to fight to the finish." And not just from the east. A short list of the peoples who have invaded or otherwise intervened in the territories of what became greater Russia would include

Cimmerians	Magyars	French
Scythians	Vikings	Japanese
Saurmatians	Alans	Germans
Sarmatians	Mongols	British
Lithuanians	Teutonic Knights	Austrians
Goths	Swedes	Finns
Khazars	Poles	Americans
Huns	Ottoman Turks	

(America's intervention occurred in 1918, when Woodrow Wilson ordered an expeditionary army to Siberia, purportedly to extricate a trapped Czech legion.)

Expansion has been Russia's equivalent of a missile shield. Until its demise in 1917, the tsarist empire grew at the formidable rate of fifty-five square miles per day over three centuries. The empire crumbled after the Bolshevik Revolution, only to be stapled together again in 1920–1921 as the Red Army retook Georgia, Armenia and Azerbaijan in the Caucasus, Crimea and the Ukraine, Belorussia, and Central Asia. Stalin partitioned Poland in collusion with Hitler in 1939 and reannexed the Baltic States the following year. The Soviet Union also acquired as booty slices of Finland in the 1940 Winter War. In 1945–1946, with the knout of occupying forces, Stalin further shielded the Soviet homeland by implanting eight satellite states in Eastern Europe, including one in East Germany, along with a socialist state in North Korea. He retook the Kuril Islands and South Sakhalin, which the tsar had lost in the 1905 Russo-Japanese War. As Vietnam, Cambodia, Laos and Cuba became part of the world's "socialist sixth," Moscow pressed outward to arm and aid leftist regimes in Syria, Egypt, Yemen, Libya, Algeria, Ethiopia, Angola, Mozambique, Nicaragua and, more fatefully, Afghanistan. Thus did Moscow acquire the "strategic depth" so coveted by apostles of expansion.

All this provides one measure of Russia's historic fears and the colossal energy of the response. A visitor to post-Communist Russia everywhere senses the long talons of memory. A few hours northeast of Moscow lies Yaroslavl, an industrial city of 650,000 inhabitants. Here it is a few minutes' walk from the eleventh-century walls that were attacked by Mongols, Norsemen and the Poles, past a statue of Lenin, histrionically gesturing in front of the city hall, to a promontory where one can see the bridge across the Volga that withstood a Nazi assault in 1941–1942. A prevalent Russian outlook is crystallized in a saying of Tsar Alexander III, inscribed on the wall of the General Staff Academy in Moscow: "Russia has only two friends in the world, her army and her navy." Even among the young this martial past seemingly retains its allure. In 2000, when Russia elected Vladimir Putin as president, students at a Moscow school were asked if they favored the restoration of the Russian empire; more than half said yes.

This imperial heritage, this wary look beyond frontiers, this concern, even fixation, with former foreign foes permeates Moscow. A great boulevard leads southwest of Moscow some sixty miles to Borodino, site of the 1812 battle remembered for its fearful losses (42,000 out of 121,000 for the Russians; 32,000 out of 130,000 for Napoleon's Grand Armée and its subject allies). Formally victorious, Bonaparte's exhausted troops then occupied Moscow, whose outskirts soon rose in flames, apparently deliberately set by Cossacks. The result was the burning of Moscow, which John Keegan calls "the single greatest material catastrophe of the Napoleonic wars, an event of European significance akin in its psychological effect to that of the Lisbon earthquake of 1755." The Cossack irregulars who butchered French stragglers were not the romantic horsemen of Tolstoy's fiction but cruel visitations of the steppe, "pitiless, pony-riding nomads whose horsetail standards," to quote Keegan again, "cast the shadow of death wherever their hordes galloped, visitations that lay buried in the darkest recesses of their collective memory." Still, as a Russian might justly ask, Who invaded whom?

Returning from Borodino, a visitor encounters Moscow's enormous new military museum in Victory Park honoring the Soviet dead (27 million by Russian count) in World War II. Elaborate dioramas recreate the major engagements of the Great Patriotic War, their scale taxing imagination—the battle of Kursk (August 1943) involved 4 million people, 69,000 guns, 12,000 warplanes and 13,000 tanks. Above, in the Hall of Memory and Sorrow, the numbed visitor encounters the names and decorations of Soviet heroes and heroines, by the tens of thousands.

At Moscow's Tretyakov Gallery, entire rooms are devoted to immense canvasses summoning the memory of gallantry past. Most striking are the works of Vasily Vereshchagin (1842–1904), a master of battle panoramas whose work is scarcely known outside Russia. He meticulously recreated past martial epics *(Napoleon on Borodino Heights),* portrayed firsthand Russian conquests in Turkestan *(At the Fortress Walls: "Let Them Enter")* and reminded those at home of the necessary toll *(The Apotheosis of War,* showing a pyramid of skulls). Through his canvasses, Russians first glimpsed the determined features and sartorial finery of their new Asian subjects. His successor in celebrating the natural and human marvels of the East was the explorer and mystic Nicholas Roerich, who from boyhood was drawn to Central Asia, its people and natural wonders. He is today a Russian cult figure, his life commemorated at a lavish Roerich Cultural Center behind Moscow's Pushkin Museum.

Music, opera and ballet all elaborated imperial themes. When Borodin's *Prince Igor* premiered in Paris, the audience gaped at Roerich's sets, with their golden skies encompassing Tatar tents, and at the costumes he designed, based on his researches into Kyrgyz and Yakut sources. During the famous saber dance, a critic reported, the entire audience "was

ready to stand up and actually rush to arms." The repertory of Serge Di-
aghilev's Ballets Russes thereafter offered a procession of Cossacks and
Golden Hordes, slaves and emirs, Samarkand princesses and love-besotted
shahs. The tradition continued into Soviet times. The highlight of the
Leningrad season in 1934 was *The Fountain of Bakhchisarei*, a ballet based
on a Pushkin poem about the Tatar abduction of a Polish princess. On-
stage, West meets East in the harem, where the Pole's charms incur the
jealous wrath of the khan's favorite. At its 1999 American debut, New
Yorkers were similarly entranced by this Orientalist farrago, performed by
the same company, with its inevitable undulating white-clad girls and
frenzied sword dancers.

Nagging apprehension of spatial vulnerability, fixation on security
and fear of the Other: countless observers have elaborated the theme. Yet
it is more than a cliché. Chekhov, a writer incapable of banality, compressed it in this passage: "In Russia, an artist's energy should be directed
at showing two forces: man and nature. On the one hand, physical weakness, nervousness, early sexual maturity, a passionate desire for life and
truth, a dreaming of a range of activity as wide as the steppe, analysis full
of anxiety, a lack of knowledge together with high conceptual flights, and
on the other hand—a boundless plain, a severe climate; a severe, gray nation with its heavy, grim history, its Tatar period, officialdom, ignorance,
poverty, the humid climate of the capitals, Slavic apathy, etc. Russian life
so threshes the Russian that he cannot collect himself; it threshes him like
a thousand-pood stick." (A pood is a Russian measure of weight, equal to
about 36 pounds.)

Russian cities, with their customary ring of walls around a central
keep, or kremlin, attest to these preoccupations. So does the Russian language, which generously offers six variations of the verb "to go," depend-
ing on frequency, means of transport and final destination. There are
different prepositions for going to an enclosed space with defined limits
(a theater or library) or an undefined space (a street). The casting and
chiming of church bells is another Russian specialty, a reminder that bel-
fries not only summon the devout but also warn of attack. It is an anxiety
that transcends historical epochs. Consider, for example, Sergei Eisenstein's published notes for *Alexander Nevsky*, his 1938 film revisiting a long
past Russian victory over the Teutonic Knights:

Bones. Skulls. Scorched fields. Charred ruins of human dwellings.

People enslaved and driven far from home. Plundered towns. Human dignity trampled underfoot. Such is the awesome picture rising before us as we think of the early thirteenth century Russia. Having laid waste flourishing Georgia with her ancient culture in the Caucasus, the Mongol-Tatar hordes of Genghis Khan skirted the Caspian from the south bringing with them horror, death and bewilderment. . . . [yet the Russian people] though enslaved by the barbarous Eastern nomads, rallied round the glorious Alexander Nevsky to rout the Teutons when the latter stretched their tentacles to grab a slice of Russian soil.

Eisenstein's obvious subtext was that a Russia beset everywhere by enemies chose to settle accounts first with the nearest and most menacing, the Germans. The climactic scene is an axe-to-axe battle on an ice-covered lake, with helmeted Teutonic Knights plunging into freezing waters in a chaotic panorama out of Hieronymus Bosch, with a frenetic score by Prokofiev. But there is also an undertone of irony and fatalism, together with defiance and anger, in Eisenstein's notes—*Alexander Nevsky* was filmed during Stalin's Great Purge, when Russian dignity was being trampled anew (and by a Georgian). Decoding what artists and writers said during Bolshevik times was and is a cottage industry. Typical of the ambiguity, the double-edged wordplay, is Alexander Blok's celebrated meditation on Russia and Asia. Blok (1880–1921) was the most gifted lyricist of his generation, and innumerable Russian students have pondered his enigmatic poem "The Scythians" (1919), with its opening stanzas:

You are but millions—we are an infinite number.
Measure yourself against us, try.
We are the Scythians, we are the Asians you call us
With slanted and greedy eyes.

Centuries of your days are but an hour to us,
yet like obedient guards
we've held a shield between two hostile races:
Europe and the Mongol hordes.

Hundreds of years go by, still you look eastward,
collecting, melting our pearls,

and laughing at us as you wait for the ripe moment
to blast our walls.

But time has come to term and the evil hour
beats its wings. Each day multiplies
offenses; soon of your lovely Paestum
there will be no trace.

(Translated by Olga Andreyev Carlisle and Rose Styron)

IN REALITY, the Scythians were not slant-eyed Asians but a warrior
people of Iranian-speaking, nomadic pastoralists whose realm extended from the Don to the Danube, and from Kiev to the north, southward to the Black Sea. Though nominally ancient history, their story is
unexpectedly topical. It reminds us that belief in a "clash of civilizations"
—the notion of sharp and invidious cleavages existing between cultures—
is as old as civilization itself. To the Greeks and Persians, the Scythians were
savages, people of no fixed address, devoted to war and mayhem, infidels
given to unspeakable rites. Yet from a wider perspective, the Scythians
loom like forebears to the Mongols and Tatars, and to the Afghans and
Chechens, and to every other people whose misfortune it is to be known
mainly at second hand, through the prism of alien prejudice.

As early as the eighth century B.C., Greeks had established outposts on
the Black Sea, the starter seeds for city-states, most of them colonized by
settlers from Hellenic Asia Minor. Over time, as on similar frontiers elsewhere, Greeks and Scythians traded and intermingled, Scythian pastoralists turned to farming, Greek colonies grew into thriving ports, and wheat
sown in the rich black Crimean soil found a lucrative market in the
Aegean. Reciprocally, the Scythians prized, acquired and emulated Attic
painted ware, while their warrior kings commissioned the superb golden
ornaments found in their hill-sized tombs, or kurgans, strewn on the
Ukrainian steppe.

To the intellectuals of Athens, Greek superiority vis-à-vis the Scythians and other rootless nomads was self-evident. Even the normally even-
handed Thucydides remarks that when the Scythians were united, no
people in Europe or in Asia could bear comparison with them, "though
of course they are not on a level with other peoples in general intelligence

and the arts of civilized life." That barbarians were irrational and capable of heinous crimes was illustrated in classical drama by the tragedy of Medea, the vengeful witch from Colchis (in present-day Georgia) who slays her own children.

Yet the Scythians proved scarcely irrational in opposing a Persian expedition in 512 B.C. led by Darius the Great. As the huge imperial army kept advancing, the Scythians kept retreating. They torched their own grazing fields, causing the exasperated Darius to send this message to his royal adversary: "Why do you keep running away?" To which, as Herodotus relates, the Scythian king responded: "You do not understand me, my lord of Persia, I have never run from any man in fear; nor do I do so now from you. There is, for me, nothing unusual in what I have been doing; it is precisely the sort of life I always lead, even in times of peace. If you want to know why I will not fight, I will tell you: in our country there are no towns and no cultivated land; fear of losing a town or seeing crops destroyed might indeed provoke us to hasty battle—but we possess neither. If, however, you are determined upon bloodshed without the least possible delay, one thing there is for which we will fight—the tombs of our forefathers. Find those tombs, and try to wreck them, and you will soon know whether or not we are willing to stand up to you. Till then—unless the fancy takes us—we shall continue to avoid a battle . . . and your claim to be my master is easily answered—be damned to you!" Bereft of food, harassed by archers on an ever lengthening supply route, Darius cut his losses and retreated, a defeat so humiliating that it went wholly unmentioned in the annals of his reign; its details would be unknown save for Herodotus's account.

The story highlights three themes that recur in the pages that follow, the first being the dangerous tendency among the technically more advanced to underestimate the military imagination and desperate daring of the supposedly less advanced. Napoleon made the point when, having barely prevailed at Borodino and having encamped in Moscow, he glimpsed the approaching conflagration from a Kremlin window. "What an appalling sight!" he was heard to exclaim. "They are doing this themselves! So many palaces! What extraordinary determination! What men! They are the Scythians! [*Ce sont les Scythes!*]"

Second, as implied in Greek accounts and verified by excavations, there were in reality no discrete fault lines between settled and nomadic peoples, who intermingled on the borderlands. Though cultural differ-

ences were indeed real, sweeping claims of superiority put forward to justify the victors in any imperial competition need to be regarded with
skepticism. A relevant authority is Arnold Toynbee, an historian steeped in
Hellenism who nevertheless singled out the nomadic empires of the
Scythians, Mongols and Turks for their "astonishingly robust and vivid
cultures."

Third, the very discipline needed to sustain a nomadic life proved in
the end a disabling limitation. Toynbee suggests that in overcoming the
formidable handicaps of nomadic life, and in undertaking the challenge of
governing scattered subject populations, the Mongols and Turks relied on
"intractable and inflexible institutions which precluded any further social
development." And so it proved when an emergent Russian empire vanquished the heirs of Jenghiz Khan and pushed outward into Siberia, Central Asia and the Caucasus.

THE RISE OF Russia is a phenomenon that could not have been predicted and stubbornly resists explanation. At the far margins of
Europe, in an unpromising physical setting, without real roots in earlier
Western empires, exposed always to invasion, an otherwise obscure forest
people managed to survive, multiply and then dominate a hundred other
warrior peoples inhabiting a sixth of the world's landmass, peoples rang-
ing from kindred Poles and Ukrainians in Europe to the little-known
Adzherians in the Caucasus and the Karakalapaks in Uzbekistan. What
was originally a conglomerate of obscure Slavic principalities originating
in the ninth century came under Mongol dominion from 1238 to 1462.
In shaking off Mongol rule, the princes of Muscovy ultimately emerged
as the tsars of all Russia, their title deriving, like *Kaiser,* from caesar.

This imperial connection, however, did not spring from Rome and
the Western empire, but from Byzantium in the East, endowing Russian
Orthodoxy with its universal, apocalyptic and autocratic strain. As the historian James H. Billington amplifies in *The Icon and the Axe*: "Following
Clement and Origen rather than Augustine, Orthodox theology spoke
less about the drama of personal salvation than that of cosmic redemption.
Whereas Augustine willed to Latin Christendom the brooding sense of
pessimism about the earthly city, these Eastern fathers willed to Orthodox

Christendom a penchant for believing that the Christian Empire in the East might yet be transformed into the final, heavenly kingdom."

We tend to forget that the empire's cradle was not Moscow but Kiev, a lofty fortress city dramatically sited in Ukraine above the mile-wide shores of the Dnieper. Here, circa 980, arrived the Russian grand duke Vladimir, having murdered his brother to secure the Kievan throne. Hard drinking and high living, he was said to have acquired numerous wives and eight hundred concubines. While in his thirties, Vladimir unexpectedly turned against the pagan gods whose crude stone effigies are still scattered in or around every Russian or Ukrainian historical museum. He was well aware, having fought and traveled in northern Europe, that the neighboring kings of Poland, Hungary, Denmark and Norway had recently converted to Latin Christianity. He did not follow suit but, as related in ancient chronicles, summoned advocates of Islam, Judaism and Christianity to make their case. His choice fell on Orthodox Christianity, since he judged the Jews too dispersed and believed his subjects would rebel against Islam's ban on alcohol. And besides, his emissaries were dazzled by Constantinople and the Hagia Sophia. "We no longer knew whether we were in heaven or on earth," they reported. In 988 Vladimir swept into Crimea, conquered the Byzantine port city of Kherson, then audaciously sought as his bride Anna, a sister of the Byzantine Emperor Basil II. Convert first, restore the city and you may wed Anna, came the reply. Vladimir was duly baptized—the presumed baptistry, recently rededicated, is shown to visitors by pious guides at the excavated site of Kherson on the outskirts of Sevastopol. Returning to Kiev with his bride, Vladimir decreed the mass baptism of his subjects as pagan idols were unceremoniously dumped into the Dnieper. In due course Kiev's own Santa Sofia Cathedral arose, completed in 1037 by Vladimir's son, Yaroslav the Wise. With its thirteen cupolas, it became the inspired prototype for monumental churches throughout tsardom, its nobility so persuasive that Santa Sofia somehow survived both Mongols and Bolsheviks.

Thereafter Kiev's glory faded. In 1223, the Mongols sacked the city, and as the Kievan state disintegrated, Russian leadership passed by increments to Moscow. When, to the horror of Eastern Christendom, the Ottoman Turks burst through triple walls to take Constantinople in 1453, Orthodox canonists, half in hope, half in despair, venerated Moscow as the third Rome and acclaimed its grand duke as successor to the Byzantine emperors. Three landmarks confirmed Muscovy's preeminence: the coronation of its first tsar, his victory over the Muslim Tatars at Kazan, and the conquest of Siberia, all occurring during the long reign of Ivan IV (1533–1584), known as the Terrible. No Russian ever left a deeper mark. Acceding as a three-year-old to the throne, surviving a lonely and parlous regency, Ivan was crowned tsar of all Russia by the Orthodox Metropolitan Makary in 1547. Not only was Ivan the first prince of Muscovy formally anointed as tsar (i.e., emperor), he likewise flouted tradition by choosing a Russian boyar's daughter—technically his slave—as empress. She was Anastasia Romanovna Zakharina, and their union joined Ivan's ancient House of Rurik, with its semilegendary ninth-century Norse origins, to the comparatively upstart House of Romanov. Mikhail, grandson of Anastasia's brother Nikita, became the first Romanov tsar in 1613, founding the dynasty that ended in a cellar at Ekaterinburg with the massacre in 1918 of Nicholas II and Alexandra and their royal brood.

For Ivan, being anointed as tsar was a symbolic coup; his conquest of Kazan, which Russians took by assault in October 1552, gave birth to an empire. Located 425 miles east of Moscow, Kazan was among the independent khanates spawned by Jenghiz Khan's Golden Horde. Remarkably, the horde had persisted for more than a century after the Great Khan's death in 1227, enduring until cumulative blows—conflicts between nomadic and sedentary Mongols, the horrific Black Death and the rise of a rival Central Asian warlord, Tamerlane—led to its dissolution. Yet even dismembered, its limbs took on a life of their own. Among successor states were the khanate of Kazan on the middle Volga, Astrakhan on the lower Volga, and the Crimean khanate at Bakhchisarai, all ethnically Mongol or Turkic, nearly all Muslim. In theory, Muscovy and other Russian principalities were vassals to the Mongols, also known as Tatars, but in practice Orthodox princes intermittently collaborated with, and even exacted tribute from, their nominal Islamic overlords. The famous "Mongol yoke" was less constricting than the phrase suggests.

Under Ivan the Terrible's predecessors, Muscovy had successfully defied Kazan by playing on Tatar disunity, and Ivan III even managed to wrest tribute from his erstwhile suzerains. However, facing an untested boy prince and buoyed by a succession of victories over Russians in recent campaigns, the khan of Kazan simply stopped paying. The new tsar rose to the challenge, called for a holy war and mobilized as many as

150,000 horsemen and foot soldiers, a force bolstered by Ivan's newly formed *stretltsy*, or musketeers, buttressed by 150 siege cannons and a corps of skilled sappers trained by a Danish mercenary. Witnessing the campaign was a visiting Englishman, Giles Fletcher, who left this graphic sketch of Russian cavalry on the attack:

> They have drums besides of a huge bigness, which they carry with them upon a board laid on four horses, that are sparred together with chains, every drum having eight strikers or drummers, besides trumpets and shawms, which they sound after a wild manner, much different than ours. When they give any charge, or make any invasion, they make a great hallow or shout together, as loud as they can, which with the sound of their trumpets, shawms, and drums, makes a confused and horrible noise. So they set first discharging their arrows, then dealing with their swords, which they use in a bravery to shake, and brandish over their heads, before they come to strokes.

In 1552 Ivan and his expeditionary army laid siege to Kazan, its walls bristling with the bows of 30,000 defenders. In a climactic assault, a forty-foot wooden platform slammed against walls weakened and then breached by ear-shattering underground explosions detonated by Ivan's sappers. For the Russians, it helped that this was a popular war against Islamic adversaries feared and despised for abducting slaves for the flesh markets at Kaffa, where husky Russian males and blond females fetched premium prices. To settle accounts, besiegers stormed into Kazan's citadel shouting "God be with us! God be with us!" as defenders were slaughtered, their wives and children flushed from houses to be sold as slaves. At day's end, the double-headed imperial eagle—another legacy from Byzantium—fluttered from the highest tower at Kazan, signaling a victory that spread Ivan's fame as far as Tudor England.

It is difficult to overstate the significance of this first territorial victory over the once invincible Tatars, a triumph of Cross over Crescent, duly memorialized with the construction of St. Basil's Cathedral facing the Kremlin. Thereafter, the Volga became a Russian river, a riparian sovereignty confirmed two years later on the Lower Volga when Ivan's armies vanquished the khanate of Astrakhan. When Ivan claimed the Volga—Europe's longest river, covering 2,325 miles on its winding course and having navigable tributaries totaling some 20,000 miles—he initiated a drive of eastward conquest that rolled on until the tsar's Cossacks met the Americans three centuries later on the Russian River in northern California.

In fewer than seventy years, Moscow became master of Siberia, a land rich in resources covering 5.3 million square miles, nearly 2 million square miles bigger than the continental United States. The instruments of conquest were the Stroganovs, mercantile barons and commercial agents of the tsar, and the Cossacks, freebooting warriors renowned for their superb horsemanship, their unquestioning fidelity and their ferocity. They fought in the pay of the Stroganovs but in the name of the tsar. A former river pirate named Ermak invaded Siberia along with some eight hundred Cossacks armed with matchlock muskets and pikes. Improbably, this small force overwhelmed vastly more numerous nomadic tribes—the Yakuts, Kirghiz, Oroks, Chukchi, Buriats and scores more—so that Ivan was able to add "tsar of Siberia" to his accumulating titles—a legacy whose geopolitical significance is even today inadequately appreciated.

That Ivan IV was a great figure is incontestable; whether he truly warranted his epithet is still in dispute. His defenders note that the Russian word *grozny*, translated as "terrible," also connotes awesome, dreadful or fearsome; in England even the nonviolent Edward VI was called "our most dread and soveraigne lord." How, his defenders ask, was Ivan worse than Catherine de Medici, instigator of the massacre in 1572 of 50,000 French Protestants on St. Bartholomew's Day? A dozen mitigating parallels from the same era have been advanced. And yet, even allowing for Russophobia, Ivan's use of systematic terror as an instrument of power proved a precedent and prototype for his successors, Romanov and Bolshevik alike. No person, lowly or noble, was immune from his wrath, exerted personally and capriciously with no possibility of appeal; he was known to execute on the spot, with his ubiquitous curved staff, solely because he was affronted by someone's expression. He formed the Oprichnina, a secret police force that he empowered to imprison, torture or murder at his command. Supporting all this is ample testimony from the foreign diplomats and merchants at his court. Even by the standards of his time, Ivan displayed contempt for rudimentary decency and (the abiding incubus in Russian life) an imperious indifference to rule of law. This judgment was anticipated in verse by George Tuberville, secretary in 1568 to Thomas

Randolph, envoy of Queen Elizabeth I (whom at one point Ivan wished to marry). Tuberville wrote:

In such a squage soil, where laws do bear no sway,
But all is at the king's will, to save or else to sway,
And that sans cause, God wot, if so his mind be such:
But what mean I with kinds to deal, we ought no saints to touch.
Conceive the rest yourself, and deem what lives they lead,
Where lust is law, and subjects live continually in dread;
And where the best estates have none assurance good,
Of land, of lives, nor nothing falls into next of blood:
But all of custom doth unto the prince redown,
And all the whole revenue comes unto the king his crown.

THE PRECEDING OFFERS a context for what follows. But note well: The past is not a matrix but a chalked sentence on a blackboard, a text for discussion rather than a mandate from some collective subconscious. On its face, Russia's asymmetric legacy, its darker history and immemorial fears, augurs poorly for a lasting relationship with the normally sunny-side-up United States. But recent events have discredited the belief that the future replicates the past. Consider events since 1989, which confounded many expectations deriving from the history I have briefly retold. To universal surprise, the Soviet Union yielded up its empire without a shot. It did nothing as the Berlin Wall fell. It peacefully withdrew 700,000 troops from the Baltic States and Eastern Europe. Then the Soviet Union itself proceeded to implode, in defiance of all precedents and prophecies. Experience has not been kind to the certitude of experts, especially geopolitical analysts. Twice in the past century Russia ruled the heartland, supposedly the key to global dominion, and twice its mastery proved chimerical. After the fact, it is now conventional wisdom that the Soviet imperial project stunted Russia's growth as a nation-state, galvanized a Western counteralliance, resulted in squandering resources on ungrateful clients and left as its legacy a bloated bureaucracy that persists as dead weight. Yet the Russian Federation, shorn of its former holdings, remains a vast country, rich in resources and promise.

Even sans empire, Russia occupies 13 percent of the earth's land surface (compared with the tsarist empire's 17 percent in 1913), encompasses eleven time zones and is nearly as large as the United States and Canada put together. Its population, estimated at 145 million in July 2001, is mostly ethnic Russian but with persisting non-Russian enclaves, notably the Islamic north Caucasian republics: Chechnya, Daghestan and Ingushetia. Moscow's protracted, agonizing and shaming war with Chechen separatists is a reminder of the costs of maintaining an empire, and it serves as an antidote to imperial nostalgia. Yet on the whole, and to the surprise of Western analysts, the break with the imperial past has been clean. "The Soviet Union resembled a chocolate bar," in the words of Nikolai Leonov, once chief analyst of the KGB. "It was creased with furrowed lines of future division, as if for the convenience of its consumers."

Viewed from across the Atlantic, in truth, Americans have much to be thankful for. Russia survived its radical transition to capitalism ("market Bolshevism," in the apt phrase of one U.S. scholar), absent the massive Western help it believed had been promised. It also carried out an unprecedented electoral transition when the erratic and ailing President Boris Yeltsin gave way to a former KGB officer, Vladimir Putin, who reassures Russians with his seeming ordinariness and impresses foreigners with his poker-faced acumen. Vastly more important, and not just to Americans, the new Russia did not brandish its doomsday arsenal but honored agreements to reduce its nuclear stockpile; nor did a mutiny of consequence break out among Russia's grumbling, underpaid armed forces, a commonly unmentioned blessing. Moreover, Putin responded mildly even to President George W. Bush's brusque insistence on scrapping the Antiballistic Missile Treaty, long lauded by Moscow as the keystone of stable nuclear deterrence. WHICH THEY REPEATEDLY VIOLATED

What once seemed unimaginable—that Russia might join NATO and eventually become part of the European Union—is now a humdrum topic for academic papers. Writing before 9/11, Dmitri Trenin, a Russian political analyst at the Carnegie Moscow Center, contended on pragmatic grounds that the era of "Eurasia" was over, and that Russia's resources, history and culture favored a turn to the West. After 9/11, not only did the "war against terrorism" bring Washington and Moscow closer together, but Americans glimpsed unexpected economic synergy in the partnership. With an air of eye-rubbing surprise in December 2001, a *New York Times* editorial commented that Russia "has quietly become a behemoth in the oil business, a development with important political and economic implications for the United States."Within two years, Russian output had jumped about 15 percent, partly the result of new technology and rising prices, so that as of January 2002, Siberian oil accounted for close to 10 percent of world production. Eager to expand its market share, Moscow began looking with greater favor after 9/11 on partnerships with foreign producers. A consortium led by Exxon Mobil announced agreement in October 2001 on developing an oil field near Sakhalin Island in Russia's Far East, with an initial investment of some $4 billion, a record high for foreign firms since the collapse of Communism. This coincided with the completion of a $2.6 billion pipeline from Kazakhstan to Russia's Black Sea port at Novorossisk. Constructed by a consortium led by Chevron Texaco, the pipeline is meant to bring oil from huge Caspian reserves through Russia into world markets at a significant level—the initial pumping capacity is 600,000 barrels a day. At the same time, Transneft, the state-owned pipeline company, announced the opening of a Baltic Sea terminal with a capacity of 240,000 barrels a day.

Though these projects have had their interruptions and disagree-ments, momentum favors further partnership, opening a fresh chapter in a story as interesting as it is unfamiliar. Russia's oil industry rose with lit-tle notice, and its past successes, ironically, helped undermine Soviet Com-munism. Though geologists as early as the 1920s found petroleum in the marshland forests of west Siberia, it was not until 1959 that serious pump-ing began. Before then, Iran was a major Soviet supplier, but as Washing-ton pulled Tehran into its sphere of influence in the 1950s and 1960s, Moscow turned urgently to its own fields. Within a decade, the USSR began to export oil, rapidly becoming the world's number two producer. After the 1973 Yom Kippur War, oil prices quadrupled, an economic coup promoted by Iran and engineered by OPEC, the Organization of Petro-leum Exporting Countries. What was an "oil shock" for the West proved a windfall for Russia. From 1973 to 1985, energy exports accounted for 80 percent of Soviet export earnings, and when OPEC prices peaked, newly rich Arab states flocked to Moscow's arms bazaar. Flush with cash, the Brezhnev regime deferred the unpopular and difficult tasks of re-forming a rustbelt economy and squandered its gains on improvident Third World clients. Lenin once remarked that Bolsheviks would sell the world's capitalists the rope with which they would be hanged; Leonid Brezhnev reversed the maxim.

Taken together, therefore, an unforeseen opportunity exists for Washington and Moscow to work together fruitfully, given mutual respect and a modicum of common sense. Plainly there is ample potential for discord. Powerful factions in both countries view with suspicion and hostility the tentative alliance that already exists. In Russia, nationalist believers in "the phoenix model" recall that twice before—during the "time of troubles" in the seventeenth century, and then again during the revolutionary turmoil after the Bolshevik takeover—Russia endured foreign intervention, only to recover and arise from the ashes bigger and stronger than ever. Can it happen again? Dmitri Trenin put forward this answer in *The End of Eurasia: Russia on the Border Between Geopolitics and Globalization*, written before 9/11:

> Russia-Eurasia is over. To the west of its borders, there lies an increasingly unified Europe, a natural place for Russia's own integration *as a European country* [author's italics] in an appropriate form. To the east lies an increasingly interconnected Asia, where Russia must either establish itself *as a country in Asia* [author's italics] or face the mounting pressure to withdraw west of the Urals. To the south, there is the challenge of Islamic activism whose source is both internal and external. All this places Russia in a highly uncomfortable position, demanding vision and the capacity for action. . . . Yet the end of Eurasia, a real catastrophe, is no tragedy. It is merely the end of a long era. But it is not the end of Russia, for which a new and potentially happier era can now start.

In effect, Dmitri Trenin calls for the completion of the epic project begun by Peter the Great (1672–1725), the six-foot-seven-inch giant whose shadow still pervades Russia. He was the supreme modernizer who, with autocratic determination, created a magnificent capital on the Baltic, and turned a primitive army and non-existent navy into a global force. He instilled values of service and merit by example and command, turning the lamp of Western learning on the backwards corners of his northern realm. Is it conceivable that Peter's vision will be carried forward by a former KGB officer who rules with consent of the governed? As of 2002, it is not conceivable.

III

IRAN

The Agonies of Non-Sovereignty

The deposed Shah of Iran and former President Nixon joke with reporters during their July 1979 meeting in Cuernavaca, Mexico—a summit between "two fallen non-angels," in the words of their good friend and defender, columnist William Safire. In the Nixon years, the Shah sought (vainly) to restore Persia's imperial glory in the Gulf, and beyond. *Photo courtesy Corbis.*

O F THE DISPARITIES that afflict foreign relations, the most diffi-cult to overcome is asymmetry of knowledge. The need-to-know highway in the much touted Information Age tends to be a one-way street. Americans can travel the world knowing little about the history, culture and language of the countries they visit. Non-Americans do not have that option with respect to the United States. Even without knowing a word of English, people everywhere ingest Yankee ways through movies, television, music, comic strips, sports and more recently Internet cafés, so that Santa Claus and "Jingle Bells" turn up seasonally in places as unlikely as the old quarter of Baku on the Caspian Sea and the muddy alleys of Manaus on the river Amazon.

Among the important places about which Americans know too little, Iran figures high. Hence the shock in November 1979, when Iranian students burst into the U.S. embassy in Tehran and violated established international law by holding fifty-two diplomats hostage, thus initiating a crisis that cost Jimmy Carter his presidency and ended with Ronald Reagan's inauguration 444 days later. The hostage crisis was a rehearsal for 9/11. Americans watched in disbelief as televised mobs screamed "Death to America!" and jeered at blindfolded U.S. captives, their insults endorsed by Iran's glowering leader, Ayatollah Ruhollah Khomeini, about whom Americans knew nothing until his triumphant return to Iran earlier that year.

The shock was understandable. Iran's deposed monarch, Mohammad Reza Shah Pahlavi, was generally perceived as a trusted ally and enlightened modernizer. He had ruled a country toasted as an "island of stability" by none other than President Carter during a visit to Tehran the year before. Some Americans recalled that the Central Intelligence Agency had once engineered a coup to restore the shah to his throne. Yet that had occurred twenty-five years earlier, when many experts contended that Moscow was trying to subvert Iran. In 1953, so instructed the consensus, vital U.S. interests were at stake, given Iran's size (628,000 square miles, two and a half times larger than Texas), its location (frontiers with the Soviet

Union, Iraq, Turkey, Afghanistan and Pakistan), its oil resources and its role as watchdog of the Persian Gulf.

In any case, what had Washington done to warrant the ayatollah's stinging epithet "Great Satan"? The wonderment persists, as does a prevailing ignorance of Iranian history. No country offers a clearer object lesson in the hazards of indirect dominion. In theory, Iran retained its sovereignty during the heyday of empire. In practice, final authority on vital matters rested with not one, not two, but three great powers, acting together or as rivals. The spirit of this rivalry was well expressed by a key participant, George Nathaniel Curzon, author of the early and compendious *Persia and the Persian Question*. "Turkestan, Afghanistan, Transcaspia, Persia," he wrote in 1892, "to many these names breathe only a sense of utter remoteness or a memory of strange vicissitudes and moribund romance. To me, I confess, they are pieces on a chessboard upon which is being played out a game for dominion of the world." Curzon did not need reminding that the word "checkmate" derived from the Persian "shah," meaning king, and "mat," meaning helpless or defeated.

Twice in the past century, the British hand-picked, and twice deposed, Iran's *shahinshah*, the king of kings. In 1907 the British and Russians formally carved Iran into spheres of influence: Russia's zone included Tehran, while the British got the southern oil fields just coming into production. Because of Iran's oil and its geography, British and Russian forces occupied this ostensibly neutral nation during both world wars. For nearly half a century, Britain decided how much Iran would be paid for its oil. When it was threatened with loss of this privilege in 1953, the British intelligence service MI6 conspired with the CIA to remove Iran's constitutional premier, Mohammad Mossadeq. This repeated the successful sabotage in 1911 of Iran's promising parliamentary system. At that time the British had acquiesced in Russia's forcible assault on the newborn National Assembly to expel an American employed by Iran to collect taxes.

So thick is the texture of collusion, so deceptive are appearances in a history seemingly coauthored by Machiavelli and Borges, that one is scarcely surprised to discover that *Iran: Past and Present*, now in its ninth edition and described by its academic publisher (Princeton University Press) as the "standard work on Iran," is by Donald N. Wilber, a scholar and archaeologist who led a double life as a CIA agent. Stranger yet, Wilber was principal architect of Operation Ajax, the 1953 coup promoted by

American and British agents to unseat Mossadeq. Nowhere in Wilber's narrative of the coup does he mention the CIA by name or even hint at the role he played in the history he helped shape.

I RAN'S PAST AND its sanitized representation in the West help explain the frustrated rage in Tehran when Jimmy Carter yielded to urgent appeals from the shah's advocates and allowed the terminally ill former monarch to enter the United States. This, we tend to forget, was what ignited the hostage crisis. The sense that nobody really cared added to the ignominy among a people, commonly misidentified as Arabs, who boast a continuous history extending over twenty-six centuries. Persians trace their ancestral origins to early settlements on their country's huge central plateau, where deserts abound and water is scarce. The need to share and conserve water favored the rise of strong rulers who led an aggressive quest for more fertile lands beyond. Persian warriors tramped southward through the snow-capped Zagros Mountains to the waters of what became known as the Persian Gulf, northward to the Caspian Sea and the highlands of Azerbaijan. This was the heartland of the first Persian empire, which pressed outward from the fifth to the third centuries B.C. under the Achaemenian god-kings Cyrus, Darius and Xerxes. At the empire's zenith, its satrapies extended from the Mediterranean to the Indus, reaching from the Caucasus to the Arabian Sea. "My father's kingdom," credibly boasted Cyrus the Younger, "extends so far to the south that men cannot live there because of the heat, and northward to where they cannot exist because of the cold."

Around this time (dates uncertain), a prophet named Zoroaster inspired a new religion stressing the duality of good and evil, an ethical precursor of later monotheisms. The Magi, the Wise Men who made their way to Bethlehem, were Zoroastrians, and in Iran today, fire worshipers true to the old faith still constitute a recognized minority. Every March, even under the Islamic Republic, Iranians observe the Zoroastrian New Year, a twelve-day fete known as Noruz whose origins predate Cyrus the Great.

The Achaemenians fell to the Macedonian armies of Alexander the Great, whose generals founded the Seleucid dynasty (323–223 B.C.), named after Seleucis, Alexander's cavalry commander. The Hellenic century ended with Persia's conquest by the Parthians, nomadic warriors whose intrepidity blocked the eastward expansion of the Roman empire. The successor Sassanian line (A.D. 208–637) nurtured the first flowering of Persia's emblematic arts: dome and vault architecture, lapidary painting and carpets of unsurpassed elegance. Then followed nearly nine centuries of alien rule, first by the Arab caliphs, whose armies overwhelmed Persia after the death of Mohammed in 632. Next came the Seljuks, a Turkic-speaking tribe from Central Asia, followed by the Mongols, whose cruelty was tempered by gestures of tolerance and humanity. The Seljuks gave way to the Timurids, the royal house of Timur the Lame, known to Europe as Tamerlane, renowned for his sumptuous court at Samarkand. Finally the Persians reclaimed their patrimony under their own warlords, the Safavids, in the sixteenth century. Then followed a decisive turn in Iran's history.

During the centuries of alien rule, Persians preserved their language and culture. Expedited by arms and trade, both took root in Central Asia's oasis cities, as well as in adjacent Afghanistan and the Mogul courts of northern India. Even though the Arab conquest proved a humiliation to the losers, who were now subordinate to semiliterate tribal nomads from backwater Arabia, the Persians nonetheless embraced Islam and with their sophistication helped bring forth the caliphate's golden age. During these early years, devout Persians turned to variants of the mainstream Sunni faith. Many were drawn to Sufism, a mystical offshoot of Islam that flourished in Central Asia and entered Persia via the Seljuks. Its teachings were immortalized by Persian poets, notably Hafez and Rumi.

In the same era, another minority Islamic sect, known as the Party of Ali, or Shiites, vied for adherents among the faithful. The majority Sunnis recognized the first four caliphs as Mohammed's rightful heirs, whereas the Shiites believed that Mohammed's closest male relative, Ali, the first imam, was the true leader of the Muslim community. Ali's successors were his sons Hassan and Hussein, the second and third imams, continuing to the eleventh imam, all of whom died violently at the hands of jealous caliphs. But the twelfth imam, Mohammed, Shiites say, escaped death by vanishing in A.D. 878 into the cave below the Great Mosque at Samarra, in what is now Iraq. He is the Hidden Imam, the Awaited One, whose reappearance as Mahdi will herald the end of time. Hence the Shiites became known as Twelvers, and their creed found its early supporters in Persia, especially in the garrison town of Qum.

Then, as if by divine approbation, Ismail (1487–1524), the young founder of the Safavid dynasty, decreed in circa 1502 that Shiism was

henceforth the religion of Persia. His decree was as enigmatic as it was astonishing. What made it more startling, remarks Karen Armstrong in her
history of Islam, is that Twelver Shiism had hitherto been an esoteric sect,
withdrawn from politics. Now it enjoyed the coercive support of a powerful shah and his successors, who soon persecuted the gentle adherents
of Sufi mysticism, supplanting their teachings with emotional dirges and
mourning rituals for Shia martyrs. As Armstrong writes, "The establishment of a Shii Empire caused a new and decisive rift between Sunnis and
Shiis, leading to an intolerance and an aggressive sectarianism that was unprecedented in the Islamic world but which was similar to the bitter conflict between Catholics and Protestants that erupted at the same time in
Europe."

From the outset, Twelvers identified with underdogs; only in Persia
did Shiites find powerful state patronage. This is still broadly the case. In
Saudi Arabia and other Gulf states, there are Shia minorities (in Bahrain,
a majority), many being oil workers. In Iraq, where some 60 percent of
the inhabitants are Shiites, its rulers have been Sunni. In southern Lebanon, an important Shia enclave, the Party of Ali has had to submit to
Maronite Christians and Israeli occupiers as well as to Sunni overlords. For
Iran, the populist strands in Shiism, together with the special aura accorded its clergy, have proved a perennial trial to secular rulers, royal or
elective. If, as some theorize, Ismail's turn to a minority faith within Islam
was a way of avenging Persia's humiliation at the hands of Arabs, his wishes
were overfulfilled. Thus the stage was prepared for Persia's complicated
encounter with Russia and the West in the nineteenth century.

For Europe, if not for the United States, to paraphrase Dickens,
the early 1800s were the best of times and the worst of times, times
of revolutionary turbulence on the French side of the English Channel
and of British conservatism on the other. Still, even in monarchical England, people were rightly proud of their civil liberties, their Houses of
Parliament, and their humanitarian impulses (at some cost, Britons led the
drive to suppress the slave trade). Then as later, Russia was an autocracy,
the tsar absolute master of an ever growing overland empire. Yet what
made England a global power, especially after the American Revolution,
was its own inexorably expanding Indian empire.

The instrument of British control was the East India Company. Chartered by Queen Elizabeth I and granted the power to issue currency and raise armies, the company was quasi-sovereign and remained so until after the Indian mutiny of 1857–1859. From its base in Calcutta, through battles and bribes, the company had by 1800 subjugated most of India, ruling directly or via princely surrogates. At that moment, the twin threats to the Raj were France and Russia, then allied. (The logistics of a joint assault on India were in fact examined by Napoleon and Tsars Paul and Alexander I.) The distance between the Russian empire and British India was then two thousand miles, but with each year the distance dwindled. At points, by century's end, only twenty or so miles separated the two empires.

Caught between these clashing powers was Persia, where a new dynasty emerged in 1785—the Qajars, who ruled until the aftermath of World War I. Descended from Turkmen chieftains in Central Asia, the Qajars sat uneasily on the Peacock Throne, as evidenced in the overblown, fiercely bearded formal portraits of the dynasty's eight shahs. British envoys, sensing this social insecurity, flattered with a trowel when bribes or bullying failed. Over the course of a century, Britain secured a privileged role in the Persian court, winning extraordinary concessions. One effective method was the creation of spurious decorations, handsomely beribboned and scattered like confetti at court. Russia was Britain's principal rival for Persian favor, though early in the competition France was a third suitor, notably after Napoleon invaded Russia, turning the latter momentarily into a British ally.

Adding to its complexity was a peculiar arrangement whereby the British sent two sets of emissaries. London was directly represented by its envoy at the Qajar court in Tehran. Meanwhile, Britain's East India Company from the 1790s also posted a Resident at Bushire (now Büshehr), an unprepossessing city on the southern Gulf coast. From the outset, successive Residents cultivated ties with nearby lesser sheikdoms that persist to the present. Soon British India's man at Bushire was dubbed the uncrowned king of the Gulf, which did not endear him to his diplomatic counterparts in Tehran.

Financiers, traders, speculators and adventurers now flocked to Persia, most of them from Britain and Russia. Markets opened in the hinterland, consulates blossomed and foreign shipping began plying Persian rivers. The most spectacular coup was perpetrated in 1872 by Baron Julius de

Reuter, a naturalized Briton born in Germany and founder of the British press agency. He obtained concessions to build railways, establish a bank, and to collect customs for twenty years. He gained exclusive rights for seventy years to operate mines, tramways and water works, to build irrigation canals and fell timber, as well as an option to found utilities, post offices and other enterprises. Lord Curzon called it "the most complete and extraordinary surrender of the entire industrial resources of a kingdom into foreign hands that has probably ever been dreamed of, much less accomplished, in history."

As Sir Denis Wright, a onetime British ambassador to Tehran, explains in his insider's account, *The English Amongst the Persians* (1977), the shah's interest was not just pecuniary: "He and his Prime Minister were worried by the Russian threat to Persian independence. They believed—or hoped—that by giving the British a large economic stake in the country they would become committed to defending that independence." Within Persia, however, the Reuter concessions provoked an outcry against foreigners—an outcry promoted by Russians and mullahs alike. The shah backed down and canceled the railway concession, but Reuter was able to rescue his banking and mining rights with the support of the British Foreign Office. Thus was launched the Imperial Bank of Persia, which soon earned a reputation for honesty. However, the smell of impropriety and groveling to foreigners was reinforced in 1890, when the shah granted a fifty-year monopoly on the production, sale and export of tobacco to a British army officer, Major Gerald Talbot, who paid the king of kings £25,000 and his prime minister £15,000 for the privilege. The deal was so flagrant that diplomats feared a massacre of Europeans as the Shiite clergy called for total abstention from tobacco. Faced with a ruinous boycott, the shah voided the concession and paid a half million pounds in compensation to Talbot's Imperial Tobacco Corporation.

Assisting in these negotiations was a figure of some interest, Sir Henry Drummond Wolff, who seemed destined by heredity to play a catalytic role in the region. His father, Reverend Joseph Wolff, was renowned for journeying from Richmond, England, to the Central Asian khanate of Bokhara in 1843–1844 to plead for the life of two British officers under death sentences as alleged spies. The son also proved an enterprising envoy and politician, remembered for bestowing his artful bogus decorations. As a former Conservative member of Parliament, he could count on influential backing at home for his causes. Sir Henry was among the first to

suspect that Persia might possess oil. He was also among the earliest advocates of a brash new strategy. Why not make a deal with the Russians to
divide up the Persian pie? Why not indeed?

B Y AN INTERESTING twist, the Anglo-Russian Convention of
August 31, 1907, a nonpareil specimen of imperial hauteur, was
the work of an ostensibly anti-imperial Liberal government. The general
election of 1906 resulted in a lopsided Liberal majority in Parliament, and
the new prime minister, Sir Henry Campbell-Bannerman, spoke for a
cabinet committed to Irish home rule and serious reforms in India.
Nonetheless Liberals like Lord Morley, now the secretary of state for
India, had long felt that the Russian menace was overblown and that accommodation was preferable to confrontation. Besides, Kaiser Wilhelm's
Germany and its dreadnoughts had replaced Russia as the likeliest potential adversary. Soundings thus began in St. Petersburg concerning a comprehensive agreement on Afghanistan, Tibet and Persia to write an end to
a century of Anglo-Russian rivalry. Sir Arthur Nicolson, later Lord
Carnock and father of the author Harold Nicolson, initiated negotiations
with Alexander Izvolsky, the Russian foreign minister. The British, in Sir
Arthur's words, approached "the Persian problem solely from the point of
view of the defense of India."

An accord was agreed on and signed. Without consulting its inhabitants, England and Russia divided Persia into three spheres of influence: a
British zone in the south, a Russian zone in the north, and a neutral zone
in which the two powers undertook reciprocally not to seek exclusive
concessions. Russia's northern third was by far the biggest and included
Tehran, reflecting Russia's proximate and superior influence. Though oil
fields in the south were already being developed, their fecundity was not
yet known. Lord Curzon, no longer viceroy of India but now an opposition leader in the House of Lords, assailed the treaty as one-sided: "We had
thrown away the efforts of our diplomacy and our trade for more than a
century." In Russia, by contrast, the Duma greeted the accord with cries
of "Bravo!"

The Persians reacted with absolute shock. News that their country
had been dismembered coincided with a constitutional revolution meant
to restore Persia's independence and self-respect. Beset by charges of cor-

ruption and misrule, an aging Qajar ruler, after a bloodless revolt in 1906, acceded to the election of a National Assembly, the first of its kind in Persia. The assembly convened in October and drafted a new constitution with fifty-one articles, which the old shah grudgingly signed before his death. From the outset, Russia and its local royalist allies did what they could to subvert a parliament that might serve as an unsettling example for others in the tsar's realm. In his careful diplomatic history of Iran, Ruhollah K. Ramazani of the University of Virginia, himself a native of Tehran, writes that Russia's intervention "destroyed the foundations of the Constitutional government twice in about four years."

The first blow came in December 1907, four months after the Anglo-Russian Convention was signed, when a newly enthroned and weirdly reactionary Qajar ruler summoned his prime minister and ordered him arrested. With money loaned by the Russian bank (his crown jewels as security), the shah hired rioters to storm the Majlis, or National Assembly. When the shah's coup failed, the Russians sent in their locally billeted Cossack Brigade to dissolve parliament and decree martial law. The Majlis building went up in flames, its records destroyed and eight Iranians killed. The Russian commander proclaimed himself military governor of Tehran. Ramazani describes the limp response of Sir Edward Grey, Britain's Liberal foreign secretary: "Prior to the 1907 convention, Great Britain acted as midwife of the new order, but despite Grey's good intentions, British performance generally favored Russia at the expense of Iran. Grey's policy toward Iran from beginning to end was nonintervention and friendship with Russia."

Then, unimaginably, a popular uprising brought together ethnic, religious and westernizing factions that otherwise agreed on little, and the insurgents overwhelmed the Cossack gendarmes, forcing the despised shah to abdicate. His twelve-year-old son was proclaimed successor, and a Qajar noble named as regent. A free press that had sprung up during the First Majlis reappeared as a Second Majlis was elected. In November 1910, the Persian foreign minister instructed his embassy in Washington to seek out a "disinterested American expert as Treasurer-General" to set up an honest tax-collecting system for Persia, which was nearly bankrupt. The choice fell on W. Morgan Shuster, a forty-three-year-old American who had already served as customs collector in the new Republic of Cuba and who reorganized tax collecting in the Philippines between 1901 and 1906. With the support of President Taft, his former chief as governor-general in Manila, Shuster agreed to serve for three years in Persia. Along with a trio of young aides, in April 1911 Shuster sailed from New York into Persia's maze of mirrors. Bad enough was the chill (which Shuster reciprocated) on the part of Tehran's European colony and the perplexities of distinguishing Persian friends from unctuous enemies. Worse was the report that, with Russian support, the ousted shah was plotting to reclaim his throne. The finale occurred in November 1911, when Treasurer-General Shuster's special police brushed past a Cossack guard to occupy the home of the ex-shah's brother. Angered by this and other incidents, Russian authorities demanded Shuster's dismissal for trespassing in Russia's sphere of influence. When the Majlis balked, Russian troops advanced on Tehran, resulting in casualties among liberals and clergy at Tabriz and the shelling of the National Assembly. On Christmas Day, the Persian cabinet formally dismissed Shuster, who returned home and wrote an impassioned account of his mission, *The Strangling of Persia*, that closed with this passage:

> The Persian people, fighting for a chance to live and govern themselves instead of remaining the serfs of heartless and corrupt rulers, deserved better of fate than to be forced, as now, to sink back into an even worse serfdom, or to be hunted down and murdered as 'revolutionary dregs.' . . . . [W]ith the exception of corrupt grandees and dishonest public servants, all desired that we should succeed. Russia became aware of this feeling, and unwittingly *paid us the compliment of fearing that we would succeed in our task* [author's emphasis]. That she never intended to allow; the rest of the controversy was detail.

Such was the fruit of the 1907 convention. As the diplomat Sir Denis Wright frankly observes, "The Persians, who had come increasingly to look upon Britain as their protector against Russia and the champion of liberal ideas, were shocked beyond measure by this alliance with the devil." Firuz Kazemzadeh, the Yale scholar and the son of a Persian diplomat, writes in his authoritative *Russia and Britain in Persia 1864–1914*: "[I]t was in September 1907 that the modern Persian image of Britain crystallized. . . . Justifiably or not, most Persians would, from then on, be prepared to believe only the worst of England." The reckoning lay a decade ahead, after the Great War.

WHAT GAVE PERSIA higher priority for the British was the pervasive new ingredient in twentieth-century diplomacy: oil. By 1900, nearly half a century had passed since E. L. Drake's drills lanced the first gusher in Titusville, Pennsylvania. By bullying and buying out competitors, John D. Rockefeller had long since transformed Standard Oil into a giant U.S. monopoly, with Royal Dutch Shell its principal global rival. In Baku, oil literally gushed from seaside derricks on the Caspian as Russia also became a world oil power. Hence Britain's anxiety about securing its own protected source of what was already perceived an essential strategic asset.

British hopes were buoyed by an entrepreneurial buccaneer, William Knox D'Arcy, a high-living millionaire who had amassed a fortune in Australia's gold rush. When reports of oil surfaced in Persia, Russia vied with Britain for concessions, but with diplomatic assists and well-placed bribes, D'Arcy's agents prevailed. For £20,000 in cash, plus shares worth the same amount and 16 percent of net profits, he wrested a concession in 1901. Valid for sixty years, it covered three-fourths of Persia (480,000 square miles); a quadrant in the north was omitted out of deference to Russia. Yet this generous concession nearly bankrupted D'Arcy, who spent upward of £200,000—a royal ransom at the time—on bringing oil to markets. What saved him was an unsung British technician, George Reynolds. As Daniel Yergin remarks of Reynolds in *The Prize*, "He was at one and at the same time engineer, geologist, manager, field representative, diplomat, linguist and anthropologist. . . . It was his determination and obstinate commitment that kept the project going when there was every reason—from illness to extorting tribesmen, to mechanical frustration, to searing heat and unforgiving winds to endless disappointment—to waver."

Thanks to Reynolds's taciturn perseverance and D'Arcy's betting instincts, the operation succeeded. On May 25, 1908, at a desperate nadir in the company's fortunes, a gusher at Masjid-i-Suleiman in southern Persia spouted fifty feet, dousing the rejoicing drillers. In violation of Persian sovereignty, a protective British umbrella instantly opened over the field as the Indian government deployed troops to guard the rigs. Sir Percy Cox, the British Resident at Bushire, persuaded the local sheik to permit a pipeline to carry the oil 130 miles to the Gulf, where it could be shipped from refineries on the offshore island of Abadan.

The speed with which this happened owed much to D'Arcy's ongoing friendship with Britain's preeminent naval "oil maniac," Admiral Sir John Fisher. They first met in July 1903 at Marienbad, the gracious Bohemian spa to which "Jacky" Fisher went regularly to rest and to indulge his lifelong passion, dancing. Fisher's great goal was to convert the British navy from coal to oil. He liked D'Arcy and, on becoming first sea lord a year later, found essential backing to keep the Persian operation going. Then all these elements—oiling the navy, Darcy's concession and British strategy—converged in 1911 when Winston Churchill, still a budding Liberal MP, became first lord of the admiralty. He was Jacky Fisher's devoted fan, and he coaxed the old admiral—who had by then retired and was twice Churchill's thirty-seven years—into heading the Royal Commission on Fuel and Engines. Together they moved a balky service forward full throttle, and conversion became a fact. On June 17, 1914, Churchill put before the House of Commons a bold matching proposal: for £2.2 million, the British government could acquire 51 percent of the shares and two seats on the board of D'Arcy's Anglo-Persian Oil Company. This could ensure the Royal Navy rock-bottom prices for its petroleum, which proved the case. (The exact prices were kept secret for decades.) On June 28, Parliament approved a bargain rivaled only by Disraeli's coup in acquiring majority shares in the Suez Canal Company. Over time, Anglo-Persian became Anglo-Iranian and then, after 1953, British Petroleum or BP, but the 51 percent arrangement stuck, surviving even Prime Minister Thatcher's privatizing drive. Oil in this instance proved thicker than ideology.

WHEN WORLD WAR I broke out, Persia immediately declared itself neutral, but this did not deter belligerents from violating its territory from the first shot until long after the last. As hostilities commenced, Russian forces occupied Tabriz, Masshad and other northern cities. Garrisoned near Tehran was Russia's fifth column: the Persian Cossack Division, organized in 1879 as a royal bodyguard, subsidized by the tsar and commanded by Russian officers. When Turkey joined up with the Central Powers in November 1914, its regiments entered western Persia to block a possible Russian incursion. Adding to the scramble was a recently formed Persian gendarmerie, whose Swedish officers were pro-German. Britain for its part reinforced cordons around oil fields, and in

1916 it formed a special local army, the South Persia Rifles. The scramble grew more desperate following the Bolshevik Revolution and the ensuing civil war between Reds and Whites in the Caucasus and Central Asia. Fearing the worst for Persia, the British ordered still another army, the North-West Persia Force (or Norperforce) into Tehran and its environs in 1919–1920. Norperforce's colorful major general was Sir Edmund Ironside, an undercover agent in the Boer War and the first British officer to land in France in 1914. A gifted linguist, he was a reputed model for Richard Hannay in John Buchan's spy novels, *The Thirty-Nine Steps* and *Greenmantle*. In Persia Ironside also became kingmaker.

Coping with this in London was Lord Curzon, at last foreign secretary. But in 1919–1920 he was frustrated at every turn by Communists and nationalists abroad and by cabinet detractors at his back. Even Curzon's critics acknowledged that he knew more than anybody else about Persia, and he was given carte blanche to draft a treaty meant to resolve the Persian question. In the first article, the British government reiterated "in the most categorical manner the undertakings which they have repeatedly given in the past to respect absolutely the independence and integrity of Persia." The Anglo-Persian Treaty then authorized posting British experts to create a national army, build railroads, supply arms and revise tariffs, with the incentive of a £2 million loan. As Harold Nicolson comments in *Curzon: The Last Phase*, the foreign secretary could have scarcely chosen a worse time to put forward a well-meant but anachronistic scheme. While British armies ranged in Persia, the Bolsheviks, in full cry against imperialism, published secret wartime pacts showing that Britain had offered tsarist Russia the Dardanelles in return for a far bigger "sphere of influence" within Persia.

This was the context as Ironside began weeding Russian officers from the Persian Cossack Division. Standing six feet, four inches himself, Sir Edmund noticed a fellow six-footer, a colonel named Reza Khan, ramrod erect under a karakul hat, tough as leather boots and nicknamed "Machine Gun Reza." He was "a man and the straightest I have met yet," Ironside recorded in his diary, "the real life and soul of the show." Reza Khan, then in his forties, was made commander of the Cossack Division. Before leaving Persia, Ironside told him that Britain would not oppose his seizing power. Sir Edmund's protégé took him at his word in 1921. Back in England, Ironside noted in his diary, "I fancy that all the people think I engineered the *coup d'état*. I suppose I did, strictly speaking."

Five days after seizing power, Reza Khan annulled the Anglo-Persian Treaty, pointedly doing so on the same day his envoys in Moscow signed the Russo-Persian Treaty. What abetted this calculated rebuff was Lord Curzon's failure to note that Persia's oft violated constitution required that treaties be ratified by the Majlis, which, given his phenomenal memory, seems an almost Freudian slip. "More serious was his misconception of the attitude of the average Persian towards Russia and Great Britain," amplifies Harold Nicolson. "He did not realize that in 1919 it was Great Britain who was regarded as the oppressor and Russia as the potential friend." Moreover, the element of force was lacking in war-fatigued Britain, and anyway, Nicolson went on, "had not President Wilson denounced all 'separated interests' all 'zones of influence'? Were not the United States today a more authoritative power than the British Empire, and was not American opinion always upon the side of those oppressed nationalities who had the good fortune to be outside the area of the Caribbean Sea?"

Reza Khan's first post was as war minister. Two years later he was prime minister. In 1925, having deposed the last Qajar shah, the eighth in an enfeebled line, he crowned himself Reza Shah. Before founding his own Pahlavi dynasty, Reza Shah had toyed with proclaiming a republic, following the example of Kemal Atatürk, the Turkish soldier-reformer he sought to emulate. But kingship was too entwined with Persia's identity, Reza Khan concluded, and so he chose the Peacock Throne. The choice measures the difference between the two. Reza Shah was an Atatürk manqué who wanted it both ways: preserving the feudal prerogatives of royalty while seeking the global prestige of being Persia's enlightened modernizer.

In the spirit of Atatürk, Reza Shah founded and energized a unifying national army. He promoted railroads (Persia's first) from the Caspian to the Gulf. He established schools and hospitals, powered cement and textile factories with new electric lines. Moreover, he sent Persians abroad to study, especially at German and French universities. He clashed with Shiite mullahs over female dress codes; in the 1930s, women wearing chadors were barred by law from hotels, restaurants, cinemas, buses and taxis. As did Atatürk, he decreed that Persians adopt a family name, and he sought glorifying links with Persia's ancient empires (his dynasty took its name, Pahlavi, from the language spoken by the Sassanians).

Reza Shah's whim was absolute, his thirst to avenge proverbial, his skin gossamer. No elective constitutional system was allowed to grow

roots under the Pahlavis, another break from Atatürk's example. To the un-
traveled shah, the concept of a free press was unfathomable. In 1937, the
New York *Daily Mirror* published a story about Iran that included the following sentence: "Reza Shah had once been employed as a stable boy in
the British Legation." His diplomats threatened to break relations with
Washington unless the Hearst tabloid instantly apologized. "Total despot
that he was," write William Dorman and Mansour Fahrang in *The U.S.
Press and Iran*, "Reza Shah could not believe that the State Department
was unable to order a newspaper to apologize to him."

An interesting glimpse from within can be found in Sattareh Farman
Farmaian's memoir, *Daughter of Persia*. One of thirty-plus children in the
harem of a Qajar noble, Sattareh attended an American missionary school
and in 1944 arrived in the United States to study social work at the University of Southern California—the first Iranian woman to undertake so
unconventional an odyssey. In her memoir, she recalls Reza Shah and his
persecution of the now powerless Qajar families: "The Shah was so big
and strong that I feared that not even God could touch him. He had taken
away our rights, stopped our mouths, suppressed our constitution and our
parliament, stolen people's property, and ruined, imprisoned, and killed
men with impunity—not only my brother and his friend Teymourtash,
the minister of court, but many others: Sadar Assad, the chief of the
Bakhtiari; Solatdoleh, the chief of the Qashqa'i; Samuel Haim, the Jewish
community's representative in the Majlis; Eshqi the poet; Modarres the
mullah, who along with [the author's father] Shazdeh's nephew, Mohammed Mossadegh, had been one of the few members of parliament to
protest his being given dictatorial powers. And these were only the most
prominent. I was terrified."

YET REZA SHAH is owed his due. On the matter of oil, his outrage
was warranted by any reasonable standard. The still extant D'Arcy
concession had been modified in 1920, but only modestly as Persians
noted, since a British Treasury official, Sir Sydney Armitage-Smith, served
as chief negotiator for Persia. When royalties from Anglo-Persian sharply
declined during the Great Depression, the defiant Reza in November
1932 unilaterally canceled the company's concession. This followed years
of inconclusive haggling over long-standing Persian grievances: the com-

pany interpreted "net profits" to apply only to its operations in Persia, evaded Persian taxes, and wrongly withheld royalties as compensation for Persia's unavoidable failure to prevent wartime attacks on its pipelines. Moreover, Reza Shah was indignant over Britain's recognition of the new kingdom of Iraq on Persia's western border, a country he viewed as an imperial concoction. All this was compounded by the oil company's quasi-governmental status. In the words of Daniel Yergin, "The management of Anglo-Persian could endlessly repeat that the company operated as a commercial entity, independent of the government, but no Persian would ever believe such an assertion."

Finally, after mediation by the League of Nations, the parties agreed in 1933 to a new contract that reduced Anglo-Persian's concession to 100,000 square miles, provided for a fixed royalty of four shillings per ton on sold or exported petroleum, assured Persia 20 percent of worldwide profits to shareholders in excess of £671,250 and guaranteed Persia annual proceeds of at least £750,000. It seemed a victory for Persia, the more so since the company also promised to recalculate royalties from prior years and speed "Persianization" of the workforce. In fact, as oil prices and profits soared in the years ahead, the company's tax payments to Britain were roughly triple its royalties to Iran. Highly skilled jobs were still reserved for expatriate technicians, and Persia was denied real access to company books, so that the Royal Navy's bargain-basement prices for its oil remained secret.

Little wonder, given his combative temper and suspicion of Britain, that Reza Shah began looking to Germany as a potential counterweight to Britain and the Soviet Union. Early in the 1920s, Germans began trickling to Tehran; friendship societies and student exchange programs followed. This accelerated in the 1930s as Reza Shah sought a sharp reduction in trade with an evermore domineering Soviet Union. In 1940–1941, commerce with Germany reached its peak; 48 percent of all imports came from the Third Reich, and 42 percent of all Iranian exports headed there. Whether Reza Shah was ideologically pro-Nazi is harder to ascertain. His son and successor, Mohammad Reza Pahlavi, insisted this was a falsehood, though his formulation is less than flattering: "My father mistrusted Hitler from the very beginning, if for no other reason than as an authoritarian ruler he was deeply suspicious of another who used such brutal methods. . . . True, we employed a number of German technicians, but their employment had nothing to do with politics."

Even so, Reza Shah came to loathe and distrust Britain and Russia alike and seemed to bet that the Third Reich would prevail. In 1935, arguably with a weather eye to Nazi racial doctrines, he changed Persia's name to Iran, meaning land of the Aryans. Inarguably, he was thrown into confusion by the Nazi-Soviet Pact of August 1939 and spoke from the heart in affirming Iran's wish to be neutral when war broke out the following month. Further confusion followed the German invasion of the Soviet Union in June 1941, which made Russians and Britons allies. That summer they issued an ultimatum to Persia (Churchill instructed his officials always to use the old name), demanding the expulsion of all German nationals. When Reza Shah demurred, British and Russian forces invaded on August 25, 1941. The shah abdicated, explaining to his son, "I cannot be the nominal head of an occupied land, to be dictated to by a minor English or Russian officer." The Majlis immediately proclaimed the twenty-two-year-old Mohammad Reza Pahlavi the new king of kings. The ex-shah was hustled onto a British ship to Mauritius in the Indian Ocean, where he was politely briefed by two veterans of the Eurasian power game, Sir Clarmont Skrine, formerly consul general at Kashgar in western China, and Sir Olaf Caroe, future governor of British India's North-West Frontier. Reza Shah was taken to Johannesburg and kept under house arrest; he died there in 1944.

It was all done so casually, this checkmating, by leaders distracted by larger matters. On August 10, 1942, while en route to Moscow, Churchill stopped at Tehran and had lunch with the new shah. The prime minister reported to Foreign Secretary Eden that the shah "expounded the principles of the allied cause with the greatest vigour and explained why he was convinced that the interests of Persia lay wholly with Britain and the United States." Yet the matter of Persia meant so little to Churchill that in *The Grand Alliance*, volume 3 of his history of the war, the changing kingship was dispensed with in a single paragraph. The old shah "went into comfortable exile" while his "gifted" young son "under Allied advice" restored "the Constitutional Monarchy." In volume 5, *Closing the Ring*, Churchill's November 1943 meeting in Tehran with Franklin Roosevelt and Joseph Stalin occupies a full four chapters, but the "gifted" host, and the plight of his invaded country, failed to make the final cut.

The shah was mortified by his treatment. "Although I was technically host of the conference," he writes in *Answer to History*, "the Big Three paid me little notice. We were after all what the French call a *quantité néglible* in

international affairs and I was a king barely 24 years old." The royal host
was allowed perfunctory audiences with FDR and Churchill, but he managed to have a serious talk with Stalin, who was "polite, well-mannered
and respectful, not even touching his tea before I had mine." One senses
something of the new shah's power-worshipping penchant in his estimate
of the Soviet leader: "However, much as I opposed him and everything he
stood for, the man was a colossus. The great victor of World War II was
neither Churchill nor Roosevelt, for all their eloquence, but Stalin. He
pulled the strings at Tehran, Yalta, and Potsdam, and he imposed a Soviet
peace on the world that has lasted thirty-five years." A decade after this was
written, the Soviet Union, like the shah's throne, became a historical expression.

As WORLD WAR II ended in August 1945, northern Iran fell on the
periphery, out of Allied sight but very much on Joseph Stalin's
mind. No thread of continuity was more durable in Soviet foreign policy
than its leader's determination to repossess every sliver of territory once
ruled by the tsar. Stalin's revolutionary career had begun in the oil fields
of Baku, where he tried to unionize oil workers. He knew the geography
of inner Asia like the back of his left hand, and he well understood the
strategic importance of oil—Hitler's assault on the Russians failed in part
because his Panzers failed to reach Soviet oil fields. Stalin also believed
northern Iran properly belonged in Russia's sphere, as provided in the
1907 Anglo-Russian Convention.

Hence the crisis over Iran that heralded the Cold War. In the Tehran
Declaration, Stalin, Churchill and FDR reaffirmed Iranian independence,
sovereignty and territorial integrity, and the Soviet Union and Great
Britain duly agreed to withdraw all their forces by March 1, 1946. As the
deadline neared, the Soviets began arming a separatist Azerbaijani movement in northern Iran, while their forces barred Iranian troops from entering the area. In Washington, Acting Secretary of State Dean Acheson
understood that America had little military leverage but ample moral authority. In December 1945, he met with the Iranian ambassador, Hussein
Ala, who told him that "Iran had more confidence in the United States
than Great Britain. Ala feared that London might cut a deal with Moscow
to split Iran into two spheres of influence." Acheson chose to respond

firmly while avoiding ultimatums and leaving the Soviets "a graceful way out." He cabled Moscow demanding its reasons for moving more troops into northern Iran; he warned of serious international complications and urged the Soviets to work out a deal with the Iranians: the honorable exit. His tactics succeeded. With a nudge from the newborn United Nations, and after Iran's promise of a possible oil concession (which never materialized), all Soviet troops withdrew by May.

The episode heightened Iranian hopes that America was different from the hated Big Two. Older Persians remembered W. Morgan Shuster's defense of their nationhood in 1911 and recalled that at Paris Woodrow Wilson supported Persia's request (denied) to address the peace conference. The more sophisticated understood that the United States had strategic ambitions in the Persian Gulf, dating from 1933, when Saudi Arabia awarded a sixty-year concession to the California Arabian Standard Oil Company, later reborn as Arabian American Oil Company, or Aramco. In the wartime year of 1944, Aramco's output reached 1,050,000 tons, compared with Iran's 13,270,000 tons. That same year, U.S. oilmen were scrambling for concessions in Tehran, their way smoothed by two petroleum geologists, A. A. Curtice and Herbert Hoover Jr., who had been employed as consultants by the government. Yet there was nothing inherently offensive in this courtship.

The postwar aura of goodwill toward America shone even brighter after the Iranian parliament in 1951 vented years of pent-up anger and voted to nationalize the Anglo-Iranian Oil Company. Even the shah approved, later telling the British author Anthony Sampson, "We were an independent country, and then all of a sudden the Russians invaded our country and you British took my father into exile. Then we were hearing that the oil company was creating puppets—people just clicking their heels to the orders of the oil company—so it was becoming in our eyes a kind of a monster—almost a government within the Iranian government." Thus to wide applause the shah named nationalization's chief proponent, Mohammad Mossadeq, as prime minister. Mossadeq (1880–1967), a wealthy landowner whose kin had served the Qajars, was also a Europeanized liberal and fiery veteran of the constitutional revolution. Skinny as a stork, suffering from ulcers, given to outbursts of passion and tears, he led the National Front, a coalition of the disgruntled: secular, tribal and religious. The old lion's fiercest enemies were on the left. Mobs organized by the Tudeh, or Iranian Communist Party, assailed him as a capitalist tool, while Britain's Labor government began to debate armed intervention. "If Persia were allowed to get away with it," warned Defense Minister Emmanuel Shinwell, "Egypt and other Middle Eastern countries would be encouraged to think they could try things on. The next thing might be an attempt to nationalize the Suez Canal."

The British closed down Abadan, imposed a trade blockade on Iran and tried to coax the United States into moving directly against Mossadeq. This elicited a firm rejection from President Truman and Secretary Acheson, who had met with Mossadeq and leaned to his side; they sought instead to mediate. But talks with "Old Mossy" proved fruitless, as did a special mission to Tehran by Averell Harriman. The fault was not entirely Britain's. Like other populists, Mossadeq excelled at attack but drew back from articulating difficult truths to his own supporters. As the space for accommodation narrowed, the British Foreign Office cast about for a radical remedy. The first spark came with the publication of an unsigned article in the *Times* of London on March 22, 1951. Written by Professor Ann Katherine Swynford Lambton, a reader in Persian at the School of Oriental and African Studies in London, it deplored Iran's instability and "the stupidity, greed and lack of judgement of the ruling classes of Persia."

This touched a nerve at the Foreign Office and led to a meeting with Professor Lambton at which she suggested changing governments by "covert means." She added that Robin Zaehner, a lecturer on Persian at Oxford, would be "the ideal man" to devise the means. "With his 'pebble glasses, squeaky voice and mad professor eccentricities,' Zaehner, a scholar and linguist, was an unlikely intelligence operative," writes the British scholar Stephen Dorril in *MI6*, a history of the Secret Intelligence Service, to which the present account is indebted. Once in Tehran, Zaehner quickly organized a network of Mossadeq haters and native Anglophiles, a special prize being the three Rashidian brothers, a banker, cinema owner and political fixer. Helping out was Anglo-Iranian's own intelligence service, the Central Information Bureau, with its extensive press contacts, its expertise in bribery and its links to the politically potent Bakhtiari tribe, now cut off from the company's subsidies.

At the British intelligence service, meantime, a new and distinguished station chief took over in Tehran, C. M. Woodhouse. During the late war he had been the colonel commanding the Allied Military Mission to the guerrillas in German-occupied Greece, and later he represented Oxford as a member of Parliament. Monty Woodhouse made his headquarters at the British embassy compound, with its patchy lawns within a walled site as big as sixteen city blocks. The necessary break occurred when Winston Churchill returned to power as prime minister in October 1951 and Dwight Eisenhower was elected president of the United States in the following year. The British approached their American cousins afresh. "When we knew what the [new team's] prejudices were," Woodhouse acknowledged, "we played all the more on those prejudices." He therefore decided "to emphasize the Communist threat to Iran rather than the need to recover control of the oil industry. I argued that even if a settlement of the oil dispute could be negotiated with Mossadeq, which was doubtful, he was still incapable of resisting a coup by the Tudeh Party if it were backed by Soviet support. Therefore he must be removed."

This fell on attentive ears in Washington. The new secretary of state, John Foster Dulles, and his younger brother Allen W. Dulles, the director of Central Intelligence, were not only fully cognizant of the Soviet threat, but they also happened to be partners in the law firm of Sullivan and Cromwell, which represented Anglo-Iranian. Allen Dulles had earned his intelligence spurs serving in Berne with the Office of Strategic Services (OSS). After the war, he helped create the CIA, recruiting the best men from elite schools, much on the British model. A star recruit was Kermit (Kim) Roosevelt, a grandson of Theodore Roosevelt, also an OSS veteran and later head of the agency's Middle East Division, based in Cairo. On June 23, 1953, Roosevelt was back in Washington with a twenty-two-page scenario for what came to be called Operation Ajax, drawing on a British draft as revised by Donald Wilber, the architectural historian and the agency's man in Iran. A full-dress meeting was arranged in Secretary Dulles's office to discuss the plan. Those attending besides the Dulles brothers included (according to Roosevelt) Loy Henderson, the U.S. ambassador in Tehran; Secretary of Defense Charles Wilson; Undersecretary of State General Walter (Beedle) Smith; Robert Bowie, director of the State Department policy planning staff; Henry Byroade, assistant secretary of state for the Near East, Africa and South Asia; and Robert D. Murphy, deputy undersecretary of state for political affairs—a who's who of the Cold War pantheon. Ajax was approved, and if Roosevelt's memoir is to be credited, as the meeting adjourned, John Foster Dulles looked around the room and said, "So this is how we get rid of that madman Mossadeq!"

The plot had fast-forwarded by the time Roosevelt arrived in Tehran on July 19. A successor to Mossadeq had been auditioned by the British and found worthy. He was General Fazlollah Zahedi, a devoted royalist who had served with the shah's father in the Cossack Brigade. To be sure, he had been arrested by the British in 1942 for his pro-Axis proclivities and had kept order with nightstick rigor during his years as Tehran's chief of police. This was offset by the usefulness of Zahedi's son, Ardeshir, who had attended college in Salt Lake City and served as liaison with British and American intelligence services. (Ardeshir would later become the shah's free-spending ambassador in Washington.)

Up to this point, Roosevelt had not yet conferred with the shah. A timely interlocutor materialized: Colonel H. Norman Schwarzkopf, the father of the Gulf War commander, who had overseen the Shah's Imperial Iranian Gendarmerie from 1942 to 1948. He was ostensibly stopping in Tehran while flying around the world. But he knew all about Ajax and urged his friend Kim to stop dealing with intermediaries and to treat directly with "H.I.M."—His Imperial Majesty—which Roosevelt did, meeting in time-honored covert fashion, in a parked car. To confirm that he truly represented Eisenhower and Churchill, Roosevelt informed H.I.M. that by arrangement the BBC announcer the following evening would say, "It is now *exactly* midnight," instead of the usual "It is now midnight." At their next meeting, the shah said, "I take it that your principals agree with my choice of Fazlollah Zahedi to replace Mossadegh as prime minister," to which Roosevelt said yes, and the wheels were locked in place.

In London, it happened by chance, Foreign Secretary Anthony Eden had fallen ill, and Prime Minister Churchill temporarily assumed his duties. Thus Britain's old lion gave final approval to what the British called Operation Boot. From the Foreign Office, Churchill urged the shah to dismiss Mossadeq and offered instructions on how to do it. His message, unearthed and published by the British writer William Shawcross in *The Shah's Last Ride*, deserves full quotation: "I should be glad if Mr. Henderson, U.S.A., would transmit to the Shah the following observation of a general character which I believe is correct and in accordance with democratic principles. Begins. It is the duty of a constitutional monarch or President when faced with violent tyrannical action by individuals or a minority party to take the necessary steps to secure the well-being of the toiling masses and the continuity of an ordered state. Ends."

Thus instructed, His Imperial Majesty did his part on August 16, sacking Mossadeq and naming Zahedi as prime minister. But alerted by an informant, Mossadeq ignored the shah and arrested his messenger. On the streets National Front and Tudeh Party demonstrators joined in shouting "Yankees go home!" Unsure how the army would react, the shah lost his nerve; he and Empress Soraya fled in a light plane to Baghdad, where his fellow monarch King Faisal proved less than welcoming, and then on to Rome. In London, even Churchill wavered. In Washington, gloom pervaded the quonset huts where the CIA was temporarily quartered. This was Kermit Roosevelt's moment. Working with Woodhouse and the Rashidian brothers, and benefiting from Wilber's extensive contacts, he dipped into the agency's slush fund ($100,000 or more; estimates differ) and flooded the streets with rented counterdemonstrators. With the outcome still in doubt, Roosevelt took to playing the song "Luck Be a Lady Tonight" from *Guys and Dolls* over and again on his phonograph.

WHAT TURNED THE tide wasn't luck but careful planning and necessary slush funds. Prime Minister Mossadeq and his supporters were out-organized, outspent and outfoxed. Tehran's streets were dominated by hired gymnasts turning handsprings, gangs of youths passing out ten-riyal notes and a supporting cast that shouted in unison the name of Mohammad Reza Shah. As army support wavered, the coup triumphed. On August 19 an excited Associated Press reporter handed the shah a news flash reading "Mossadeq overthrown. Imperial troops control Tehran. Zahedi Premier." In his suite at Rome's Excelsior Hotel, the shah's face went white and he declared, "I knew that they loved me." After his victorious return to Tehran, the shah effusively thanked Roosevelt, saying, "I owe my throne to God, my people, my army—and to you!" Roosevelt quickly adds in his account, "He meant me *and* the two countries— Great Britain and the United States—I was representing. We were all heroes."

Skeptics noted that after the coup, the first official U.S. visitor to Tehran was the oil expert Herbert Hoover Jr., the son of the former president. As Secretary Dulles's special representative, he was to negotiate, as per a prior understanding with Britain, a new oil consortium agreement that would open Iran to American companies. Purportedly, the shah told Hoover that any favor the CIA had done for him would be paid for in oil. After arduous negotiations, assisted by the Dulles brothers' law firm, a new agreement emerged that marked a change in oil diplomacy. Chastened by Mexico's nationalization of oil and pressed by a Truman-initiated Justice Department antitrust suit against the international petroleum cartel, the big oil companies showed a more prudent regard for local sensibilities. Under the arrangement, Iran would own all the country's oil resources, yet it would not interfere in the decisions of independent operating companies, with Anglo-Iranian qualifying for 40 percent of the consortium, Shell 14 percent, each of five major U.S. companies 8 percent and a French company 6 percent. Later, a "little consortium" was added, giving aggrieved smaller American companies a share of the pie. In Daniel Yergin's view, set forth in his history of the oil business from which these details are taken, there was a bigger bottom line: "With the establishment of the Iranian consortium, the United States was now *the* major player in the oil, and the volatile politics, of the Middle East." As if to underscore its succession to Britain's role in Iran, Washington expeditiously advanced loans it had refused to Mossadeq: $60 million in 1954, $53 million in 1955 and $35 million in 1956.

As for Mossadeq, his supporters were jailed, his foreign minister executed, and the deposed firebrand tried for his alleged political crimes. But "the Old Bugger" (his CIA code name) turned the tables by using his trial to make the best and most eloquent case for his doomed administration. He was found guilty, imprisoned for three years, and kept under house arrest at his ancestral estate until his death in 1967. In *Daughter of Persia,* Sattareh Farman Farmaian offers this tribute, noting that he was falsely portrayed in the press as half mad: "Mohammed Mossadegh, I knew, had lost neither his sanity nor his dignity; and it was the American press that was indecent. He had represented a true mobilization of our national will. His twenty-eight months in office had been one of the few times Persians had ever cooperated and achieved something together. He had been obstinate, made many mistakes, and once even resorted to unconstitutional trickery. But he had not failed because of the way he looked, or because of his eccentricities and mannerisms. He had failed because he struggled too hard and too uncompromisingly against a superpower."

Having recovered his throne, Mohammad Reza Pahlavi seemed a different sovereign. His previous uncertainty gave way to certitude, his shyness to love of limelight, his deference to boldness. He rejoiced when his third wife, Farah, produced the essential male heir; always self-conscious about his height, he now wore elevator shoes as well as a chestful of medals on state occasions. In 1967, on his forty-eighth birthday, he formally crowned himself king of kings in a fete featuring a 101-gun salute, a coronation hymn ("You Are the Shadow of God") and a citywide shower of 17,532 roses for each day of his life, scattered over Tehran by the Royal Iranian Air Force. The shah broke with tradition by also crowning Empress Farah with bejeweled headgear designed by Van Cleef and Arpels. He appeared more certain than ever that he was destiny's child, having survived assassination attempts, British guile and Soviet efforts to dismember Iran.

This was followed in 1971 by an even more stupendous gala at Persepolis, the ancient seat of the Achaemenian god-kings, to mark the supposed 2,500th anniversary of the founding of the Persian empire, at a cost of more than $100 million. Here the shah's youthful tastes, developed at La Rosey, the exclusive Swiss boarding school he had attended, came to the fore. Despite widespread drought that year in Iran, notwithstanding student protests and the prudent misgivings expressed by Empress Farah, fifty tents designed by Jansen of Paris bloomed at Persepolis to accommodate as many dignitaries, whose lavish meals were prepared by chefs from Maxim's and washed down by 25,000 bottles of French wine. "The Shah of Iran established himself tonight as one of the world's great party givers," reported Charlotte Curtis in the *New York Times*. "For sheer grandeur, his gala in a silk tent will be hard for any nation to surpass." The shah himself set the tone, with this coda to the welcoming address to his guests, including the emperor of Japan and nine other monarchs: "Sleep easily, Cyrus, for we are awake!"

In a further bold gesture, the shah in 1976 decreed that the traditional Islamic calendar be supplanted by the Pahlavi calendar, its first year marking the putative foundation of Persian kingship. This move was directed expressly at the Shiite clergy, with whom the shah had quarreled since 1963, the year the land reforms in his much touted "White Revolution" began to take effect. Faced with clerical criticism at that time, the shah angrily dismissed objections by "lice-ridden mullahs," whereupon Islamic anger swelled, notably in the religious center of Qum, where Ayatollah Ruhollah Khomeini first attracted attention with his wrathful attack on the shah. Khomeini's jeremiad at Qum's Great Mosque all but invited arrest:

Let me give you some advice, Mr. Shah! Dear Mr. Shah, I advise you to desist. . . . I don't want the people to offer up thanks if your [for-

eign] masters should decide one day that you must leave. I don't
want you to become like your father. . . . During World War II the
Soviet Union, Britain and America invaded Iran and occupied our
country. The property of the people was exposed and their honor
was imperiled. But God knows, everyone was happy the Pahlavi had
gone! . . . Don't you know that if one day some uproar occurs and
the tables are turned, none of these people around you will be your
friends.

Widespread riots followed the sermon and led to the ayatollah's arrest, conviction and imprisonment until his release nine months later.
Soon after Khomeini's release, President Lyndon Johnson offered the shah
U.S. military advisers and a credit line of $200 million for weapons, pro-
viding Iran adopted the Status of Forces Agreement (SOFA) giving American personnel immunity from local laws. The SOFA measure was
rubber-stamped by the Majlis, now a caricature of its former self, its two
parties having earned the popular nicknames "Yes" and "Yes, Sir." There
followed this thunderclap from Qum:

> Does the Iranian nation know what has happened in recent days in
> the Assembly? Does it know what crime has occurred surrepti-
> tiously? . . . Does it know that the Assembly, at the initiative of the
> government, has signed a document for the enslavement of Iran? It
> has acknowledged Iran is a colony, it has given America a document
> attesting that a nation of Muslims is barbarous, it has struck out all
> our Islamic and national glories with a black line. . . . If the Shah
> should run over an American dog, he would be called to account but
> if an American cook should run over the Shah, no one has any claims
> against him. . . . I proclaim that this shameful vote of the Majlis is in
> contradiction to Islam and has no legality. . . . If the foreigners wish
> to misuse this filthy vote, the nation's duty will be clearly specified.

For this, Ayatollah Khomeini was banished, finding asylum first in
Turkey, then in Iraq and finally in France before his tumultuous return in
February 1979. His jeremiad against the Status of Forces Agreement crystallized outrage over America's indirect dominion and stoked the fires of
retribution.

STILL, *pace* the ayatollah, the shah was nobody's tool; his greatest follies were self-generated. Having launched his "White Revolution," he called his next Iranian project the "Great Civilization," a process whereby Iran would leapfrog into the modern era. The propellant would be oil, whose price soared dramatically as a result of the oil embargo that followed the Yom Kippur War in October 1973. The price of oil quadrupled within two months, meaning that Iran's yearly petroleum revenues of $5 billion could potentially rise to $20 billion. At a news conference in Tehran in late December, the Polish journalist Ryszard Kapuscinski was struck by the shah's excitement as he talked grandly about Iran's becoming the world's fifth greatest power. A few days later, in an interview with the German news magazine *Der Spiegel*, the shah was still in thrall. "In ten years we will have the same living standard that you Germans, French and English have now," he said.

So Iran plunged forward, and billions were lavished on imports. Kapuscinski describes what happened when ships full of merchandise began steaming toward Iran:

> When they reach the Gulf, it turns out that the small obsolete ports are unable to handle such a mass of cargo (the Shah hadn't realized this). Several hundred ships line up at sea and stay there for up to six months, for which delay Iran pays the shipping companies a billion dollars annually. Somehow the ships are gradually unloaded, but then it turns out there are no warehouses (the Shah hadn't realized). In the open air, in the desert, in the nightmarish tropical heat, lie millions of tons of all sorts of cargo. Half of it, consisting of perishable foodstuffs and chemicals, ends up being thrown away. The remaining cargo has to be transported into the depth of the country, and at this moment it turns out there is no transport (the Shah hadn't realized). . . . Two thousand tractor-trailers are thus ordered from Europe, but then it turns out there are no drivers (the Shah hadn't realized). . . . The trucks, unused to this day, still sit, covered with sand, along the Bandar Abbas–Tehran highway.

The bungling culminated in the tardy discovery that Iran lacked sufficient technicians to assemble the factories and the machinery, which eventually reached their interior destination (the shah didn't realize).

Of all the imports, the most costly were high-tech American weapons.

The shah's appetite for military hardware, whetted by the Johnson administration, became voracious during the Nixon-Ford years, partly owing to the monarch's friendship with Secretary of State Henry Kissinger. A grand strategic vision had mutual appeal: Let Iran assume guardianship of the Persian Gulf, thereby easing Washington's military burdens in the region, in return for American arms and training expertise. Despite Pentagon misgivings, the shah was given unrestricted access to the most advanced U.S. arms, excluding nuclear weapons.

From 1972 to 1976, Iran spent $4 billion on American military equipment, making it Washington's leading foreign customer. When the Democrats took over the White House in 1977, the strategic partnership continued to prosper under Jimmy Carter. In his meetings with the shah, the president pressed for moderating oil prices and broadening human rights, which the shah interpreted as a swap—join the Saudis in restraining price hikes, keep buying arms and expect a waiver on human rights. Yet even as the two leaders met in the Oval Office in November 1977, Washington police fired tear gas at clashing Iranian demonstrators on the nearby Ellipse; clouds of the stuff drifted above Carter and the shah as they posed for cameras in the Rose Garden.

Ineluctably, the demonstrations spread to Iran, in defiance of the hated Savak (the Shah's omnipresent secret police) and his huge military establishment. A thousand grievances—the inequities of a boom economy, the insolence of Westerners in their compounds, the affronts of bizarre female fashions and infidel missionaries—welded a coalition of the dispossessed and disenchanted, of secular radicals and theocratic reformers. The bubble burst in January 1979, when the armed forces mutinied and the shah once again fled his country. On February 1, an Air France jetliner bearing Ayatollah Khomeini landed in Tehran.

Also on the plane was a press party including Elaine Sciolino, then a *Newsweek* correspondent based in Paris. Years later, she learned that the shah's generals, including the commander of the air force, had prepared a plan to shoot down Khomeini's plane. They put their proposal to Zbigniew Brzezinski, the national security adviser, who took it to the president. Brzezinski told Sciolino that Jimmy Carter would have nothing to do with it. Did that mean the Carter administration rejected the idea of letting the Iranians do it on their own? There was nothing to stop them, Brzezinski went on, yet one of the problems with Iranians "is that they often talked more than they did anything." Was the presence of Western journalists, among them ABC's Peter Jennings, a factor? "The issue simply didn't arise," was Brzezinski's frosty reply.

Sciolino's strange story, which she relates in her book, *Persian Mirrors*, attests to the perils of this misalliance. For the shah's generals, there was no impropriety in asking for White House permission to carry out an act of terrorism by slaying an entire planeload of civilians to kill a venerated Muslim cleric. Had the deed been executed, imagine the reaction after someone talked, as someone would have, and it transpired that the United States had been an accessory, or appeared to be an accessory, to an ineffaceable affront to Islam, Iran and American values?

Instead, the ayatollah landed, kissed the ground, and Iran's Islamic revolution began.

FOR ALL HIS austerely spiritual demeanor, the ayatollah soon evinced a ruthless craftiness and an absolutist temper, with tragic consequences. Having dissembled and outwitted the secular leftists who came with him from Paris, he loosed a reign of virtue and terror that claimed many of their lives. His regime's police proved bloodier and crueler than the shah's. His wrath was aimed at dissidents of every stripe, including adherents of Baha'i, a religion notable for its esteem of learning and advocacy of human rights but deemed a heretical offshoot of Islam. More than a million lives were lost in the eight-year Iran-Iraq war that the Islamic Republic was unable to win or shorten. It was started in 1980 by the Iraqi leader Saddam Hussein, who feared Iran would make common cause with his own oppressed Shiite majority. When mutual exhaustion led to an armistice in 1988, the ayatollah spoke of peace as a "poisoned chalice." He then changed the subject by issuing a fatwa calling for the murder of a British author, the Indian-born Salman Rushdie, who had "defamed" Islam in his novel *The Satanic Verses*. After Khomeini's death in 1989, his clerical heirs veered from absolutism to grudging concessions to a young, restless and unhappy majority in an inconclusive struggle that continues as of this writing.

In its region, Iran has limited powers as a leader but considerable leverage as a spoiler. Its collaboration is essential on urgent matters—the legal status of the Caspian Sea, the stability of Afghanistan, an Israeli-Arab accord, Gulf energy politics and the future of Iraq. In my view a necessary

precondition for a thaw in Washington's relations with Iran is a mutual acknowledgment of wrongs perpetrated by both countries, by the United
States in lawlessly promoting the 1953 coup and by Iran in its no less law-
less detention of American hostages in 1979–1981. A precondition to the
precondition is a greater American awareness of Iran's recent past.

That past has been ill served by American journalism. Seemingly, not
a single U.S. newspaper at the time examined critically the covert sources
of the 1953 coup. It was only years later that the CIA's role became
known. Timid and protective reportage predominated in the succeeding
decades. The shah was lauded in print and on the television screen, as
shown in a year-by-year scrutiny undertaken by William A. Dorman, a
professor of journalism at California State University, and Mansour
Fahrang, revolutionary Iran's first envoy to the United Nations, who resigned during the hostage crisis. The authors single out a few exceptions,
most notably a 1974 article for *Harper's* magazine by Frances FitzGerald,
titled "Giving the Shah Everything He Wants."

Yet fallible messengers are not the chief culprit in America's troubled
relations with Iran. The underlying blame rests on the tendency of successive administrations, Democratic and Republican, to treat an ancient
and resentful country as if it were a satrapy, employing the methods of indirect rule long practiced in the Caribbean and Central America. The relationship found its galling symbol in the virtual cantonments inhabited
by U.S. military and civilian personnel, who were immune to local laws.
In Iranian eyes, for over a generation, Americans exercised power without
responsibility, in the process dissipating a heritage of goodwill by seeming
to prove that Washington was little different from London or Moscow. It
is instructive (if unflattering) that America's stock in Iran has recovered,
indeed has touched new highs, at a time when America's physical presence is to all intents null.

IV

PAKISTAN

Sins of Partition

In regal ermine and with enviable aplomb, Viceroy Lord Louis Mount-batten and his lovely Vicereine, Lady Edwina, pose for posterity, summer 1947, before they departed newly sovereign India. It was certainly not "Dickie" Mountbatten's intention that as many as a million former British subjects might perish as a result of India's partition. But perish they did.   *Photo courtesy Corbis.*

W E HAVE LEARNED at cruel cost that nations are not born but made. Recent scholarship has shown how myths and modern fabrications fertilize the taproots of even the proudest and oldest nations. Thus the British perennially look back to the notional reign of King Arthur. By a useful coincidence, the first English printer, William Caxton, published Malory's *Morte d'Arthur* in 1485, the very year the War of the Roses ended in victory for Henry Tudor, who claimed kinship with Britain's fabled monarch. As King Henry VII, he saw to it that his heir, also named Arthur, was baptized in 1486 at Winchester, which Sir Thomas Malory had identified as the site of Camelot. Prince Arthur, however, never ascended the throne, dying of consumption at the age of fifteen. His brother, Henry VIII, forged his own legendary reign, but he also harked back to Camelot. In 1522 Henry showed the visiting Emperor Charles V the thick oaken table, complete with place names, that was said to be the actual Round Table. Genuine or not, it still hangs in Winchester Castle. Yet curiously, the most heartfelt Arthurian revival coincided with the Victorian and Edwardian heyday of the British empire. These were the decades when Tennyson wrote his *Idylls of the King*, and when infatuation with chivalry pervaded schoolrooms and the newborn Boy Scouts. This was when Britain's viceroy, Lord Edward Lytton, proclaimed Victoria empress of India in 1876 at an assembly in Delhi that evoked Camelot with tents, shining lances and silken banners designed by Lockwood Kipling, Rudyard's father. In the empire's late afternoon, the governing elite formed an exclusive study group called the Round Table, which was also the name of its journal. Its leading light was Prime Minister Balfour, known half jokingly as "King Arthur."

But only half jokingly. Winston Churchill reflected the mood in a rhapsody about Camelot in his *History of the English-Speaking Peoples*: "It is all true, or it ought to be, and more and better besides. And wherever men are fighting barbarism, tyranny and massacre, for freedom, law and order, let them remember that the fame of their deeds, even though they themselves be exterminated, may perhaps be celebrated as long as the world rolls round." What took centuries on the British Isles happened figuratively overnight in the New World. On June 7, 1776, the Continental Congress resolved that "these United Colonies" ought to be free and independent. On July 4, less than a month later, Jefferson's pen magically changed the name to "the Thirteen United States of America." Not long after the Treaty of Paris formally ended hostilities in 1783, Americans had contrived the half-mythical ingredients of nationhood: Old Glory, "Yankee Doodle," Paul Revere's ride, Valley Forge, Betsy Ross, the Boston Tea Party, Nathan Hale, and Washington crossing the Delaware (later imagined with nautically improbable details by a German artist an ocean away). By 1800 the consolidation of American national identity was complete. What made this possible was an exceptional skein of circumstances—a gifted generation of rebels, British preoccupation with France, the swift adoption of an elastic federal system, and George Washington's decision to retire after two terms as president, thereby sparing Americans a senescent liberator-for-life.

This occurred in the innocent, prelapsarian era, before nation makers added the toxic ingredients of ethnicity and religion. During the late eighteenth century, beginning with the philosopher Johann Gottfried von Herder and other precursors to German nationalism, the idea ripened that nations derived from a deeper unity of language, blood and culture. Soon enough, linguistic and archaeological discoveries lent the simulacrum of science to theories of an exalted Aryan superrace, one of its symbols being the swastika. Nobody expressed the notion with more energy and eloquence than the French diplomat and author Comte Joseph-Arthur de Gobineau (1810–1882), who believed that the Nordic branch of the Aryan race was destined to rule the world. A fluent writer and indefatigable traveler, Gobineau had served as France's envoy to Persia, where besides spinning folkloric Oriental tales, he acquired the gloss of learning for his long work *Essai sur l'inégalité des races humaines* (1853–1855). Alexis de Tocqueville, who valued Gobineau as a friend but rejected his racial theories, feared the worst once his *Essai* found readers in Germany. As Tocqueville warned in 1856, "I think your book is fated to return to France from abroad, especially from Germany. Alone in Europe, the Germans possess the particular talent of becoming impassioned with what they take as abstract truths, without considering their practical consequences; they may furnish you with a truly favorable audience whose opinions will sooner or later re-echo in France, for nowadays the whole civilized world has become one."

An ocean of blood has since been spilled for what Tocqueville recognized as a dangerous and specious doctrine. Indeed, all the world's nations are in varying degrees "imagined communities," in the inspired phrase of Cornell University's Benedict Anderson. None of the four "commons" deemed essential to nationhood—common ethnicity, language, territory and religion—are in fact essential. A major language, it has been aptly said, is a dialect with an army behind it. Thus the Holy Roman Empire, the supposed matrix for a reborn Germany, was three-fourths non-German speaking, while in Prussia at least five languages were spoken besides German: Polish, Lithuanian, Estonian, Sorbish and Dutch. As Patrick Geary recounts in *The Myth of Nations*, at most only half the French population in 1900 spoke standard French as a native language. The rest first learned Celtic, Germanic and Romance dialects. "Across Europe," Geary writes, "the pernicious effects of the philological method of identifying people by language were myriad. First, the infinite gradations of broad linguistic groups in Europe were chopped up by scientific rules into separate languages. Since the spoken and written realities never corresponded exactly to these artificial rules, 'official' forms—usually systemized versions of a local dialect, often of a politically powerful group or important city— were invented and imposed through state-sponsored education systems. . . . Not surprisingly, proponents of these 'standard' languages tended initially to ascribe them to real or desired political boundaries."

The test of ethnicity is equally fallible. The foreign affairs columnist William Pfaff reminds us in *The Wrath of Nations* that the British monarchy's present incumbents are by blood German, before that Dutch, and before that Scottish. Pfaff adds, "There has been no 'English' king since the eleventh century." With this in mind, Daniel Defoe wrote "The True-born Englishman" (1701) to counter prejudice against kings of foreign origin. After itemizing Europe's long caravan of invading and conquering peoples, Defoe remarks of "that heterogeneous thing, an Englishman":

In eager rapes and furious lust begot,
Betwixt a painted *Briton* and a *Scot:*
Whose gendering offspring quickly learned to bow,
And yoke their heifers to a *Roman* plough;
From whence a mongrel half-bred race there came,
With neither name nor nation, speech nor fame,
In whose hot veins new mixtures ran,

Infused betwixt a *Saxon* and a *Dane;*
While their rank daughters, to their parents just,
This nauseous brood directly did contain
The well-extracted blood of Englishmen . . .

Precisely because of this prevalent heterogeneity, nation makers turned to other devices to bond and inspire. Experience confirmed the efficacy of symbolic extrusions of statehood (e.g., flags, anthems, uniforms, passports, medals, national museums, Olympic teams). Their emotional impact was articulated by the Austrian-born Theodor Herzl (1860–1904), the founder of modern Zionism. Herzl had the especially difficult task of persuading a widely dispersed people to reestablish a wholly defunct state. In a letter unearthed by his Israeli biographer Amos Elon, Herzl in 1895 spoke enthusiastically about designing a flag: "You might ask mockingly:'A flag? What's that? A stick with a rag on it?' No sir, a flag is much more. With a flag you lead men . . . for a flag, men live and die. In fact it is the only thing for which they are ready to die in masses, if you train them for it. Believe me, the politics of an entire people—especially a people scattered all over the earth—can be manipulated only through imponderables that float in thin air. Do you know what went into the making of the German Empire? Dreams and songs, reveries of black, red, and gold banners, all in a very short time. Bismarck merely shook the tree that the visionaries had planted."

If symbols fail, there remains the appeal to hatred, prejudice and primal blood lust, achieved by assailing a common enemy or a vulnerable internal minority, preferably of a different religion. The results can be found throughout Asia: southward from the Caucasus to Sri Lanka, eastward from the Persian Gulf to the remote borderlands of China. In the pages that follow, we focus on Pakistan, Afghanistan and the five former Soviet republics of Central Asia. Put at its simplest, the story goes like this.

At the heart of the region's disorder is Pakistan, whose rise arguably constitutes the most grievous failure of Britain's colonial unraveling. Pakistan is the archetypal imagined community, an offspring of precipitate partition. Its frontiers are porous, its polyglot population exceptionally diverse. Its chief claim to unity is Islam, on which its authoritarian rulers have relied, inordinately. This has contributed to three wars and a nuclear confrontation with India, chiefly arising from an unresolved dispute over Kashmir, as well as the cesarean birth of Bangladesh in 1971. A melancholy casualty has been the Red Shirts, a nonviolent, democratic, and secular liberation movement that once dominated the Pashtun areas on Pakistan's North-West Frontier. There occurred a recent and depressing sequel, the election in October 2002 of an Islamic religious alliance whose radical leaders vowed to expel the American military from the province, whose border areas shelter Al Qaeda chieftains who escaped from Afghanistan. On taking office, new members of the provincial assembly set the tone by pausing to pray for Mir Aimal Kasi, the Pakistani who had just been executed in America for killing two CIA employees in 1993 at the agency's main entrance in Langley, Virginia.

W HERE DID IT all begin? My own sense is that it originated in a misbegotten faith in partition among imperial rulers and their diverse subjects. Dividing the body politic has repeatedly served as a fatal means of obtaining short-term relief. Outwardly, partition seems a pragmatic way of splitting the difference, thereby honoring the principle of self-determination and separating antagonistic peoples. Yet on closer inquiry, with rare exceptions, the postcolonial and post-Communist division of countries into separate states has uprooted millions of people, fomented internecine wars, degraded the citizenship of trapped minorities and perpetuated ancient grievances, closing both minds and frontiers. Give or take a little, this has been true of Pakistan, Kashmir, Ireland, Palestine and Cyprus, as well as, most recently, former Yugoslavia. That the United States should condone or encourage partition seems especially ironic, since Americans fought a civil war to preserve a federal union that remains a beacon for others.

The unintended consequences of territorial surgery were evident for all to see after the first contentious partition of the imperial age. In 1905, during Lord Curzon's final, troubled year as viceroy of India, he won London's approval for slicing Bengal into two provinces: East Bengal, comprising 18 million Muslims and 12 million Hindus, and West Bengal, whose 47 million inhabitants were overwhelmingly Hindu. The purpose, Curzon insisted over and again, was simply administrative efficiency—Bengal had grown too populous—yet his own advisers were well aware of the political implications. "Bengal united is a power," one of them counseled. "Bengal divided will pull several ways. That is what the Congress leaders feel; their apprehensions are perfectly correct and they form one of the great merits of the scheme. . . . One of our main objects is to split up and thereby weaken a solid body of opponents to our rule."

Furious protests resulted in West Bengal when the British announced the partition plan in 1903. Hindus saw it as giving needlessly enhanced status to East Bengal, whose peasant inhabitants had converted to Islam to escape their lower-caste status as Hindus (or so many indignantly claimed). Anger was most vehement among leaders of the bar and press in Calcutta, capital of both Bengal and the British Raj. Opponents mounted a mass boycott of British goods (known as the Svadeshi or indigenous products movement), mobilized clamorous rallies, signed enough petitions to fill a landfill and sang patriotic Bengali songs, some written by the future Nobel laureate Rabindranath Tagore. By contrast, in East Bengal, Muslims relished their new empowerment in a territory whose boundaries foreshadowed those of present-day Bangladesh. The Hindu reaction was recalled by the late doyen of Bengal letters, Nirad C. Chaudhuri, in his *Autobiography of an Unknown Indian*: "It was from the end of 1906 that we became conscious of a new kind of hatred for the Muslims, which sprang out of the present and showed signs of poisoning our personal relations with our Muslim neighbours and school-fellows. If the spouting enmity did not go to the length of inducing us to give up all intercourse with them, it made us at all events treat them with a marked decline of civility. We began to hear angry comments in the mouths of our elders that the Muslims were coming out quite openly in favor of partition and on the side of the English."

So impassioned was the protest, and so persevering, that on the occasion of the great Durbar in 1911 celebrating his accession to the throne, George V announced both the rescinding of partition and the transfer of the Raj's capital from Calcutta to Delhi. Yet as the historian Stanley Wolpert has observed, even if Curzon had no obvious political motives for partition, its political aftereffects were monumental: "Svadeshi and boycott, national education and svaraj [self-government], the major planks of India's independence movement, assumed nationwide significance for the first time in the scheme's wake." In his presidential address to the Indian National Congress in December 1905, Gopal Gokhale expressed the mood: "The whole country has been stirred to its deepest depths of sorrow and resentment, as had never been the case before."

No less important, the seeds of India's future division were sown.

THREE PERSISTENT QUESTIONS haunt the founding of Pakistan. Did the British deliberately inspire Hindu-Islamic enmity to divide and rule? Was partition inescapable? Did Britain's precipitate withdrawal from India in 1947 contribute to massacres that claimed hundreds of thousands of lives? Regarding the first question, the British editor and imperial veteran H.V. Hodson offers the standard yet credible rejoinder in his account of the Raj's final months, *The Great Divide*: "It is not possible to divide and rule unless the ruled are ready to be divided. The British may have used the Hindu-Muslim rivalry for their own advantage, but they did not invent it. They did not write the annals of Indian history, nor prescribe the conflicting customs of her communities, nor foment the murderous riots that periodically flared between Hindus and Muslims in her villages and cities. They were realists, and if they did use India's divisions for their advantage, the divisions themselves were already real."

Nonetheless, even if one grants Hodson's point, the jury remains out on the second question. Concerning the third, there is fresh evidence that British haste and surreptitious conniving made a bad outcome worse. Certainly only a decade prior to India's division, partition was but the dream of visionaries. The name "Pakistan," in the consensual version, was coined by a thirty-five-year-old Punjabi Muslim, Choudhary Rahmat Ali, who said he spoke for three other Muslims at Cambridge University. In 1933, Ali published a pamphlet titled *Now or Never* "on behalf of the thirty million Muslims" living in the five northern units of India. Subsequently Ali offered this explanation for his invented acronym: "PAKISTAN is both a Persian and an Urdu word, composed of letters taken from the names of our homelands: that is, Punjab, Afghania (N.-W. Frontier Province), Kashmir, Iran, Sindh, Tukharistan, and Baluchistan. It means the land of the Paks, the spiritually pure and clean."

What gave propulsion to Ali's idea was the widening schism between the Hindu-dominated Indian National Congress and the Muslim League, the twin engines of India's liberation movement. Their alliance cracked after the British Parliament adopted the Government of India Act in 1935. The act established a federal system that granted substantial autonomy to eleven provinces, of which Muslims comprised the majority in four: Bengal, Punjab, Sind and the North-West Frontier Province. When the first elections were held in 1937, Congress ran up majorities in six provinces and became the biggest single party in Assam. The Muslim League, however, lagged badly in four Muslim-majority provinces, owing to factional disputes, Muslim support for the interfaith Unionists in the Punjab and the popularity of the Red Shirts, a movement allied with Congress, in the North-West. Disappointed Muslim Leaguers proposed a compromise: form coalitions in those provinces where they had finished a strong second. But the predominantly Hindu Congress would agree to power sharing only if Muslim Leaguers gave up their separate identity.

"In other words," writes Penderel Moon, formerly of the Indian Civil Service, in his classic account, *Divide and Quit*, "Congress were prepared to share the throne only with Muslims who consented to merge themselves in a predominantly Hindu organization. They offered the League not partnership but absorption. This proved to be a fatal error—the prime cause of the creation of Pakistan—but in the circumstances it was a very natural one. There was nothing in parliamentary tradition requiring Congress on the morrow of victory to enter into a coalition with another party; and a coalition with the League, which the Congress leaders looked upon as a purely communal organization, was particularly distasteful to them."

To Muslim leaders, it seemed a portent of likely humiliation under a "Hindu Raj"—already a popular epithet. Exacerbating political differences were the conflicting personalities of Mohammad Ali Jinnah, the unchallenged head of the Muslim League, and Mohandas K. Gandhi, the unquestioned mentor and conscience of the Indian National Congress. Both were lawyers, and both supported the Allied cause during World War I, in the vain belief that freedom would be India's reward for suffering substantial casualties. Jinnah was born in Karachi, circa 1875, and trained as a barrister in London at Lincoln's Inn. Soon after returning to India in 1896, he made his mark both at the Bombay bar and within the National Congress, becoming renowned as "the ambassador of Hindu-Muslim unity." This itself was unusual. His family belonged to the minority Ismaili community led by the Aga Khan, not to mainstream Sunni Islam. "Anglicized and aloof in manner," Rajmohan Gandhi writes of him, "incapable of oratory in an Indian tongue, keeping his distance from mosques, opposed to the mixing of religion and politics, he yet became inseparable, in that final phase, from the cry of Islam in danger."

Jinnah was a constitutionalist and secularist who shunned advertising his faith on his tailored sleeves. Indeed, his rift with Gandhi after World War I stemmed in part from the Mahatma's turning to *satyagraha*, or nonviolent resistance, using Hindu doctrine to energize mass support and adopting his universally recognized trademarks, the dhoti and spinning wheel. In *The Idea of India,* the Delhi-born historian Sunil Khilnani has succinctly stated Jinnah's own program:"Jinnah saw the Muslims as forming a single community, or 'nation,' but he envisaged an existence for them alongside a 'Hindu nation' within a united, confederal India. The core of his disagreement with Congress concerned the structure of the future state. Jinnah was determined to prevent the creation of a unitary central state with procedures of political representation that threatened to put it in the hands of a numerically dominant religious community. As such, this was a perfectly secular ambition. *But the contingencies of politics and the convenient availability of powerful lines of social difference pushed it in a quite contrary direction.*" (Emphasis added.)

Whatever hope remained for compromise lay in the hands of Britain's last viceroy, Louis, Earl Mountbatten of Burma, great-grandson of Queen Victoria, nephew of the tsar and tsarina of Russia and cousin of King George VI. Empowered by Britain's Labor government with man-on-the-spot discretion to free India, Lord Mountbatten arrived in Delhi in March 1947. By then, the communal breach that developed after the 1937 elections had widened appreciably during World War II, when Gandhi and Congress, unable to obtain unequivocal pledges of independence, launched a provocative "Quit India" campaign. The British responded by jailing thousands of Congress officeholders, to the advantage of the unjailed Muslim Leaguers. Yet it needs stressing that Gandhi was wholly opposed to partition. As he wrote in 1939 to a Muslim correspondent, "Why is India not one nation? Was it not one during, say, the Moghul period? Is India composed of two nations? If so, why only two? Are not Christians a third, Parsis a fourth, and so on? Are the Muslims of China a nation separate from the other Chinese? . . . How are the Muslims of the Punjab different from the Hindus and the Sikhs? Are they not all Punjabis, drinking the same water, breathing the same air and deriving sustenance from the same soil? . . . And what is to happen to the handful of Muslims living in the numerous villages where the population is predominantly Hindu, and conversely to the Hindus where, as in the Frontier Province or Sind, they are a handful? The way suggested by the correspondent is the way of strife."

One reads this with wonder and sympathy. Certainly Gandhi foresaw the calamities ahead more clearly than the pragmatic surgeons of partition. For this he paid with his life; Gandhi had begun a hunger strike protesting communal violence and was planning to visit newborn Pakistan when he was shot mortally in January 1948 by a Hindu fanatic who believed him too partial to Muslims. So who, or what, was responsible for the breakup of India?

As VICEROY, Mountbatten was given broad discretionary authority by Prime Minister Clement Attlee, who also agreed, at his insistence, on a swifter transfer of power than the Labor government envisioned. With minimal deliberation, Mountbatten from the first rejected confederal proposals as unworkable and acceded in principle to partition. Still, even if division was unavoidable, it is difficult to praise its execution. As viceroy, Mountbatten surreptitiously assisted the Hindu side. His method for demarcating frontiers was at best arbitrary, at worst reckless. His timetable for separation left the Indian army on the sidelines when communal slaughters began.

Gandhi and Jinnah emerge with greater credit. In his first meetings with the viceroy, the Mahatma advanced the bold idea of offering Jinnah the prime ministership of India, while providing for a truncated Pakistan within India with the possibility of expansion. In the words of Rajmohan Gandhi, in his fair-minded biography of his grandfather: "No student of this episode can fail to be struck by the exertions of the Viceroy's office against the scheme. The staff, and the Viceroy too, seemed to resist a solution emanating from Gandhi, an encroachment on their prerogative by an unrepentant foe of the Raj." Gandhi's offer was never put to Jinnah, and instead Mountbatten moved pell-mell to partition.

To demarcate frontiers, the viceroy established the Boundary Commission, winning agreement from Jinnah and Jawaharlal Nehru (the Congress leader) on Sir Cyril Radcliffe, a distinguished British barrister, as its chairman. It was a curious choice. As Radcliffe's former private secretary, Christopher Beaumont, later remarked in an interview, the chairman had never traveled east and "was a bit flummoxed by the whole thing. It was a rather impossible assignment, really. To partition that subcontinent in six weeks was absurd." Only when he arrived in India did Radcliffe learn from Mountbatten that he had thirty-six days to draw boundaries that bisected the Punjab and Bengal, dissolving Hindu-Muslim-Sikh communities rooted in centuries of history. Radcliffe was given a pile of maps, figures from a 1943 census, and the assistance of four judges, two Hindus and two Muslims. "They were totally useless," Beaumont recalled. "They simply took the communal line, so he was left on his own."

Radcliffe completed his top-secret labors by August 13, two days before India's freedom was proclaimed at midnight. The morning after independence, writes Stanley Wolpert, the tireless biographer of Gandhi and Nehru as well as Jinnah, the Boundary Commission's awards were revealed, and the celebration gave way to slaughter: "In and around Amritsar bands of armed Sikhs killed every Muslim they could find, while in and around Lahore, Muslim gangs—many of them 'police'—sharpened their knives and emptied their guns at Hindus and Sikhs. Entire trainloads of refugees were gutted and turned into rolling coffins, funeral pyres on wheels, food for bloated vultures who darkened the skies over the Punjab." Partition uprooted more than 10 million people, and estimates of the number slaughtered range from just under 200,000 to at least 1 million. These are estimates; having agreed to the carve-up, its perpetrators had little incentive to reckon its mortal cost.

In 1966, W. H. Auden wrote a twenty-six-line poem, "Partition," that was a judgment on both Viscount Radcliffe (as he became in 1962) and the hasty surgical statecraft he exemplified. It reads in part:

> Unbiased at least he was when he arrived on his mission,
> Having never set eyes on this land he was called to partition
> Between two peoples fanatically at odds,
> With their different diets and incompatible gods . . .
> Shut up in a lonely mansion, with police night and day
> Patrolling the gardens to keep assassins away,
> He got down to work, to the task of settling the fate
> Of millions. The maps at his disposal were out of date
> And the Census Returns almost certainly incorrect,
> But there was no time to check them, no time to inspect
> Contested areas. The weather was frightfully hot,
> And a bout of dysentery kept him constantly on the trot,
> But in seven weeks it was done, the frontiers decided,
> A continent for better or worse divided.

The controversy did not abate with Radcliffe's death in 1977. From the moment of partition, critics challenged the viceroy's avowals that the Boundary Commission operated with total independence, claiming he

had secretly interceded to rig the results in India's favor. Mountbatten's
defenders categorically dispute the accusation. For his part, Radcliffe on
winding up his work destroyed all confidential records, refused thereafter
to discuss the commission's work and never visited India or Pakistan.
There matters stood until 1992, when Christopher Beaumont, Radcliffe's
former aide and the last surviving principal, learned that his grandson had
been given the partition of India as an honors subject at Cambridge University. The onetime private secretary now concluded "that the event had
passed into history, and that the time had come for the truth to be revealed."

Beaumont provided the *Daily Telegraph* with a memorandum he had
prepared many years earlier on the commission's deliberations, an essay
that formed the basis for a detailed article in the staunchly Conservative
paper. He had already entrusted the document to All Souls College at Oxford and had confided its substance to Penderel Moon, also of All Souls
and then completing his history of the Raj. Thus in a very British way,
Beaumont confirmed that frontiers had been secretly redrawn to Pakistan's disadvantage. The most important reversal involved Ferozepore, an
area of some four hundred square miles, important because its canal headwaters controlled the irrigation system in the princely state of Bikaner.
Forewarned by a leak of Ferozepore's award to Pakistan, Nehru joined
with the Maharajah of Bikaner in appealing to the viceroy. After a private
lunch with Mountbatten—Radcliffe's second and last meeting with the
viceroy—the chairman bowed to pressure and altered the Punjab line.
"This episode reflects great discredit on Mountbatten and Nehru," Beaumont's memorandum concluded, "and less on Radcliffe."

P ARTITION AND THE massacres it provoked were part of a conti-
nental-scale upheaval that attended the British withdrawal. When
the Hindu maharajah of predominantly Muslim Kashmir dithered before
choosing accession to India, the Indian army and Pakistani irregulars mo-
mentously clashed in October 1947 under circumstances still disputed
more than a half century later. The harshest words about divide-and-quit
were uttered not by the enemies of the outgoing Raj but by its appalled
indigenous allies. Nirad Chaudhuri spoke for them in *Thy Hand, Great
Anarch!*, the second volume of his autobiography:

By what the British administrators *did* and also what they did *not*, they stultified two hundred years of British rule in India by disregarding two of its highest moral justifications: first, the establishment and maintenance of the unity of India; secondly, the enforcement of *Pax Britannica* to save the lives of Indians. . . . Then an apologia emerged *ex post facto* which is the most shameless sophistry I have read anywhere. It was argued and is still being argued that if the British had not left—the manner of their leaving being conveniently glossed over—there would have been uprisings and therefore loss of life far exceeding what was seen. Now, the conjuring up of hypothetical bogeys which no one can prove or deny is the first defence of every coward who yields at the first sign of trouble.

A further arresting passage from Chaudhuri concerns Jinnah, whose generally negative reputation in the West was mirrored in the Oscar-winning 1982 epic, *Gandhi*. In the film, Jinnah slinks in the shadows wearing an ill-fitting suit, thereby adding sartorial insult to historic injury in a work that skittishly fails even to make clear the Hindu identity of Gandhi's assassin. Chaudhuri expresses the contrary view: "I must set down at this point that Jinnah is the only man who came out with success and honour from the ignoble end of the British Empire in India. He never made a secret of what he wanted, never prevaricated, never compromised, and yet succeeded in inflicting unmitigated defeat on the British Government and the Indian National Congress. He achieved something which not even he could have believed to be within reach in 1946."

The interesting question is what might have happened had Jinnah not been terminally ill. Weighing only seventy pounds, he died of cancer on September 11, 1948, when his creation, Pakistan, was barely a year old. It is hard to believe that Pakistan's *quaid-i-azam* (great leader) would have approved his offspring's glum clerical cast, its support for Islamic zealots in Afghanistan and Kashmir, its oligarchic rule by generals or feudal landlords—and yet all these things were byproducts of Pakistan's violent birth and synthetic nationhood. When on August 11, 1947, Pakistan's constituent assembly met in Karachi for the first time, Jinnah spoke these words from the chair:

You will no doubt agree with me that the first duty of a Government is to maintain law and order, so that the life, property and religious beliefs of its subjects are fully protected by the State. [He followed with an appeal to forget the past and cooperate regardless of color, caste or creed.] I cannot emphasize it too much. We should begin to work together in that spirit, and in the course of time all these angularities of the majority and minority communities, the Hindu community and the Muslim community—because even as regards Muslims you have Pathans, Punjabis, Shias, Sunnis and so on, and among the Hindus you have Brahmins, Vashnavas, Khatris, and also Bengalees, Madrasis, and so on—will vanish. Indeed if you ask me this has been the biggest hindrance in the way of India to attain freedom and independence and but for this we would have been free peoples long ago. . . . Now, we should keep in front of us our ideal . . . that in the course of time Hindus would cease to be Hindus, and Muslims would cease to be Muslims, not in the religious sense, because that is the personal faith of each individual, but in the political sense as citizens of the state.

Jinnah spoke in his capacity as first governor-general of soon to be sovereign Pakistan, and his words honor his memory. Yet the difficulty of respecting his scruples was soon apparent. Pakistan is less a country than a jumble of discordant peoples and places. After a half century, it still has a provisional, unfinished quality. Its successive rulers, braided or civilian, have governed under seven different constitutions, and not one has completed his or her term of office or managed an orderly transfer of power. The official language, Urdu, is the first language of only 8 percent of its people, the other mother tongues being Punjabi (48 percent), Sindhi (12 percent), Siraiki, a variant of Punjabi (10 percent), Pushto (8 percent) and Baluchi (3 percent). A visitor senses the same cultural and political bewilderment in Islamabad, whose construction began in 1961 to replace the former capital at Karachi. All that seems Asian about Islamabad is its impressive setting on a plateau below the Himalayan foothills. Otherwise, with its late International Style buildings Islamabad is like an alien implant grafted on adjacent Rawalpindi—an impression enhanced by Shah Faisal Mosque, among the world's largest, designed by a Turk, built with Saudi petrodollars, its four sleek minarets resembling rockets. Following Pakistan's nuclear bomb test in 1998, a futuristic granite simulacrum of the weapon rose in Islamabad, illuminated at night in a warning glow of orange.

Pakistan's miseries have been compounded by its geography, its loser's share of the Raj's spoils and its antipathetic diversity. A thousand miles of foreign territory separated West Pakistan with its 50 million inhabitants from the 45 million people in what was East Bengal, later East Pakistan, now Bangladesh. Not only did India inherit most of the Raj's transportation system, irrigation canals and top universities, but of the thousand indigenous officers in the elite Indian Civil Service and the national police, only a hundred were Muslims. This was the overworked skeleton staff, bolstered by fifty British civil servants and eleven Indian army officers, that overnight had to create Pakistan's administrative, judicial and diplomatic systems. Adding to the challenge were the millions of *mohajirs*, or refugees, flooding the country. Nor did it help that the only bond uniting the inhabitants of West Pakistan and physically remote East Pakistan was Islam. Eventually and in unhappy wartime circumstances, the Bengalis went their own way in 1971, founding Bangladesh and loosing a fresh flood of refugees. Equally problematic was Baluchistan, the most westerly of Pakistan's provinces, with its beehive of fierce tribes on both sides of the frontiers with Iran and Afghanistan. Descending dramatically from the mountains to the Arabian Sea, Baluchistan terminates in what the British geographer Sir Thomas Holdich called "a brazen coast, washed by a molten sea." The Baluchis were (and are) as volatile as their setting. Their chiefs defiantly opposed accession to Pakistan, precipitating an invasion a year after independence, followed by martial law and the arrest of their khan, who was charged with conspiring with Kabul to hatch a full-scale uprising (a charge denied by the Baluchs and never proven).

And everywhere lie minatory memorials to the region's former glories. The Grand Trunk Road, the impressive thoroughfare connecting Kabul and Calcutta built centuries ago by the Mogul emperors, passes west of Rawalpindi. Its aging signposts still optimistically announce distances north to Kabul and south to Amritsar and Delhi. But freedom of movement vanished with partition. Although India and Pakistan pledged themselves to unfettered passage of trade, people and ideas, within a year after independence, amid mutual recrimination, frontiers were closed and have remained so. The present writer remembers a candlelit dinner (the power was out) at Mrs. Bhandari's Guest House in Amritsar, the Sikh capital in the Indian Punjab, when our innkeeper recalled how easy it once was to make a day trip to Lahore, which she had not been able to visit for more than forty years. She nostalgically recalled Lahore's great Mogul forts, the sparkling fountains in Shalimar gardens and the massive cannon known as Kim's Gun, in front of the Lahore museum with its riches of Gandharan sculpture. For ordinary Indians, all could be on another planet.

Just as evocative is Sind, a southwestern province named after the Indus River, the cradle of the Harappan civilization, where large-scale agriculture originated five thousand years ago. Sind provided the gateway to conquest by Alexander the Great, the Arabs and then the British. In 1843, General Charles Napier on his own authority annexed the area to the Raj, telegraphing his deed, so the well-worn story goes, in a single word, *peccavi* (I have sinned). In touring the province, Napier kept asking, "Whose lands are these?" And nearly everywhere the answer came, "Bhutto's lands." It was still the case when Pakistan was born. Sir Shah Nawaz Khan Bhutto founded the first political party in Sind during the 1930s; his son, Zulfikar Ali Bhutto, served as Pakistan's leader from 1971 until his ouster six years later by General Mohammad Zia al-Haq, who approved Bhutto's execution and reinstituted martial law. Bhutto's daughter Benazir grew up on the family estate in Larkana, not far from the ruins of Mohenjo-daro, the greatest of Indus Valley sites, enhancing the sense of reflexive entitlement that marked her own turn as Pakistan's ruler, after General Zia was killed in a still-mysterious air crash in 1988. With Benazir Bhutto, one encounters another major recurring theme—the persistence of a powerful landowning elite that collides repeatedly with the meritocratic military, a competition that gives bargaining leverage to the third major force in Pakistan, the Islamic establishment, with its political parties and its ubiquitous religious schools.

The importance of that third force was evident in the most arresting of Pakistan's pre- and postindependence dramas, the struggle for mastery in the North-West Frontier Province. Here the last British governor and the Muslim League jointly sidetracked the Red Shirts, a brave, promising and inconvenient popular movement.

O F ALL THE PEOPLES on the subcontinent, few have more infallibly impressed outsiders than the mountaineers known to the British as the Pathans, today the Pashtuns or Pushtuns. After 9/11, Americans were dazzled by the interim Afghan leader, Hamid Karzai, with his confident if wary expression, his regal cape and bold karakul hat made from the skin of a sheep fetus. The pity is that Americans did not get to know such notable Pashtuns as the guerrilla commander Abdul Haq, slain in a treacherous 2001 ambush in Afghanistan, and Sayd Bahauddin Majrooh, a poet and philosopher assassinated in 1987, almost surely on orders of a U.S.-assisted Afghan rival. These friends of freedom were drawn from the same gene pool that gave Afghanistan (where Pashtuns form the dominant ethnic group) its great warrior-emperors, as well as its poets, smugglers and assassins.

Among the first Westerners to assess the contrariness of the Pashtuns was Mountstuart Elphinstone, the Scotsman who in 1809 led the first British mission to Kabul. In his travel account, he writes that "their vices are revenge, envy, avarice, rapacity, and obstinacy; on the other hand, they are fond of liberty, faithful to their friends, kind to their dependents, hospitable, brave, hardy, frugal, laborious, and prudent; and they are less disposed than the nations in their neighborhood to falsehood, intrigue, and deceit." Equally impressed was Lord Curzon. "I know these men," the viceroy wrote. "They are brave as lions, wild as cats, docile as children. . . . It is with a sense of pride that one receive the honest homage of these magnificent Samsons, bearded instinct with loyalty, often stained with crime."

That the Pashtuns were indomitable was confirmed by Britain's defeat in the First Afghan War (1838–1840), a humiliating debacle that ended an unbroken succession of victories by the Raj's armies. In 1846, having concluded they could not change or pacify the Pashtuns, two British political officers, Henry Lawrence and Harry Lumsden, struck on the idea of recruiting them. Thus originated the Queen's Own Corps of Guides, an elite irregular force whose colors and emblems—crossed tulwers (or curved sabers) and the slogan "Rough and Ready"—became the most celebrated in British India. Initially, Lumsden startled his superiors by garbing the Guides in a dun-colored local fabric called khaki (from Persian for dust) instead of the regulation scarlet. The shock wore off, the use of khaki proliferated, and the Guides proved their military worth, becoming the prototype for Britain's Special Forces and America's Green Berets.

The British romance with the Pashtuns deepened after the Second Afghan War (1878–1881), which ended in a standoff. Despite the recurrent raids and counterraids on the frontier, the scuffles that inspired reams of Kipling's verse, there followed an interlude of relative calm during the eighteen-year tenure of Sir Robert Warburton as warden of the Khyber

Pass, beginning in 1879. Warburton's mother happened to be an Afghan princess—a niece of the renowned Emir Dost Mohammed—and thus he spoke the languages and understood the mores of Pashtun tribes. It was Warburton who established the Khyber Rifles, still garrisoned by Pakistan on the far side of the pass. As a biographer notes, his camp became the rendezvous of mutually hostile clans, and he traveled with no weapon but a walking stick: "Able to converse freely with the learned in Persian, and with the common folk in the vernacular Pushto, he succeeded by his acquaintance with tribal life and character, in gaining an influence over the border Afghans which has never been equaled."

Warburton's era was drawing to an end in 1897, when an uprising broke out in the Swat Valley on the North-West Frontier, threatening a British garrison on the Malakand Pass. General Sir Bindon Blood, a commander famous for his "butcher and beat it" raids, mobilized a British field force of three brigades. Among the officers flocking to the Malakand field force was a young subaltern, Lieutenant Winston Churchill. It was his first military engagement, and he doubled as a correspondent for the *Daily Telegraph*. As he wrote to his mother, Lady Randolph Churchill, "The danger & difficulty of attacking these active fierce hill men is extreme. They can get up in the hills twice as fast as we can—and shoot wonderfully well with Martini Henry rifles. It is a war without quarter. They kill and mutilate everyone they catch and we do not hesitate to finish their wounded off. I have seen several things wh[ich] have not been very pretty since I have been up here—but as you will believe I have not soiled my hands with any dirty work—though I recognize the necessity of some things. All this however you need not publish."

S TILL, IT IS TOO FACILE to stereotype the Pashtuns, now numbering some 12 million or more, most of them living in the squat stony villages straddling the Durand Line, which nominally demarcates Pakistan from Afghanistan. No foreigner has ever subdued them, and Islamabad's writ effectively ceases where the so-called Pashtun tribal areas begin. They are indeed devout Muslims, and central to their way of life is a code of honor so exacting that vendettas persist for generations. It is no less the case that mobs in Peshawar screaming "Death to America!" after 9/11 were recruited from Pashtun clans, with names resounding like a drumroll: Afridi, Khattak, Oraksai, Bangash, Wazir, Mahsud, Yusufsai. Certifiable as well, generations of exasperated colonial officers found their quarrels impenetrably irrational, centering on *zar, zan* and *zamin* (gold, women and land).

Yet this is scarcely the whole truth. Forgotten is the paradoxical fact that the foremost Pashtun leader in the struggle against British rule was a dedicated pacifist, Abdul Ghaffar Khan, once famous as the "frontier Gandhi." His followers, nicknamed the Red Shirts, had first to swear, "I shall never use violence. I shall not retaliate or take revenge, and shall forgive anyone who indulges in oppression and excesses against me." For upwards of two decades Ghaffar Khan and his Khudai Khidmatgar ("Servants of God") fought alongside Mahatma Gandhi and the Congress Party for a united, democratic and secular India. Nearly everybody who has looked into this history has been fascinated, moved and astonished. Mukilika Banerjee first heard of the Red Shirts in the 1990s while a graduate student in New Delhi. Impressed and curious, she settled on the frontier, learned Pushto, and managed to interview seventy surviving ex-Servants of God for her study, *The Pathan Unarmed*. She found that Ghaffar Khan's pacifism derived from his concept of jihad, or holy war: "Nonviolent civil disobedience offered the chance of martyrdom in its purest form, since putting one's life conspicuously in one's enemy's hands was itself the key act, and death incurred in the process was not a defeat or a tragedy: rather the act of witness to an enemy's injustice. . . . In his recruiting speeches, therefore, [Ghaffar Khan] was offering to each and every Pathan not the mere possibility of death, but rather the opportunity of glorious sacrifice and martyrdom."

Like her incredulous predecessors, Banerjee discovered that Ghaffar Khan, starting in the 1920s, managed to recruit a nonviolent army of 100,000 followers, who shared a uniform frugally stained with brick dust. The army's power was confirmed in 1930, when its general strike paralyzed Peshawar, the provincial capital, for five days, its supporters having braved arrest and torture by the Raj's police. Initially, because they were deemed so intractable, Pashtuns were denied even the limited franchise granted in the early 1900s elsewhere in British India, but this changed with the passage of the 1935 Government of India Act. In successive elections, the Red Shirts prevailed, forming provincial governments under Chief Minister Dr. Khan Sahib (as he is usually styled), the British-educated physician brother of Ghaffar Khan. Meanwhile, Ghaffar, standing six feet, three inches, instantly recognizable with his nobbly nose and homely features, became an arm-in-arm companion to Mahatma Gandhi, who pronounced the Red Shirt movement a miracle. Notwithstanding his pacifism and his liberal views on secularism and women's rights, Ghaffar Khan became a Pashtun folk hero, acclaimed as Badshah Khan, or khan of khans. This is documented in a recent book by the Indian historian Parshotam Mehra, *The North-West Frontier Drama, 1945–1947*. Combing through long unexamined records, the author found that in 1932, the NWFP, with a population of just 3 million, accounted for 5,557 convictions for civil disobedience compared with 1,620 in the Punjab, which had five times as many inhabitants.

Muslims constituted so overwhelming a majority on the frontier that the Muslim League's cry of "Islam in danger" failed to resonate. This helps explain why a movement allied with Gandhi's Hindu-led Congress took root. No less important, Ghaffar Khan had tapped into a sense of frustrated common identity among Pashtuns living on both sides of the Afghan border. He and his movement talked of a "Pashtunistan," an independent or quasi-autonomous Pashtun homeland, the content of the idea varying from time to time. It was this aspect of the movement that most troubled the British and, even more, the Muslim League. It led to Ghaffar Khan's encounter with another important if forgotten figure, Sir Olaf Caroe.

CAROE WAS TYPICAL OF his generation of Indian civil servants, specifically those Britons who came of age during the Great War who were dubbed the "Guardians" by his colleague and historian of the Raj, Philip Mason. By the time Caroe entered the elite Indian Civil Service in 1919, by way of Winchester and Oxford, he and his cohort did not need to be warned that the empire was mortal. This was implicit in news reports of anticolonial rebellions and in the British loss of nerve evident in the clouded expressions of aging imperialists like Caroe's idol, Lord Curzon. Thus even as the empire reached its territorial zenith between the two wars, its Guardians began peering anxiously down the road, glancing sideways at America and thinking hard about the possible decline to come. Like Curzon, Caroe was by instinct a Russophobe, the more so in the unnerving wake of the Bolshevik Revolution. During the 1920s, when Soviet forces retook Central Asia and the Caucasus, Comintern leaders ominously threatened to set the East ablaze. Caroe's first postings were in the Punjab, the North-West Frontier and Baluchistan, where the young political officer witnessed the gathering nationalist uprising among Hindus, Muslims and Sikhs. A stint on the Persian Gulf added to his stock of knowledge about Islam, oil and great power rivalry. When he moved on to New Delhi, becoming British India's foreign secretary during World War II, Caroe began to implement his strategic views. To preempt contested borderlands, he quietly extended India's frontier eastward into Tibet by recalling the Raj's official compendium of treaties and reissuing a new edition, under the old date, that included a frontier agreement repudiated by China, thereby sowing the seeds for India's 1962 border war with Beijing.

At the end of World War II, in what seemed a well-earned finale, Caroe was named governor of the North-West Frontier Province, which fittingly had been created during Curzon's viceroyalty. The match had an emotional resonance. Like other political officers, Caroe adhered to the Forward School, believing that Britain and its imperial charges needed to take the initiative against potential adversaries. Along with other frontiersmen, he had striven to erect a firewall against the Soviet Union. And the idea of a separate Muslim state was already in the air. While researching his biography of Jinnah, Stanley Wolpert came upon this clairvoyant testimony to a parliamentary committee in 1933 by Sir Michael O'Dwyer, who had been Caroe's chief as governor of the Punjab, saying that if the Hindu majority "endeavors to force its will on provinces with a Muslim majority, what is to prevent a breakaway of the Punjab, Sind, Baluchistan, and the NWF, *as already foreshadowed* and their possibly forming a Muslim federation of their own?" (Wolpert's emphasis.) Had O'Dwyer actually read Rahmat Ali's obscure, recently published Cambridge pamphlet, or, as Wolpert asks, "Could he perhaps have helped inspire it?"

An essential component of the Forward School mystique was the "martial races" thesis—the conviction that the best fighters in the Indian army came from the mountainous north (e.g., the frontier Pashtuns, the Nepalese Gurkhas, the Punjabi Sikhs and the highland Rajputs). The thesis was energetically popularized by Lord Roberts of Kandahar, winner of a Victoria Cross during the mutiny, a hero of the Second Afghan War, and later commander in chief of the Indian army. "The notion of 'martial races' drew sustenance from a variety of elements in the cultural baggage of late Victorian England," writes Thomas R. Metcalf in *Ideologies of the Raj*. "As the Aryans had once conquered northern India, it was assumed

that those races descended from them possessed superior military capa-
bilities." Some even claimed that the blue eyes and fair hair found among
Pashtuns proved they retained intact genetic traces of Alexander the Great's
armies. The Pashtun delight in sports and their high-spirited camaraderie
on the frontier also argued for their superiority vis-à-vis the supposedly
effeminate Bengali shopkeepers and pen-pushing civil servants.

Caroe admired the Pashtuns to the point of idolatry. The scholarly
crown of his retirement years was a 521-page treatise, *The Pathans:
550 B.C.–A.D. 1957* (1961), whose general tenor is signaled in the first paragraph: "This is a book I was bound some time to write, having had the
fortune to spend half a lifetime among Pathans." What follows is a full-
scale history, including elaborate pullout maps indicating tribal areas,
translations of the Pashtun bard Khushal Khan Khatak and photographs
meant to underscore the kinship between Alexander the Great and contemporary Pashtun militiamen. Caroe dedicated his book to the first president of Pakistan, General Iskander Mirra, who also was the first (in 1958)
to dissolve parliament and impose martial law, paving the way for the dictatorship of Field Marshal Ayub Khan, the initiator of Islamabad's strategic ties with Washington.

All this lay ahead in 1946 when Caroe took up the reins as governor
in Peshawar. His predecessor, Sir George Cunningham, at that point
found little enthusiasm for joining Pakistan. In his diary, the outgoing
governor quoted a Muslim visitor as saying that for "the average Pathan
villager, a suggestion of Hindu domination was only laughable." The
Muslim League's weakness was confirmed in March provincial elections.
Though Muslim League candidates inveighed against the Hindu Raj, Dr.
Khan Sahib's Congress Party nonetheless carried thirty of fifty legislative
seats. As independence loomed, the North-West Frontier was India's only
Muslim-majority province not governed by a Muslim League ministry.
This put its last British governor in a delicate position. When Nehru proposed a tour of the frontier to rally his Congress allies, Caroe warned
vainly against the trip on security grounds. On his arrival in September
1946, Nehru was greeted at the airport by thousands of jeering Islamic
militants waving black flags and, as Caroe had predicted, the trip proved a
humiliation. The stage was set for months of communal thuggery as Muslim gangs attacked Sikhs and Hindus in the province's Settled Areas (as
they were formally known). To the Khan brothers, the import was plain—
that Sir Olaf was promoting the tumult to discredit them. On May 6, 1947,

Ghaffar Khan accused Caroe of joining "an open conspiracy with the Muslim League to bathe the province in blood" by condoning "the murder of innocent men, women and children."

The charge was delivered in anger. Doubtless Dr. Khan Sahib's rattled provincial government made its own overzealous mistakes, and I find it hard to believe that Caroe connived in murder. Yet he did have a record of surreptitiously promoting his strongly held views and leaving few fingerprints. Some thumb marks, however, survived. While scavenging State Department files in the National Archives in Washington, my wife came on a report made by a visiting U.S. official of his interview with Caroe in May 1947: "Sir Olaf indicated that the Foreign Office tended too much to look upon India as a peninsular unit like Italy. . . . He felt it did not sufficiently realize the great political importance of the Northwest Frontier Province and Afghanistan, which he described as 'the uncertain vestibule' in future relations between Soviet Russia and India." Caroe expressed regret that his own government played down Soviet penetration of frontier areas like Gilgit, Chitral, and Swat, adding "he would not be unfavorable to the establishment of a separate Pakhistan [*sic*]."

Nehru and the Khan brothers thus had valid grounds for doubting Caroe's impartiality when the viceroy took the unusual step of approving a plebiscite on the future of the frontier province—elsewhere the choice between India and Pakistan was made by provincial ministries or princely rulers. As a gesture to Congress, Mountbatten also determined that Caroe was "suffering badly from nerves" and asked him to request a leave as provincial governor until the transfer of power. Caroe complied. A deputy presided as the referendum took place on July 17, its one-sided judgment in favor of joining Pakistan marred by charges of fraud and intimidation and by a boycott that kept half the 5 million eligible Pashtun voters from the polls. On August 17, as Pakistan came into existence, Dr. Khan Sahib refused to resign as chief minister. He and his cabinet were peremptorily dismissed, and a Muslim League ministry installed. Dr. Khan Sahib was subsequently jailed and later made his peace with Islamabad, serving briefly as a Pakistani minister before he was slain by an unforgiving Pashtun in 1957 in Lahore.

Of the leaders, the greatest loser was Ghaffar Khan. In newborn India he was all but abandoned by his former Congress Party allies, while in newborn Pakistan he was charged with sedition and promoting separatism. It made no difference that he took an oath of allegiance to the new state, or that he repeatedly insisted he sought autonomy for Pashtuns within Pakistan. He was repeatedly jailed or kept under house arrest until his death in Peshawar in 1988 at the age of ninety-eight. At his request, he was buried in the Afghan city of Jalalabad. His memory was honored by a cease-fire in the ongoing Afghan war as 20,000 mourners formed a cortege extending through the Khyber Pass into Afghanistan. Otherwise, the khan of khans was simply scrubbed from history—so wholly forgotten that even in the post–9/11 deluge of dispatches from Pakistan, the sole reference to Ghaffar Khan this writer noted in any American publication lay deep within a *New Yorker* article by the British journalist Isabel Hilton.

A FURTHER TWIST in the quixotic saga of the Frontier Gandhi is that Afghanistan, whose cause he always defended, helped consign Ghaffar Khan to obscurity. His memory was clouded by the protracted dispute over the validity of the Durand Line. This boundary between British India and Afghanistan, with its erroneously authoritative name, was demarcated in 1894–1896 by Sir Mortimer Durand, a frontier officer known for his battlefield valor in Afghanistan, his knowledge of inner Asia and his love of games. By agreement between the British Raj and the Afghan emir, Durand and his team of surveyors sought to end the uncertainty over control of contested Pashtun areas. But the tribes were not consulted, nor was the demarcation based on sound topography. The line became a nebulous buffer within a buffer. As a result, writes the Indian frontier historian Parshotam Mehra, tribal brawls proved an enduring problem for the British: "[They] could neither abandon the frontier nor occupy the tribal areas and thus found themselves, for most part, engaged in an interminable war with the tribes. Afghanistan, however, got a measure of respite, for its rulers found it easy to maintain contact and exercise influence with the tribes in the British sphere, across the Durand Line."

The resulting skirmishes and recurrent uprisings persisted through the 1930s and (with clumsy Axis encouragement) during World War II. In 1944, sensing the approaching demise of the Raj, the Kabul government sent a note reminding the British of Afghan interest in the fate of the Pashtuns. As Louis Dupree writes in his encyclopedic history of Afghanistan, the British replied that "since, in their opinion, the Durand Line was an international boundary, it should not concern the Afghans." Later, leading up to independence, Lord Mountbatten tacked on a vague addendum: "Agreements with the tribes on the North-West Frontier will have to be negotiated with the appropriate successor authority." Pakistan thus inherited the intractable British "problem." In 1947 the Afghan king, Mohammad Zahir Shah (astonishingly, the same monarch who returned from exile to Kabul in 2002 as a symbol of putative continuity), notified the Pakistanis that his government viewed the Durand Line as an imperial anachronism, overdue for overhaul. Pakistan spurned the overture, and in riposte Afghanistan became the sole dissenter at the United Nations in opposing Pakistan's accession to the world organization. Thus recommenced a quarrel that over time has proved calamitous for both countries.

Each made inflated charges and each promoted unrest across the disputed frontier. Both resorted to mutually crippling sanctions that closed ports and highways. Both embraced policies that were inconsistent or impenetrable. Pakistan, for example, has favored a plebiscite to resolve the dispute with India over Kashmir but rejects out of hand a similar resolution for the Pashtuns, who are also divided by an arbitrary boundary. All seemed fair in a dispute waged without quarter: Pakistan's Radio Free Afghanistan beamed incendiary words across the Khyber, while Afghanistan gave covert encouragement to the Waziri insurgent, Mirza Ali Khan, notorious on the frontier as the Faqir of Ipi. During the 1930s he held off 30,000 British troops and turned to the Nazis for help during World War II before taking up arms against Pakistan; he was a tireless troublemaker until his last breath in 1960. Well-intended mediators soon came to dread entanglement in the flypaper of the "Pashtunistan" dispute. Always there was the suspicion of perfidy and dark plots, as in the 1951 assassination of Pakistan's first prime minister, Liaqat Ali Khan, the politician who had been to Jinnah what Nehru had been to Gandhi. A confirmed secularist, Liaqat Ali Khan was killed at a public meeting in Rawalpindi by an Afghan exile. Kabul denied all involvement, and its disclaimer was formally accepted. But the stain of doubt endured.

From this detritus of empire emerged a new alignment that persisted for decades. When Pakistan blocked Afghanistan's access to the Western trading system, Kabul began looking north to the Soviet Union for favorable trade deals, development aid and military assistance. As the Cold War advanced, Afghans became expert at coaxing aid from rival suitors, obtaining U.S. help for roads and schools in the south and Russian aid in the north. Cautiously but not egregiously, Kabul tilted to Moscow in the 1960s. Its leaders turned to the international system for resources to expand the modern sector in their capital without confronting rural oligarchs. This equilibrium persisted even after the 1973 ouster of King Zahir Shah by his envious and ambitious cousin, Mohammad Daoud, who proclaimed a republic. (In the Pashtun language, the same word doubles for enemy and cousin.)

In short, it seemed a vindication of Olaf Caroe's global strategy. Afghanistan was to all appearances a stable buffer, with Pakistan a solid firewall protecting the Persian Gulf. After returning to Britain in 1947, Caroe continued as an influential counselor on the region's affairs. He sketched his thoughts in an essay appearing in *Round Table* (March 1949), the imperial house organ. There he approvingly noted the formation of NATO, adding that the common interests linking the North Atlantic nations also converged in the Persian Gulf. He elaborated his thesis in *Wells of Power: The Oilfields of South-Western Asia* (1951), which called on Washington to take up its great power responsibilities and erect a "northern screen" around the Persian Gulf's oil fields, the prospective partners being Iran, Afghanistan, Iraq and Pakistan. He offered a paean to Pakistan as the potential leader with a special mission: "In politics, as in things of the spirit, a marriage of forces, themselves destined to perish, may generate a fresh force of greater power. It is not too much to hope that, through Pakistan, some new strength of this kind may animate the Muslim world."

Alas, Caroe's marriage came unstuck, and what he had assumed would be the glue—the appeal of Islam—proved over time its solvent. Under General Zia's military dictatorship, Pakistan bet heavily (with covert U.S. support) on evicting the Soviets from Afghanistan in the 1980s by arming an international Islamic brigade to do the job. From frontier training camps arose the Taliban and Osama bin Laden, and after 9/11 the United States turned to Pakistan as a critical ally in the war against the forces it helped father. The result was a shaky alliance with a nation deeply at odds with itself. Just how shaky became clear in October 2002 after national and regional elections meant to stabilize the rule of President Pervez Musharraf, the former army chief of staff who had seized power three years earlier. The votes resulted in an unwelcome surge of support for a coalition of anti-American Islamic parties known by the initials MMA, whose leader, Qazi Hussain Ahmed, assured an exultant rally in Peshawar, "It is a revolution. We will not accept U.S. bases and Western culture."

The outcome was a sobering setback for the self-effacing and secular-minded General Musharraf, whose own career encapsulates the theme of this chapter. He was born in New Delhi in 1943 to a father who was a diplomat in the colonial foreign office. At four years of age, he was among the millions of Muslims forced by partition to move west into Pakistan. "It was early August," his mother, Zarin, recalled in an interview with the *New Yorker*'s Mary Anne Weaver, "and the communal riots had already begun. We fled for our lives. We took the last train out of Delhi for Karachi. . . . The train passed through entire neighborhoods that had been set to the torch. Bodies were lying along the rail tracks. There was so much blood. Blood and chaos were everywhere. The train journey took us three days, and we used to halt at night. We were terrified of the Hindus and Sikhs, who were massacring people in the trains moving west. We had no water, no food. It was summer and it was terribly hot. I had three small children. We could take nothing with us. We had to leave everything behind—our house, my father's house, my mother's house. We had to start over from scratch."

Young Pervez climbed upward like other bright Pakistanis via the armed forces, where he spent most of his career battling India. Now he faces a more ambiguous adversary in the form of an Islamist rising, especially in Baluchistan and the North-West Frontier. It is difficult to conjure a politically more difficult border area. Along the North-West Frontier, there are said to be 7 million Kalashnikovs, or one for every grown man. Peshawar is the hub of a thriving black market in drugs and weapons, its slums and refugee camps the recruiting ground for jihadists who would happily kill every infidel anywhere. The flavor is suggested by Weaver's account in her recent book *Pakistan: In the Shadow of Jihad and Afghanistan*. She describes her visit to the largest *madrassa* (or seminary) in the frontier province, which is among the most militant in Pakistan. "What do you think of Osama bin Laden?" she asked the seminary's chancellor, Maulana Sami ul-Haq. "What do you think of Abraham Lincoln?" came the response. It is obvious that America's encounter with the Pashtuns, the remarkable people living on both sides of the Afghan frontier, has barely begun.

V
AFGHANISTAN
In a Dark Defile

Soviet soldiers bid adieu to Afghanistan in 1989, ending a fateful decade of intervention in behalf of an incompetent Marxist regime in Kabul. "It'll be over in three or four weeks," Communist Party chief Leonid Brezhnev promised his dismayed ambassador to Washington in 1979. Defense Minister Ustinov warned military dissenters to "stop reasoning" and start shooting. *Photo by Stuart Franklin, courtesy of Magnum.*

WHY, PLEASE TELL US why, do they hate us? No question was asked more anxiously by Americans in the weeks after September 11. Why, more particularly, would educated Saudi Arabians from well-to-do families turn themselves into human guided missiles in collaboration with an antediluvian regime in Afghanistan? What had the United States ever done to Saudi Arabia except buy its oil and defend its territory during the Gulf War? And why Afghanistan? Americans had, after all, cheered and armed the Afghan resistance after the Soviet Union invaded in December 1979 to rescue a tottering Communist regime in Kabul. The Central Intelligence Agency orchestrated massive arms shipments via Pakistan, including state-of-the-art Stinger surface-to-air missiles. Three U.S. administrations promoted a bipartisan policy of covert aid that persisted through a decade of occupation. Presidents Carter, Reagan and Bush *père* hailed the mujahedin as "freedom fighters," and their acclaim was echoed on Capitol Hill and by editorial boards coast to coast.

The strategy worked. Bowing to battlefield realities, Mikhail Gorbachev agreed in April 1988 to a complete Soviet withdrawal, an unprecedented retreat under fire that heralded the passing of the Cold War. CIA officers uncorked the champagne as the last Russian soldier crossed the Friendship Bridge out of Afghanistan in February 1989. Yet sadly, from that moment nothing went right for the freedom fighters. They brawled among themselves and failed, in their first major offensive, to liberate Jalalabad. When they finally managed in 1992 to dislodge the abandoned Communist regime in Kabul, they shelled one another, devastated their own capital and pillaged its treasures. Desperate Afghan farmers beset by anarchy turned as never before to their only sure cash crop—poppies. Output soared and, according to informed U.N. estimates, Afghanistan was soon exporting three times more opium than the rest of the world combined. Warlords of every description, battening on the drug traffic and aided by a dozen foreign patrons, carved the country into fractious enclaves, dispelling hopes that more than 5 million Afghan refugees, mostly in Pakistan but with as many as a million wasting in Iran, might finally return home.

No wonder Afghans in 1994–1995 turned gratefully to a new movement, the Taliban, meaning "students" or in some renderings, "The Seekers." These soldiers of Allah—young, incorruptible and burning with primordial piety—stormed Kabul in 1996. Flouting the rules of asylum, they entered the U.N. compound and seized Najibullah, the fallen Communist leader. Taliban executioners castrated and lynched the despised former president, then hoisted his corpse in a public square. Decrees followed that mandated beards for men and banished women from schools, workplaces and even the streets unless escorted. Adulterers and other alleged trespassers were stoned to death in the soccer stadium, soccer having been banned. Out went television, movies and music, along with all other innovations not condoned by the Koran, as rigidly interpreted by the Taliban's hermetic leader, the one-eyed Mullah Muhammad Omar, who scorned even a handshake with non-Muslims.

As the Taliban conquered all but the northern fringe of Afghanistan, it became apparent that The Seekers also had an export agenda. According to the Pakistani journalist Ahmed Rashid, who was present in Kabul when Soviet tanks first rolled in and again when the Communist regime fell, some 35,000 Muslim militants from forty Islamic countries signed on as volunteers in the Afghan jihad. Inviolate Kabul became the cynosure for soldiers in this foreign legion as they turned homeward across a great crescent extending from the Russian Caucasus and former Soviet Central Asia, through India's troubled Kashmir, then eastward via Southeast Asia to the Philippines and the most populous Muslim nation, Indonesia. As detailed by the veteran Middle East correspondent John K. Cooley, Afghan-hardened militants also made their way back to predominantly Muslim oasis cities in western China and into the hovels of Egypt and Algeria. Crossing the Atlantic, Islamic radicals in 1993 truck-bombed the World Trade Center in lower Manhattan, a dress rehearsal for 9/11. Caught and convicted, the truck bombers proved to be disciples of a blind Egyptian prayer leader, Sheik Omar Abdel Rahman, who had been an honored visitor to Afghan training camps in Peshawar, facilitating his visa clearance by the CIA.

THIS WAS SURELY NOT what William Casey, President Reagan's director of Central Intelligence, had in mind. Nor was it the epilogue envisioned by Zbigniew Brzezinski, President Carter's national security adviser, who initiated the clandestine Afghan aid program. Seen in hindsight, as elaborated by Cooley in his prescient book, *Unholy Wars* (1999), this backlash was in part the outcome of "a strange love affair that went disastrously wrong" between Washington and "some of the most conservative and fanatical followers of Islam." The ardor was real and the motives high-minded. The well-traveled American writer Robert D. Kaplan aptly subtitled his book *The Arabists* as *The Romance of an American Elite.* "Arabists" is insider shorthand for an older cadre of State Department officers smitten with Islam in general and Arabs in particular. Many were the offspring of missionaries or had attended American schools in Beirut and Cairo with strong missionary roots; others were Ivy Leaguers who came to the Middle East steeped in the mystique of Richard Burton, Charles Doughty and Lawrence of Arabia.

Their mentor and champion in the State Department was the formidable Loy Henderson, unknown to the laity but in the judgment of his colleagues the consummate career officer, fully deserving of his honorific title, "Mr. Foreign Service." Henderson's initial postings in Eastern Europe and the Soviet Union in the 1930s persuaded him that Communism was irretrievably amoral and expansionist, and his World War II service as U.S. envoy in Baghdad convinced him that Islamic states were essential frontline partners in an already developing global competition. Subsequently, as director of the State Department's Office of Near Eastern Affairs, he helped forge the Baghdad Pact in 1955, a defensive alliance between Turkey and Iraq supported by Iran, Pakistan and Great Britain. As ambassador to Iran earlier in the 1950s, he helped turn Tehran into a strategic Western anchor. Like the Arabists he tutored and promoted, Henderson viewed Israel as at best a distracting nuisance, at worst a state that compromised U.S. interests in the Middle East. Like most senior Foreign Service officers, Henderson and his Arabists had vainly opposed President Truman's decision in 1948 to recognize the state of Israel.

Among Henderson's disciples and admirers was Archibald Roosevelt, grandson of Teddy and cousin of Kermit, who served as a military attaché in Baghdad and Tehran, and then after World War II as a high-ranking CIA officer. Archie Roosevelt was the quintessential Arabist: elite schooling (Groton and Harvard), a fluent linguist and aspiring translator of classical

Arabic texts. Like others in his cohort, he had an Arab spouse. His wife was the Lebanese-born Selwa Showker, who, as "Lucky" Roosevelt, served as the State Department's chief of protocol in the Reagan years. Roosevelt's memoir, *For Lust of Knowing*, is a basic text in the covert courtship of Araby, replete with references to Kipling, Doughty and T. E. Lawrence, its title drawn from these lustrous lines by James Elroy Flecker:

> We travel not for trafficking alone;
> By hotter winds our fiery hearts are fanned;
> For lust of knowing what should not be known,
> We take the Golden Road to Samarkand.

Underscored in Archie Roosevelt's reminiscences is a notion that ripened within the CIA and the State Department: Islam was the vulnerable underbelly of the Soviet empire. He felt strongly that America erred in its anti-Soviet strategy: "We have tended to side with the Soviets in forcing our Western allies to give up their colonies but the subject races of Russia's Asian empire have continued to languish without any encouragement from us." The "true front line," Roosevelt contended, remained the northern rim of the Khyber Pass, where one could feel "the chill winds of the Cold War blowing over those forbidding mountains." Farther north lay the ancient Muslim centers of Bokhara and Samarkand, still prisoners of Kipling's ever smiling, never changing Russian bear. In substance, images and tone, this was the battle song of Great Britain's Forward School, and with historical symmetry Afghanistan was once again at the vortex of the struggle—as it still is.

In a stroke that a novelist would hesitate to contrive, the pivotal mover in bringing America into "the true front line" was Kermit Roosevelt, Archie's first cousin, who had directed the 1953 coup that restored Shah Mohammad Reza Pahlavi to power in Iran. A Harvard-educated Arabist with wartime service in the Office of Strategic Services (OSS), Kermit was also a Kipling devotee. His nickname was Kim, a distinction he shared with the British arch-traitor Kim Philby and with Kipling's eponymous boy spy. Philby later described Roosevelt as "a courteous soft-spoken Easterner with impeccable social connections, well-educated rather than intellectual, pleasant and unassuming. He was the last person you would expect to be up to his neck in dirty tricks."

Like his cousin Archie, Kim Roosevelt viewed Afghanistan as the springboard for sowing discord in Soviet Central Asia and the Russian Caucasus. As early as 1949, in a spirited and revealing book, *Arabs, Oil and History*, Kim urged a payback for Soviet exploitation of minority discontent in the West:

> Someday the opponents of Soviet Russia may tire of doing nothing but replying to endless repeated attacks on them. They may realize that you do not even win a propaganda war by staying on the defensive. If and when they do take the offensive, this southern border and its minorities offer the most promising targets. Besides the Turkomans, Uzbeks and Tajiks there are Armenians, Kurds, Circassians and a host of others. . . . The Union of Soviet Socialist Republics has Achilles' heels—ideologically and practically—in a profusion rivaled only by a centipede. Our ability to exploit these weaknesses will depend directly on our ability to give these peoples—Turkomans, Kurds, Armenians and their neighbors—confidence in our intentions, our discretion and our power. The history of Afghanistan, like the history of countless small countries, is full of object lessons of what happens when two big powers start fighting over or through it.

In the years after this was written, a dramatic concatenation of events—the shah's restoration to power in Iran, the American debacle in Vietnam, the itch to lure Moscow into its own quagmire, the disorders in Kabul, Pakistan's own Forward Policy and the river of gold that flowed into Iran after the OPEC "oil shock"—all combined to put into practice the essential strategy that Kim Roosevelt proposed in 1949. The cost in blood was borne by the people of Afghanistan, the porous buffer state at the heart of Asia.

Few countries boast a more eclectic fan club than Afghanistan. Its stark landscape, its contentious medley of peoples—principally Pashtuns, Tajiks, Baluchis, Uzbeks, Hazaras and Turkmen—and its martial history have fascinated foreigners for centuries. Whenever the globe-trotting novelist James A. Michener was asked which country he would prefer to revisit, he invariably named Afghanistan. "I remember it as an exciting, violent, provocative place," he said. "Almost every American or European who worked there in the old days says the same." Writing in 1963, Michener recalled his visit a decade before to Bamian ("one of the compelling sights of Asia"), with its colossal statues of Buddha (since demolished by the Taliban), its five hundred caves and its magnificent corridors: "From one room at the highest level of caves I counted 61 snow-covered peaks in midsummer, all over 15,000 feet high."

Kabul, with its great bazaar, mosques and forts, long rivaled the Tibetan capital, Lhasa, among travelers as a prize to die for, sometimes literally. Sir Aurel Stein, the Hungarian-born explorer of the Silk Road, spent much of his life striving to reach Afghanistan; when he finally won permission in 1943, he died peacefully at age eighty in the diplomatic residence of his friend and advocate, Cornelius Engert, the first U.S. envoy accredited to Kabul. (Stein's grave somehow survived three decades of unremitting strife, as its seekers discovered after the collapse of the Taliban regime in 2001.) The British author and traveler James Morris found Kabul picturesque but baleful, an archaic Islamic city of the kind that Richard Burton liked to sneak into. "Her history is streaked with bloodshed, bigotry and jealousy," he reported in 1963, "and though her people are usually kindly enough nowadays, she can feel a frightening city still. . . . Her people are dizzily variegated, slit-eyed or shaggily bearded, smooth like conkers or layered like pine-cones, huge, strapping frontiersmen or slinking mountaineers, Pathans and Uzbegs, Persians and Sikhs, men in every degree of social maturity, from the mediaevally austere to the padded-shoulder progressive."

Iowa-born Roseanne Klass, fresh from the University of Wisconsin, went to teach and live there in 1951–1954. For her, Afghanistan was the entrancing land of high flags. "Each of us makes his own Eden, and out of strange clay," she wrote in 1964, describing her idyllic farewell bus ride through the Khyber Pass. (After the Soviet invasion, Klass worked at Freedom House in New York as its liaison with the Afghan resistance.) Similarly enamored was the British author Doris Lessing, who befriended several Afghan refugees in the 1980s. "Before the catastrophe, all visitors to Afghanistan fell in love with the Afghans, as if with their own fabled past, when we were proud, brave, independent, and witty and generous as well," she writes in *The Wind Blew Away Our Words*.

Yet on this infectiously likable people, the facts of geography intrude like a primal curse. Fifteen percent bigger than France and totally landlocked, Afghanistan inhabits an exceptionally difficult neighborhood, hemmed to the west by Iran and Turkmenistan, to the north by Uzbekistan and Tajikistan, to the east and south by Pakistan. In a gratuitous added kick, Afghanistan is joined to China by a narrow strip known as the Wakhan corridor, inflicted by imperial mapmakers so that Russia and British India would share no common frontier. Afghanistan occupies the strategic hub of Central Asia. For centuries, lumbering caravans on the Silk Road plied its valleys and passes, and its territory nowadays offers a promising pipeline route to the Persian Gulf for Caspian natural gas—a modern Silk Road—whenever (or if ever) all concerned agree to the project.

The Afghan author Sirdar Ikbal Ali Shah has compared his own country to Scotland with its highlands and clans, but Afghanistan evokes *Macbeth*, not the Scottish Enlightenment. Sir Percy Sykes in his history calls Afghanistan "the Switzerland of Southern Asia," which makes sense only if one speaks of its mountains, its lack of access to seas and its linguistic diversity. Switzerland's neighbors decided long ago that Swiss neutrality and stability best served their interests, and by unwritten accord they have not invaded, bribed or bullied its cantons. No such self-denying abstinence has deterred Russia, Britain, America, Pakistan, Iran, India, China, Germany, Saudi Arabia, Egypt or more recently Uzbekistan, Tajikistan and Turkmenistan. Most have pursued their own Afghan ends, suborning ethnic, religious or ideological allies, cultivating the fringes at the expense of the center, while professing the profoundest respect for Afghan territorial integrity, sovereignty and independence, a formula as sincere as the boilerplate compliments adorning diplomatic notes.

And yet foreigners complain of the duplicity, cynicism and treachery of Afghan chieftains. Who, one wonders, has taught Afghans these dark arts? During the decade of Soviet occupation, an Afghan clerk found a note in the Kabul archives dated February 20, 1922, from Soviet Ambassador Roskolnikov to the Afghan Ministry of Foreign Affairs. The letter, gleefully disseminated by the resistance, thus replied to Afghan protests over the entry of Bolshevik forces into Khiva and Bokhara, thereby ending their brief interlude as independent Muslim states in Central Asia:

> Concerning the question of the independent status of Khiva, and Bukhara, this has been provided for in the treaty agreed to and signed by the two governments of Russia and Afghanistan. . . . The

Government which I represent has always recognized and respected the independence of the two Governments of Khiva and Bukhara. The presence of a limited contingent of troops belonging to my Government is due to temporary requirements expressed and made known to us by the Bukharan Government. This arrangement has been agreed to with the provision that whenever the Bukharan Government so requests, not a single Russian soldier will remain on Bukharan soil. The extension of our friendly assistance in no way constitutes an interference against the independence of the sovereign State of Bukhara. If the Government of Bukhara should cease to formulate its request and should prove dissatisfied with the continuation of such brotherly assistance, then the Government that I represent shall most immediately withdraw its troops.

Could anything be clearer?

TRUE ENOUGH, never in the modern era has any foreign power managed to conquer and colonize this prickly country. Afghanistan is to mountain warfare what France is to high fashion and Italy is to art. Poor in resources, barren in landscape, and home to a scramble of quarrelsome tribes, Afghanistan from the outside looks like a pushover for an invading army with modern weapons. Yet Afghan irregulars, even lacking a unified command, twice proved that imperial Britain at the height of her power could not master their country, a feat they repeated against Soviet invaders. As a result, Afghanistan was never colonized but continued as an amalgam of tribes under rulers at Kabul skilled at coaxing lavish bribes from foreigners to buy or impose peace at home. This was the essence of the rough bargain that shaped the peculiar character of this astonishing quasi-country.

The system took root under Abdur Rahman Khan, Britain's compromise choice as ruler in 1880 following the military standoff in the Second Afghan War. Known as the Iron Amir, he defined his dilemma precisely in an autobiography commonly believed to be genuine: "How can a small Power like Afghanistan, which is like a goat between these lions [Britain and tsarist Russia], or a grain of wheat between two strong millstones of the grinding mill, stand in the midway of the stones without being ground to dust?" The amir's solution was to make the best of being a buffer. He accepted the loss of contested border areas to British India, he acquiesced grudgingly to the Durand Line and the Wakhan corridor, he agreed to let Britain determine Afghan foreign relations. In return, the amir received 1.2 million Indian rupees in annual subsidies, increased to 1.85 million rupees after he bowed to the imposed borders, obtaining at every point a bonus in British weaponry. With this aid, the Iron Amir created a standing national army. He continually challenged tribal chieftains until his death in 1901 but never wholly secured their submission. While the amir approved of modern arms, he drew the line at modern schools and modern rails. He refused to open the windows to modern ideas—the real weapons for transforming traditional societies.

The contrast is with India. To overlook the nation-building legacy of the British Raj (however self-serving its builders' motives) is to view the imperial past in flat-earth terms, bereft of its compensating angularities. In a wise and neglected book, *The End of Empire*, John Strachey put the matter fairly. The British empire in India, he wrote, "was both iniquitous and beneficent; it was founded by violence, treachery and insatiable avarice, but also by incomparable daring and sustained resolution: it united India; it partitioned India; it industrialized India; it stunted India; it served India; it ravaged India; it created modern India; it was selfless and selfish, ruinous and constructive, glorious and monstrous." The radical scion of an Anglo-Indian dynasty, Strachey spoke with an insider's perception. An ancestral Strachey was private secretary to Clive of India, cofounder of the Raj. A squadron of Stracheys thereafter served the Victorian empire that cousin Lytton Strachey mocked and that John helped dismantle as a Laborite war minister.

Afghanistan had its best chance to catch up after World War I, when Abdur Rahman Khan's grandson, the reforming Amanullah Khan, seized power. Styling himself a king rather than an anachronistic amir, he forced a weakened Britain in 1919 to acknowledge Afghanistan's independence and then strove to transform a tribal-peasant society into a nation-state. Having forfeited the British subsidy, Amanullah turned to Soviet Russia for assistance, carefully calibrated, since his orientation was Western and his model Atatürk. Unlike the Iron Amir, however, Amanullah neglected his armed forces and thus proved no match for the regional warlords whom he affronted by exacting taxes, essential to compensate for the lost British subsidy. He further provoked traditionalists, especially the clergy, by establishing Western-style schools and tentatively promoting the emancipation of women. Amanullah's reform program, in the judgment of Vartan Gregorian in *The Emergence of Modern Afghanistan*, "suffered from the same weaknesses that had characterized the much more limited programs of his predecessors. The tragic fact is, he undertook the enormous task of rapidly transforming Afghan society without a definite plan, without the necessary financial resources, and without the requisite technological skill and manpower." In 1928 tribal rebels deposed Amanullah.

His successors did not attempt anything as bold but marked time, cautiously moving Afghanistan toward the modern state system while deferring to tribal power brokers at home. In the mid-1930s, Afghanistan joined the League of Nations, renewed its friendship treaty with Moscow, gained American diplomatic recognition and signed a regional security pact with Turkey, Iran and Iraq. But like Reza Shah in Iran, the Kabul leadership misjudged Nazi Germany and too eagerly assented when Berlin proposed Lufthansa air links and offered to send hundreds of German engineers to assist public works. Most unwisely, after World War II broke out, the Afghans went along as Germany and Italy promoted an anti-British uprising led by the irrepressible Faqir of Ipi on India's North-West Frontier, a strategy that backfired when Germany invaded Russia in June 1941. Now imperial Britain was Russia's ally. Bowing to an Anglo-Soviet démarche, the Kabul authorities expelled German diplomats and most of the technicians, but the Faqir of Ipi and other rebels continued to harass British India.

This set the stage for a confrontation over frontiers when Pakistan attained statehood in 1947. Afghanistan alone opposed Pakistan's membership in the United Nations and pressed afresh its attack on the Durand Line as an illegal imperial relic. "The conflict inevitably made the Royal Government of Afghanistan seek ways to circumvent its dependence on Pakistan for access to the international market, on which its fragile cash economy and meager government revenues depended. Transportation through eastern Iran was very poor, so the only alternative outlet was Soviet Central Asia," writes the American scholar Barnett R. Rubin, the outstanding authority on this period, in *The Fragmentation of Afghanistan*.

Step by step, Afghanistan became entangled militarily and financially with the Soviet bloc as the Cold War reshaped alignments in southern Asia. In the watershed years 1954–1955, Washington approved the first U.S. arms sale to Pakistan while refusing an Afghan request for military

aid, prompting Kabul to turn to Moscow for guns and training. Thus on
security questions, India and Afghanistan found new friends and warm
favor in Moscow, while Pakistan looked to the United States and subsequently China for military and diplomatic support. Meanwhile foreign
aid of every description flowed to Afghanistan, turning the country into
a rentier state (in Rubin's phrase), whose leaders in Kabul veered and
tacked to accommodate the whims of absentee patrons. From 1958 to
1968, more than 40 percent of Afghanistan's expenditures accrued from
overseas, most of it in the form of earmarked foreign aid. A major Soviet
project was the highway linking Kabul to Central Asia, a road wide and
strong enough, so prescient diplomats noted, to sustain Soviet military vehicles. Meanwhile, higher education was parceled out. France supported
the medical faculty, West Germany the police academy, the United States
agriculture, engineering and education, and so forth—but the training of
the Afghan officer corps remained the province of the Soviet bloc.

THE PREDICTABLE DENOUEMENT came in 1973, when former
Prime Minister Muhammad Daoud Khan ousted his cousin
Zahir Shah, abolished the monarchy, established a republic and proclaimed himself president, doing so with the vital support of Soviet-
trained officers. Like Amanullah, his reforming predecessor, Daoud
excelled in impulse, not performance. Yet had he possessed Machiavelli's
guile and FDR's charm, he could hardly have mastered the testy Bedlam
he nominally ruled. To the traditional divisions of tribe, clan and faith were
overlaid schisms within the politically potent Afghan Communist Party
and its military allies: one wing fanatic, the other pragmatic, one faction
aligned with the Soviet KGB, the other with the GRU, or Soviet military
intelligence. At this precarious moment, a seismic shift in regional geopolitics occurred. The shah of Iran, bolstered by the quadrupling of OPEC
oil prices and warmly encouraged by President Nixon and Secretary of
State Henry Kissinger, aspired to exclude Soviet influence from neighboring states and to establish a modern version of the old Persian empire.

No American writer tracked these events more closely than Selig
Harrison, a longtime student of Asian nationalism who shuttled regularly
to and from Kabul during these years. Beginning in 1974, he writes in *Out
of Afghanistan*, "the Shah launched a determined effort to draw Kabul into

a Western-tilted, Tehran centered regional economic and security sphere embracing India, Pakistan and the Persian Gulf states. The United States actively encouraged this rollback policy as part of its broad partnership with the Shah in the economic and military spheres as well as in covert action throughout Southwest Asia." For Kabul, the first tangible fruit was a $40 million easy-terms loan in 1974, the down payment in a projected $2 billion, decade-long development scheme. Not only was Iran seeking to replace the Soviet Union as Kabul's principal foreign donor, but Tehran Radio stepped up broadcasts to Afghan Persian speakers as part of a pervasive propaganda offensive. Less noticeably, the shah's secret police, Savak, collaborated with the CIA in establishing ties with radical Islamic groups in Afghanistan, seemingly the first step in a Forward Policy campaign to unsettle Soviet Central Asia.

As the petrodollars flowed to Kabul, President Daoud significantly moderated his political message. Having earlier assailed his royal cousin for being too soft on frontier disputes, Daoud now muted his call for a "Greater Afghanistan" and began accommodating Iran and Pakistan on sensitive ethnic and frontier issues. To lessen dependence on Moscow, the Kabul regime sent its officers for military training in Egypt, India, the United States and Turkey. As Harrison recounts, Saudi Arabia approved a $500 million aid package for Afghanistan, while further loans and grants flowed in the pipeline from China, the Islamic Development Bank, the Kuwait Fund and the OPEC Special Fund. His course, Daoud insisted, constituted "true nonalignment," as underscored by his well-noted criticisms of Communist Cuba and his two visits to Cairo, the second in 1977, soon after President Anwar Sadat returned from addressing the Israeli Knesset.

Divided on other matters, Afghan Communists were united in their alarm over Daoud's new course. They were seconded by tribal leaders and nationalists who feared the sale of Afghan honor for Cold War pottage. Finally the scales were tipped by the president's placatory visits with Pakistan's military dictator, General Mohammad Zia ul-Haq. At their second meeting, at Islamabad in March 1978, Daoud retreated from Afghanistan's long-avowed goal of liberating Pashtun and Baluch peoples in Pakistan, or so it looked to angry Afghans. They were not assuaged when, being asked at a news conference if the Durand Line was discussed, Daoud responded that "everything was discussed, and with the passage of time everything would fall into place." Fears of betrayal quickened when a third meeting with Zia was scheduled that summer. In Kabul, from bazaar to barracks, alert Afghans braced for a struggle. What followed was the first engagement in a war that still continues. It began when persons or groups unknown assassinated a prominent Afghan Communist. Mass demonstrations swelled into an armed rebellion as tanks and warplanes attacked the presidential palace on April 27, 1978.

The Soviets seemed as surprised by the coup d'état as President Daoud, who but for bungling, accidents and ill-luck (his palace's electronic defense system malfunctioned) would probably have survived. Trapped in his chambers, Daoud refused to surrender and was executed forthwith, along with nineteen members of his family and his personal guard. Daoud's critical misstep was his failure to imprison Hafizullah Amin, the Communist militant who organized the coup and emerged as foreign minister in the new regime. A zealous nationalist, Amin later informed Selig Harrison that he favored the "unity of all Afghans from the Oxus to the Indus," emphasizing that "the Afghan revolution and the issue of Pushtunistan are related." A similar ardor marked the new regime's domestic program: it abolished rural debts and mortgages, made school attendance obligatory, jailed Islamic clergymen and proclaimed President Nur Muhammad Taraki "the guide and father of the April Revolution." In succeeding months, at least 15,000 Afghans perished in purges ordered by Taraki and Amin. As outrage spread among political moderates and rural traditionalists, so did a budding resistance.

INITIALLY, NEITHER MOSCOW nor Washington knew what to make of the Afghan Marxists. In 1978–1979, the sclerotic Brezhnev leadership was troubled by disorders on the Soviet Union's southern border, but it was receiving conflicting assessments from KGB and GRU operatives allied to different factions in the divided Afghan party. Unsettling to both capitals was the February 1979 kidnapping and murder of the U.S. ambassador in Kabul, Adolph Dubs, a specialist in Soviet affairs known and respected by the Russian leadership. Dubs had been snatched from his embassy car at gunpoint and held hostage in a hotel by Tajik separatists demanding the release of jailed comrades; he died in the shootout when Afghan police precipitately stormed the hotel room. Amin half grudgingly apologized, blaming his Communist rivals for the failed rescue, while his defenders lamely explained it would have been political suicide for Amin as a Pashtun to negotiate with Tajik separatists—indicating that for the new, ostensibly Marxist leadership, tribalism trumped dialectics.

In Washington the hardest and clearest line was put forward by President Carter's national security adviser, Zbigniew Brzezinski, a professor-turned-strategist favored with daily access to the Oval Office. With his commanding eyebrows and forceful jaw, Brzezinski exuded certitude, and he had no doubts that the 1978 coup was the prelude to total absorption of Afghanistan into the Soviet bloc, opening the way to the old tsarist dream of reaching warm Gulf waters and dominating Southwest Asia. Less clear and more tentative, Secretary of State Cyrus Vance seconded the view of his regional deputy officer, Harold Saunders, who argued in a memorandum dated April 30, 1978, "We need to take into account the mix of nationalism and Communism in the new leadership and seek to avoid driving the new regime into a closer embrace with the Soviet Union than it might wish."

The Soviet leadership was likewise hesitant at first. Anatoly Dobrynin, the long-serving Soviet ambassador in Washington, recalls in his memoirs that the new Afghan government "attempted to impose on a virtually medieval peasantry radical reforms in land tenure, education, and even dowries, which played an important role in rural areas. This was done without proper knowledge of the countryside and inflamed the local mullahs." Not only mullahs; by autumn and winter, disaffected soldiers joined in the fight, and in March 1979 army rebels took control of Herat, a city of 200,000 inhabitants, mostly Persian speakers, located near the Iranian border. This occurred, ominously for the Kabul Marxists, only weeks after the fall of the shah and the triumph of Ayatollah Khomeini. Taraki turned to Moscow for immediate armed intervention, prompting a three-day Politburo debate. According to a secret transcript that became public in 1991, during the trials following the failed coup against Mikhail Gorbachev, Prime Minister Alexei Kosygin expressed the prevailing view: "Instead of sending our troops there, we should tell Taraki and Amin to change their tactics. They still continue to execute those people who disagree with them." Foreign Minister Andrei Gromyko agreed. "The Afghan army is unreliable and our army would become the aggressor. With whom will we fight? With the Afghan people! Our army would have to shoot them! To be blunt, the Afghan leaders have made many mistakes and haven't got the support of their own people. . . . This would place us in a very difficult position in the international arena. We would ruin everything we have constructed with such difficulty, détente above all. The SALT II talks would be ruined. And this is the overriding issue for us now."

Wisely, the Politburo decided against sending troops and, less wisely, agreed to continue sending advisers and providing advanced weapons to the very partners whose excesses the Soviet leaders decried, thereby repeating the split-the-difference, choose Option B, incremental escalation that had pulled the Kennedy and Johnson administrations into the Vietnam quagmire. What happened at Herat remains unclear—how many died or whether MIG fighters based in Russia bombed the city, as some accounts claim. It would appear that at least nine and possibly as many as forty Soviet advisers and their families died, along with as many as three thousand Afghans. According to the dissident Vladimir Bukovsky, Soviet aid in March 1979 comprised 140 artillery pieces, 90 armored vehicles, 48,000 pistols and rifles, about 1,000 grenade launchers and 680 aerial bombs—a considerable arsenal for an unreliable ally. If Bukovsky is to be believed, the Afghans also requested poison gas and chemical weapons, attesting to the moral as well as political vacuity of the Kabul commissars.

As with President Kennedy and the floundering Diem regime in Saigon, Soviet exasperation bred the belief that a regime change would somehow cure what ailed their rattled clients. In a conspiracy so murky that even today it is not clear who did what to whom, Soviet officials intrigued with Taraki to oust Amin and form a more broad-based government, but Amin was tipped off. He evaded a fatal rendezvous and struck first by executing Taraki, who was officially said to have died of a "serious illness." Thus the man Moscow wanted to oust emerged as Afghan chief— a turn the more worrisome to the Politburo since Amin, who had once studied at Columbia University, was rumored to be secretly seeking U.S. aid and might even have been a CIA agent. The latter hypothesis was very likely bolstered by Soviet awareness that in July 1979 Jimmy Carter had signed a presidential finding authorizing the CIA to undertake a covert program of encouraging Afghan insurgents with propaganda and medical aid. Such was the background when, on December 12, 1979, key members of the Politburo met in the Kremlin and recommended the invasion that proved catastrophic for Afghanistan and in time infected the rest of the world.

IN DECEMBER 1979, Soviet Ambassador Anatoly Dobrynin left Washington for his annual medical checkup in Moscow. On the morning of December 28, he was awakened by a curt radio announcement that Soviet troops had entered Afghanistan "at the request of its government." Dobrynin was not merely a high-ranking Soviet envoy—he was then the longest-serving ambassador in the Washington diplomatic corps—but was also a member of the Central Committee of the USSR Communist Party. Yet so secret was the operation that even he was not forewarned and had to call the Foreign Ministry for details of an act with obvious implications for his own job.

He was informed that the Soviet embassy in Kabul had opposed the invasion, which he found to be the project of a narrow circle within the Politburo—Foreign Minister Gromyko, Defense Minister Dmitri Ustinov, chief party ideologist Mikhail Suslov and KGB chief Yuri Andropov. They believed that Afghan instability jeopardized the security of the USSR's southern frontiers, a menace that would be magnified if an unfriendly regime in Kabul got help from Iran, China or the United States. Gromyko acknowledged in discussions among Politburo insiders at a December 12 meeting that an invasion risked international condemnation, like the outcry that followed the Soviet-led invasion of Czechoslovakia in 1968. Yet he felt security concerns outweighed the risk. After a cursory discussion, Leonid Brezhnev, the ailing, half-alert party chief, "briefly proposed approving the plan for the dispatch of Soviet troops to Afghanistan," Dobrynin noted in his memoirs. Dobrynin was not consulted by Gromyko, though he was in Moscow at the time, because he apparently felt the American reaction, whatever it might be, was not a major factor to be taken into consideration. Defense Minister Ustinov, who lacked combat experience, brushed aside opposition by his own general staff and by officers familiar with Afghanistan. Ustinov ordered dissenters to "stop reasoning" and prepare for the invasion.

On December 13, the full Politburo ratified the decision of its inner circle and signed on to the official explanation that the Soviets were invading "to carry out the missions *requested* [Dobrynin's emphasis] by the leadership of Afghanistan and exclusively aimed at repulsing the outside aggression." Thus some 50,000 troops entered Afghanistan on December 28. Following Amin's murder the same day by KGB operatives teamed up with Afghan secret police, the initial Tass statement was amended to say that the invaders arrived "at the request of the new government" headed by Babrak Karmal, the Politburo's first choice as successor. Karmal needed three days to reach Kabul from his ambassadorial post in Prague. It was a vintage Orwellian moment. Not even Dobrynin was able to determine why the doubts expressed in March were forgotten or ignored by December. There was no grand strategy, he concluded, but instead vexation over a difficult local situation, enhanced by the (not entirely groundless) fears that Afghanistan would become "another U.S. forward base against the Soviet Union lying right against our 'soft underbelly' in our Central Asian republics." "It'll be over in three or four weeks," Brezhnev assured Dobrynin.

For Dobrynin, the Afghan invasion proved to be a professional calamity. "The deeply erroneous Soviet action," he writes in his memoirs, "provided the American right with a solid political pretext for another spiral of the arms race and renewed assaults on détente, and of course helped the standard-bearer of those attacks, Ronald Reagan, defeat Jimmy Carter for re-election. As for Carter himself, he deliberately and vehemently reduced the whole scope of U.S.-Soviet relations, including nuclear issues, to the Afghan question, thus blocking progress anywhere else," the most significant blow being the decision to postpone indefinitely ratification of SALT II, the Strategic Arms Limitation Treaty.

Yet Carter's outrage did not erupt in a vacuum. It was buttressed by the day-in, day-out influence of Zbigniew Brzezinski, the year-long Iranian hostage crisis and the American presidential campaign.

FOR PRESIDENT CARTER, the fall and winter of 1979 proved "the most difficult period of my life." Hard upon the November occupation of the U.S. embassy by radical students in Tehran came the Christmas-week assault on Afghanistan: "I sent Brezhnev on the hot line the sharpest message of my Presidency, telling him that the invasion of Afghanistan was 'a clear threat to the peace' and 'could mark a fundamental and long-lasting turning point in our relations,'" Carter recalls in his memoirs. His anger swelled on receiving a devious reply from Brezhnev repeating the specious claim that the Kabul regime requested help to counter "armed incursions from without into Afghanistan territory." Within weeks the United States embargoed grain shipments to Russia and announced a boycott of the Moscow Olympics, canceled various planned meetings with the Soviets, tightened restrictions on the transfer of technology. Carter explains that "we also assessed the feasibility of arranging for Soviet-made weapons (which could appear to have come from the Afghan military forces) to be given to the freedom fighters in Afghanistan, and of giving them what encouragement we could to resist subjugation by the Soviet invaders."

This was Zbigniew Brzezinski's hour, an opportunity to strike at the Russians he loathed. His rival for Jimmy Carter's ear was the high-minded Cyrus Vance, proponent of the now sidetracked policy of détente, while the president, whom Brzezinski briefed every morning, felt he had been played the fool by Brezhnev. Not given to self-doubt, eager to prove himself the match for his famous émigré predecessor, Henry Kissinger, Brzezinski seized the first possible opportunity to implant an immovable anti-Soviet strategy. Brzezinski readily won approval from a shaken Carter for covert aid to the Afghan resistance. As he put it to the president, "Now we can give the USSR its own Vietnam." Or as he more pithily asserted later on, this was the chance "to finally sow shit in their own back yard." In a sweep through the "crescent of crisis" (Brzezinski's phrase, popularized by an alarming *Time* magazine cover story), the national security adviser persuaded Saudi Arabia to match America's covert aid dollar for dollar, and he won President Anwar Sadat's agreement to rush Egypt's leftover stocks of Soviet arms to the Afghans. Brzezinski flew to Pakistan, met with President Zia, and toured the Khyber Pass, where he grabbed a Pakistani frontiersman's rifle and aimed it northward at Afghanistan.

In Islamabad, Brzezinski agreed to an arrangement that determined what followed. Its key provision was that all arms for the resistance were to be covertly channeled through Pakistan and not directly from the United States. On this matter, Zia was adamant: Pakistan's Inter-Service Intelligence agency was to receive and distribute all weapons. His terms were accepted in Washington without serious debate. Heading into a national election, and with the hostage crisis dominating the evening news, Carter wished to avoid even a hint of waffling on aggression. In effect, Washington let Islamabad dictate its Afghan policy. What was a disaster for Afghanistan thus proved a deliverance for Zia. Overnight, disputes over Pakistan's nuclear ambitions were brushed aside, along with Washington's admonitions about Kashmir and human rights as Zia became a strategic partner of the United States and the rest of the West.

There was more. As the frontline state in a holy war, Pakistan in a decade harvested more than $3 billion in aid from Saudi Arabia and other Gulf sheikdoms, even as Islamabad turned to the godless Chinese for supplemental help. Materially, this enabled Pakistan's armed forces to deduct its tithe in weapons and cash. Moreover, as soon became evident, President Zia's military intelligence service had its own agenda. Here was its long-sought opportunity to acquire "strategic depth" by installing a new regime in Kabul that would be under Islamabad's influence. Here was a chance to train militants for the ongoing fight in Kashmir. Finally, once a friendly fundamentalist regime took root in Afghanistan, the sword of Islam could be directed at Soviet Central Asia.

The prime beneficiary of American aid among the seven resistance groups based in Peshawar was the faction led by Gulbuddin Hekmatyar, an Islamic extremist belonging to a new cohort, modern in knowledge, medieval in faith, known generically as the "bearded engineer." Imperiously intolerant and viscerally anti-American, Hekmatyar (according to Barnett Rubin, a firsthand observer in Peshawar) was also a drug smuggler, counterfeiter and opportunist who later joined with a Communist warlord in assailing Kabul with American-supplied rockets. Yet through most of the Soviet phase of the Afghan war, Hekmatyar was to all intents our man in Afghanistan.

Enter Diego Cordovez, undersecretary-general for special political affairs at the United Nations from 1981 to 1988, who commuted from capital to capital in an eventually successful effort to bring about a Soviet withdrawal. Prospects brightened with the advent in 1985 of Mikhail Gorbachev as leader of the Soviet Union. Not being party to the original decision to invade and eager to press ahead with his domestic reforms, Gorbachev signaled his wish for a face-saving exit from Afghanistan. Yet over and again, Cordovez found that Pakistan undermined him when he pressed for creation of a transition regime headed by the deposed Afghan monarch, Zahir Shah, then living in exile in Rome. The king was willing, and a poll taken by the respected Afghan writer and poet, Sayd Majrooh, showed that 70 percent of Afghan refugees in Pakistan preferred Zahir Shah to any resistance leader. After publishing this survey in February 1988, Majrooh was assassinated with American-supplied weapons on the orders, or so it was generally believed, of Hekmatyar.

Still, the greater moral and political failure lay in Washington, where the internal debate following Ronald Reagan's 1981 inaugural was between "bleeders" and "dealers"—those who wished to prolong indefinitely the Soviet Union's Afghan torment and those who wished to strike a hard-headed deal. On the evidence of Rubin, Harrison and Cordovez, Islamic fundamentalists were not taken seriously by the Reagan White House, nor by the secretaries of defense and state, nor by William J. Casey, the director of Central Intelligence. Harrison reports that Casey wanted to "stick it to the Russians," to the extent of carrying the war into Soviet Central Asia. Responding to a question about the fundamentalists put by Harrison, Defense Secretary Caspar Weinberger admitted that "we knew they were not very nice people" but "we had this terrible problem of making choices." Washington believed that once the Soviets withdrew, everything would fall readily into place (so Harrison was assured by CIA officers the day of the pullout). Hence the opposition to any transition regime and the willingness to supply Islamic militants with the latest heatseeking Stinger surface-to-air missiles when they weren't needed, Harrison argues, since Gorbachev had already signaled his willingness to call it quits.

Hence, worse yet, the American decision to move the goalposts at Geneva in 1988. Before the peace conference, Washington had agreed to stop sending arms if the Soviets went home. But at Geneva, scenting Gorbachev's desperation, American negotiators switched from "negative" to "positive symmetry," that is, letting all sides continue to arm their respective allies. In January 1989, the incoming Bush administration finally saw to it that no weapons paid with U.S. funds would go to Hekmatyar. But it made no difference, Pakistan and Saudi Arabia continued to shower arms on the fundamentalists. "In practice," writes Rubin in *The Search for Peace*, "U.S. maintenance of the arms pipeline continued to strengthen the Afghan groups that U.S. policy had allegedly abandoned." By then all Afghan exile factions were groping in the surreal maze of Pakistani politics. When Zia was killed the previous year in an aircraft explosion (along with U.S. Ambassador Arnold L. Raphael), the suspects included the Pakistani military, the KGB, every Afghan faction and the CIA. The explosion remains a mystery, and there is an absence of curiosity about its causes.

Viewing the entire melancholy outcome, Rubin remarks that no ally paid more dearly for the victory in the Cold War than the people of Afghanistan: "The maneuvers of party leaders may inspire cynicism or repulsion, but millions of unknown people sacrificed their homes, their land, their cattle, their health, their family and their lives, with barely a hope of success or reward, at least in this world." Yet once the Soviets were gone, Washington all but literally walked away, abandoning the wounded, closing purses and hearts, sending no special emissaries to help form a transition regime. It was a triumph for what I have called the Buchanan syndrome in American foreign policy, after Daisy and Tom Buchanan in F. Scott Fitzgerald's *The Great Gatsby*, the careless people who "smashed up things and creatures and then retreated back into their money, or whatever it was that kept them together."

To fight the Soviets, the CIA provided weapons and funds exceeding $3 billion to the Afghan resistance; after the Russians vacated, U.S. aid dwindled to a pittance. Anger at being treated like discarded mercenaries turned thousands of resistance fighters into easy converts for Islamic jihadists. No American has followed this conversion more closely than Mary Anne Weaver of the *New Yorker.* In her *Portrait of Egypt* (1999) she recounts a conversation with Sheik Omar Abdel Rahman, the blind Egyptian clergyman jailed for his role in the truck bombing of the World Trade Center. In 1985, Sheik Omar journeyed to Peshawar, where he was driven in a U.S.-supplied vehicle to a mujahedin training camp. There he fell under the spell of Gulbuddin Hekmatyar. "My strongest emotion was pride," he recalled. "I felt so proud of my religion, so proud of the power that Muslims had. And I knew that Allah would aid these people and this religion, and that Islam would be victorious in the end."

In practice, Weaver found, the CIA helped train and fund what eventually became an international network of highly disciplined Islamic militants, the "Arab Afghans" or the "Children of Jihad," a new breed of terrorists. "When the Soviet Union left Afghanistan and the CIA closed down its pipeline to the mujahideen," she writes, "Washington left behind tens of thousands of well-trained and well-armed Arab, Asian, and Afghan fighters available for new jihads." One portent was the machine-gun attack in Addis Ababa on Egyptian President Hosni Mubarak during a 1995 state visit. The attempt failed and the putative assassins were caught and executed; they had fought in Afghanistan. Other harbingers the same year were the truck bomb attack on the Egyptian embassy in Islamabad, the first of its kind, killing seventeen, and the car bombing in Riyadh, the Saudi capital, of a U.S. military training center, killing five Americans and wounding forty—the precursor for the still unsolved 1996 bombing of a U.S. military housing complex in the Saudi city of Dhahran, killing 19 and wounding 240 U.S. airmen.

What did Washington's politicians and experts make of this legacy of the covert Afghan strategy? It is hard to say. There was never a real debate, in Congress or in the press, about letting Zia dispense American largess. Nor was there serious discussion of Washington's failure to press for a broad-based transition regime in Kabul, headed by the willing former Afghan king, Mohammad Zahir Shah. The absence of debate and accountability is, in these circumstances, an unavoidable cost of bipartisan foreign policy. Since both Democratic and Republican lawmakers were complicit, neither had any political incentive to reopen the matter.

Among the silent were the two members of Congress who had clamored most insistently for aid to the Afghan resistance, Senator Gordon Humphrey, a New Hampshire Republican, and Representative Charles Wilson, a Texas Democrat. As a member of a House subcommittee on appropriations, Wilson succeeded in quadrupling the $30 million requested by the CIA in 1984 for the Afghans, which rose from $120 million to $250 million in 1985, $476 million in 1986 and $630 million in 1987, each increment matched by the Saudis. It was Wilson who in 1986 overcame resistance from the Pentagon, CIA and State Department to supplying the mujahedin with the high-tech, shoulder-fired Stinger missile, capable of downing helicopters or—as opponents noted—civilian airliners. In all, a thousand missiles and 250 launchers were provided to Afghan fighters. (Years later, the CIA attempted to buy back leftover Stingers at twice their original cost, but according to Harrison, citing intelligence estimates, from two hundred to four hundred remained unaccounted for.) Wilson, lanky and likable in the Lyndon Johnson mold, now a lobbyist for defense industries, had no greater fan than the president of Pakistan. As Zia glowed in a *60 Minutes* interview, "If there is a single man who has played a part in the war that will be recorded in golden letters, it is the Right Honorable Charley Wilson. Wilson did it." Years later, in another *60 Minutes* interview in 2002, Wilson finally voiced second thoughts about Washington's abrupt termination of aid after the Soviet withdrawal from Afghanistan; otherwise, like Senator Humphrey, he has adhered to the British upper-crust maxim: Never apologize, never explain.

For his part, and with enviable sangfroid, Brzezinski proffered this response to a French political weekly when asked if he regretted favoring extremist Muslims or training future terrorists: "What was more important in world history? The Taliban or the fall of the Soviet empire? A few over-excited Islamists, or the liberation of Central Europe and the end of the Cold War?" This wintry realism has an earlier parallel. In April 1917, the German General Staff debated a scheme to knock Russia out of World War I. A popular uprising in February had forced the abdication of Tsar Nicholas, but the new provisional government decided to continue fighting an unpopular war. Why not play the Bolshevik card? Germany for years had secretly cultivated, in fact helped finance, radical Russian exiles who vowed to seek peace once they took power. So the German generals, noses held and eyes averted, let Lenin and thirty other Bolsheviks pass through Germany on a train bound for Russia, precipitating the October Revolution that gave Germany seven months of peace in the East, and the world seventy years of Soviet Communism.

VI

THE CAUCASUS

A Bedlam of Identity

Mountaineer warriors in Imam Shamil's Islamic uprising in the North Caucasus. Nobody fought longer or harder against Tsarist dominion.

Courtesy Shareen Blair Brysac.

LIKE MANY AMERICANS, I owe my first visual impression of the Caucasus to ubiquitous television commercials in the 1970s showing ingratiating old-timers in Georgia who claimed to be 137 years old or thereabouts, thanks, the sponsor hinted, to a regular diet of yogurt. It later turned out that many highlanders had routinely faked their birthdays, adding decades to their age to evade being conscripted into Russian armies. Hence the twinkling eyes and wonderful grins among oldsters who were unexpectedly reaping a windfall from the global consumer culture.

I recalled the yogurt story during a visit to Georgia because it seemed to epitomize the disorders afflicting newborn nations in which confounding authority remains a way of life. Call it iceberg nationalism. On its surface Georgia possesses the formal attributes of nationhood: flags, passports, embassies, anthems, dance companies, Olympic teams and so forth. Lurking hugely below, less visible, are compacted attitudes about government and taxes (to be ignored), political compromise (besmirches honor), the role of religion (the savior of identity), responses to adversity (fatalism) and clan loyalties (never to be betrayed) that during a difficult transition combine to bewilder outsiders and defy exorcism. Much of this is embodied in rites and legends, with their encoded themes about foreign overlords, a pattern that with variations can be discerned in many long repressed nations (e.g., Armenia and Greece, Ireland and Scotland, Israel and Palestine, Poland and the Baltic States).

Georgia seems an archetypal example. That it even exists is a wonder. Its 4 million or so inhabitants speak an ancient language of unknown origin, using a slithering script that has endured with little change for eleven centuries. After the conversion of King Mirian III in the fourth century, Georgia became the second Christian state (Armenia was the first). Georgians have preserved their distinctive culture despite conquest and colonization by Greeks, Romans, Mongols, Byzantines, Persians, Arabs, Turks and Russians. Georgia has two pasts. One is visible everywhere in and around Tbilisi, the capital since the twelfth century—the cone-roofed churches rising on the encircling hills; the splotched Soviet-era hotel on the main street, which provides temporary shelter for Georgians displaced by two ongoing civil wars; the crypt in the national museum, with its Colchis gold and its darkened upper galleries, closed for want of funds; the art museum with a telltale blank space on its walls where a plaque formerly noted that Joseph Stalin studied as a seminarian in the same building; the old city, with its maze of wooden houses and their shabby balconies, redolent of genteel decay.

The less visible past is internalized. In Soviet times, party leaders professed their admiration for Georgian culture and cuisine. Ordinary Russians flocked to Georgian holiday camps, some still intact, now silent and desolate, on hills above the capital. Tbilisi grew to 1.5 million inhabitants, becoming the cosmopolitan hub of the Caucasus, renowned for its theaters and orchestras, its song and dance. (George Balanchine was among Georgia's famous emigrants; his brother, the eminent composer Andria Balanchivadze, stayed home.) A succession of visitors have expressed their delight. In 1932, while still a half-believing Communist, Arthur Koestler arrived as a literary pilgrim, having traveled the celebrated Georgian Military Highway. "I loved Tiflis more than any other town in the Soviet Union," Koestler recalled in a memoir, *The Invisible Writing,* describing the city as irresistible, neither European nor Asian but a happy blend: "It has a carefree and leisurely rhythm of life which is Bohemian rather than Oriental; but its fastidious architecture and the courteous poise of its citizens make one constantly aware that it is the product of one of the oldest Christian civilizations."

Like other visitors, Koestler discovered that Russian affection was unrequited. Georgians bridled at Soviet crudeness and condescension and plainly hoped that one day Russian rule would end. Discontent was not always passive. After a 1924 rebellion, Stalin vowed that "all of Georgia must be plowed under," and in the Great Purge of 1935–1938 he liquidated virtually the entire party leadership. The purge was carried out by the future NKVD chief, Lavrentii Beria, a Mingrelian, one of the lesser peoples in the South Caucasus (as Georgians like to emphasize). During his 1932 visit, Koestler sensed the tension when he took part in a Bolshevik ceremony at the National Opera House. He noticed that all speeches were pointedly delivered in Georgian. When Koestler apologized to his neighbor, an elderly poet, for speaking in Russian, the poet whispered back, "Your Russian is so awful they'll like it."

Given this past, it was commonly assumed Georgia would prosper when it achieved independent statehood. It seemed blessed with productive farms and fine vineyards, with ample water power, an extensive network of roads and rail, and an educated workforce. Georgian institutes for mathematics and physics were deemed outstanding in Soviet times. Yet these advantages were negated in the first years of nationhood as South Ossetians, with apparent Russian encouragement, initiated a separatist rebellion, followed by an uprising by another non-Georgian minority, the Abkhazians. Still, Moscow was not responsible for the messianic tantrums of Georgia's first president, Zviad Ghamsakhurdia, a onetime political prisoner who now jailed his rivals. He proposed a blood and language test for Georgian citizenship, claimed the Holy Grail lay hidden in Tbilisi's cathedral, and denounced both Russia and the West while condoning the Communist hard-liners who attempted in August 1991 to depose Mikhail Gorbachev. After eight months as president, violence and chaos swirling around him, Ghamsakhurdia fled the capital and died in disputed circumstances.

Hence the relief in 1992 when Eduard Shevardnadze returned to Georgia to become chairman of the State Council. Known in the West as the soft-spoken Soviet foreign minister who negotiated the orderly Soviet withdrawal from Central and Eastern Europe, Shevardnadze had earlier served as Georgia's party chief and was familiar with the local ravines. He succeeded in brokering pragmatic cease-fires with the separatist rebels, sought to mollify Moscow and struck intricate deals with clan warlords. Elected president in 1995, Shevardnadze won a second term five years later. Yet despite his emollient skills and unquestioned courage—he has survived two assassination attempts—Shevardnadze presides over a country sinking into quicksand.

As elsewhere in the Caucasus, Soviet-style censorship is no more, but the information void persists. Nobody knows for sure the size of Georgia's population (estimates range from 3 million to 5.5 million), nor can anyone say with any authority how many Georgians work abroad, or how much money they send home in remittances. Nor can anybody credibly estimate the size of Georgia's underground economy or explain how Georgian pensioners survive on the equivalent of $15 a month. Despite all its water resources, there are chronic power cutoffs, owing partly to management incompetence and partly to the recurrent cutoffs in Russian natural gas to penalize Georgia for an unpaid debt reckoned at $200 million or so.

All this has happened despite more than $1 billion in U.S. economic aid over a decade, making Georgia the third or fourth largest per capita recipient (depending on who counts) behind Israel, Egypt and Armenia. Corruption is as shameless as the traffic police flagging down motorists to exact fines for spurious offenses. "We live in a country without receipts," laments a Georgian working for an American nongovernmental organization. "That's half true," comments an AID official, "you can get receipts for almost anything—if you want to prove you have low blood pressure, sure, your doctor will write it out for you." Graft comes in all sizes. American passengers on buses from Turkey are routinely asked to pay a $3 "computer fee" at a frontier post conspicuously lacking a computer.

Yet corruption is manifestly the legacy of empire. In the words of David Usupashili, the U.S.-educated lawyer who chaired Georgia's anti-corruption commission, as he remarked to the journalist Anatol Lieven, "People were utterly cynical about Communist laws and rules, but unfortunately that fed a nihilistic mentality in which under independence they still do not respect any laws or rules at all. . . . Corruption is a way of life. People don't believe that the state will ever provide services or enforce the law, so they don't pay taxes. There are only two ways to survive here. To become financially strong yourself, or to place yourself under the protection of someone who is stronger. But there is no sense of being a citizen, only a kind of feudalism, in politics, government, business." Or in the terse summary of a U.S. aid official: "In the old days, Georgians became expert at stealing Russian silver. But now, guess what? Georgians own the silverware, and the thefts continue." Cynics question the seriousness of periodic anticorruption campaigns, noting that the president himself sets a deplorable example by awarding choice jobs to members of his own family. Moreover, in obtaining evidence of corruption, investigators use the threat of publicizing their findings to obtain favors for themselves. Cynics note that two hundred law schools have sprung up in Georgia, but as an attorney noted, "People study law to be part of the problem, not of the solution." In a wider perspective, corruption is the flip side of the intrepidity that enabled Georgians to sustain their identity for twenty-one centuries. Contempt for authority is a staple in the popular myths of the Caucasus. In Azerbaijan, the traditional mentality has been traced to an eleventh-century epic, according to the literary scholar Hikmet Hadjy-Zadeh. As set forth in *The Book of My Grandfather Korkut,* its code (paraphrased by Hadjy-Zadeh) runs essentially like this: "Winner takes all, valor over profit; defeat is worse than death; request of help is disgracing; thrift is stinginess and prudence is cowardice."

THE SPECIAL CHARACTER of the Caucasus owes much to the profligacy of nature, compounded by the combative hand of man. Nowhere else are so many nations, tribes, clans and subclans crowded testily together in so inhospitable a space—a craggy isthmus between the Caspian and Black Seas, much of it a maze of steep valleys and menacing gorges, crowned by forty-three peaks higher than 14,000 feet. Culturally and physically, Caucasia is the prototypical borderland. Its mountains, stretching six hundred miles from sea to sea, not only form the divide between Europe and Asia but also separate the two earliest Christian kingdoms (Armenia and Georgia) from Islam's two major branches, the dissenting Shias, mostly inhabiting what is now Azerbaijan, and the majority Sunnis who predominate in the North Caucasus. And around these fault lines lie the half-hidden rock pools whose prickly denizens have for two millennia frustrated and baffled intruders, starting with Greeks and Romans, proceeding more recently with Turks, Persians, Russians and now including forward scouts from an expanding America. Perhaps nowhere else are so many of the unintended consequences of empire on such generous display.

Arab geographers deservedly called the Caucasus the "Mountain of Languages." It is said that tsarist generals needed a hundred interpreters when their armies thrust into Caucasia early in the nineteenth century. Travelers reported that seventy languages were heard in the markets of Tbilisi, capital of Georgia. In Yerevan, capital of Armenia, a visitor in 1928 spotted street signs in five different alphabets—Cyrillic, Armenian, Georgian, Arabic and Latin. If these accounts smack of exaggeration, it is a prosaic fact that in Soviet times Daghestan alone recognized eleven official languages among a million people inhabiting a province no bigger than Virginia. Post–Soviet Union, diversity persists. Like its neighbor Chechnya, Daghestan lies officially within the Russian Federation, but it is the only constituent republic without an executive president. It is governed instead by a collective state council on which fourteen ethnic groups are represented. Moreover, beginning in the late 1980s, Daghestan's Communist authorities determined that each "major nation" (i.e., a group com-

prising more than 70,000 persons) might have its own "national movement," a policy that thirty-odd groups zestfully executed.

However bewildering, the result in Daghestan has been a live-and-
let-live stability that has survived repeated attempts by militant Chechens
to embroil Daghestanis in their own separatist uprising (still true, as of December 2002). And this despite Daghestan's historic role as the instigator
of the longest continuous rebellion against tsarist rule, the insurgency led
by Imam Shamil, the "Lion of Daghestan," an austere and devout disciple
of Sufism. To this day, Shamil is the iconic hero of the North Caucasus,
where his great black beard and accusing eyes stare everywhere from photographs. What pictures cannot capture is his eloquence; as a disciple once
said, "Flames darted from his eyes and flowers fell from his lips." Even in
translation, his verbal power is evident. Told by the Russians that they
could benefit his people by building roads, the imam replied: "You say my
roads are bad and my country impassable. It is well: that is the reason the
powerful White Tsar with all his armies who march on me ceaselessly can
still do nothing against me. I do not venture to compare myself to great
sovereigns. I am Shamil—an ordinary Avar. But my bad roads, my forests
and mountains, make me stronger than many monarchs. I should anoint
my trees with oil, and mix my mud with fragrant honey, and garland my
rocks with laurel and bay, so much do they aid me in my battle for Caucasian freedom."

Shamil began his holy war in the 1820s, and its major phase ended in
1859 with the Lion's voluntary surrender. "I am very happy that you are
here in Russia," Alexander II reputedly assured Shamil, with a gallantry
that did credit to the victor. "I wish it could have happened sooner. You
will not regret it. I shall look after your interests and we shall be friends."
(The tsar honored his promise; the exiled imam died peacefully in 1871
on a pilgrimage to Mecca.)

Alas, such chivalric episodes are anomalies in the Caucasus. Excess on
all sides is the common curse of this lofty isthmus. Its mountains have har-
bored clerical extremists and mass killers, audacious patriots and Mafia
thugs, desperate outsiders and romantic rebels of every description, real or
mythical—the way fittingly led by Prometheus, who for his transgressions
was chained by Zeus on the Caucasian peak of Kazbek (16,540 feet). The
Murid wars (as Shamil's uprising was called) were the fiercest by any subject peoples in the tsarist era. The horrors and redemptive gallantries of
the uprising are preserved in the tales of Tolstoy and Lermontov, who wit-

nessed them as young officers. When the wars broke out, the Russian garrison numbered roughly 50,000 men. But when Shamil assumed command and united the mountaineers of Daghestan and Chechnya in a sustained guerrilla war, Russia needed 200,000 troops to replenish losses incurred through battle or disease. In 1828, a senior officer presciently forewarned his superior, General Alexei Yermolov: "The Caucasus may be likened to a mighty fortress, strong by nature, artificially protected by military works, and defended by a numerous garrison. Only thoughtless men would attempt to take such a stronghold by storm. A wise commander would see the necessity of having recourse to military art, and would lay his parallels by sap and mine, and so master the place."

By adopting this arduous strategy, the Russians in the end prevailed, if at appalling cost. Tsarist armies all but denuded the mountains to deprive rebels of forest cover, leading to a sanguinary finale in the 1860s after Shamil's surrender. "The last phase of the Caucasian war can only be described as genocide," writes the Yale scholar Firuz Kazemzadeh. "Under the new commander, Grand Duke Mikhail Nikolaevich, troops systematically combed the mountains, valleys and the forests of Circassia, flushing out Cherkes tribesmen, driving them into the plains and to the seashore, or killing masses of them. Death, emigration to Turkey, or settlement in the plains under the guns of Russian forts in a ring of Cossack villages was the fate of the Mountaineers." Or as the grand duke laconically phrased it, "It was necessary to exterminate half of the Mountaineers to compel the other half to lay down its arms."

What, one wonders, could have prompted so determined and merciless a campaign? Was there a grand design animating Russia's continuous expansion, of which the Caucasian wars were but a part? Such questions were examined anxiously in Western Europe, especially in Great Britain. From the start, Russophobes like Lord Palmerston contended that tsarist advances into the Caucasus and Central Asia foreshadowed a frontal assault on British India. "Russia has advanced specially because nobody observed, watched and understood what she was doing," Palmerston wrote in 1835 to his colleague and brother-in-law, the Whig grandee Lord Melbourne. "Expose her plans and you half defeat them. Raise public opinion against her and you double her difficulties. . . . Depend upon it, that is the best way to save you from the necessity of making war against her." Beginning in the 1830s, there ensued a drumroll of press attacks on Russia, promoted but not wholly manufactured by politicians. British car-

toons depicted Russia as a marauding bear, menacing valiant Poles, bullying Afghans, lusting for Turkey's straits and bravely opposed by Caucasian
highlanders.

The attacks finally elicited a spirited response from Prince Alexander
Gorchakov, the tsar's long-serving foreign minister. In a circular letter to
his embassies in 1864, Gorchakov explained Russia's forward policy in cadences that reflected the spirit of an expansionist age. Russia's position, he
said, was the same as that of all civilized societies "brought into contact
with half-savage, nomad populations." In such cases, he maintained, "it always happens that the more civilised State is forced, in the interest of the
security of its frontiers and its commercial relations to exercise a certain
ascendancy" over neighbors of a turbulent and unsettled character. "First
there are raids and acts of pillage to put down," he went on. "To put a stop
to them, the tribes on the frontier have to be reduced to a state of more
or less perfect submission. . . . It is a peculiarity of Asiatics to respect nothing but visible and palpable force. . . . Such has been the fate of every
country which has found itself in a similar situation. The United States in
America, France in Algeria, Holland in her colonies, England in India—
all have been irresistibly forced, less by ambition than by imperious necessity, into this onward movement, where it is difficult to know where to
stop." Hence Russia's need to extend fortified posts deeper and deeper
into nomad territory. Even so, no matter how provoked, Gorchakov reas-
suringly concluded, Russia would act with moderation and respect the
independence of its neighbors.

Conspicuously unaddressed in his circular was Russia's reliance on
Cossacks, a separate estate of warrior-farmers serving as colonizers of
Russia's borderlands. "Moderation" was not a term that would normally
apply to Cossack hosts. Moreover, in contrast with the other countries he
listed, Gorchakov's government was answerable only to the tsar under an
absolutist system sans constitution, parliament, elections, free press or independent judiciary—how else to explain popular passivity during fifty
years of bloodletting in the Caucasus? Nor did the Russian cabinet operate collectively; each minister reported independently to the tsar, so that
it was never clear who spoke for the government. At the moment Gorchakov assured the British that the Russian empire had reached its limits,
headstrong commanders were extending them. This was the tsar's wish.
"Konstantin Petrovich, take Khiva for me," exhorted Alexander II in bid-
ding farewell in 1867 to the new military governor of half-conquered

Turkestan. Within five years, General Kaufmann did as asked—sending 13,000 men and 14,000 camels across an unforgiving desert to subdue the khanate of Khiva, 475 miles west of Tashkent. Yet perhaps the foreign minister's loudest silence in his famous circular was his failure to mention Islam.

FOR FIVE CENTURIES, Islam constituted a riddle to which Russia's leaders were unable to find a satisfactory answer. Radically different regimes—imperial, Communist and republican—attempted different strategies for winning over Muslim citizens: tolerant coexistence and generous incentives for assimilation; or forced conversion, draconian suppression and in extreme cases starvation, slaughter and expulsion. These strategies implied a common assumption of Russian superiority, a reluctance to take Islam seriously and the recurrent suspicion that non-Christians were "ignoble savages and unfaithful subjects," in one tsarist official's phrase. The impression conveyed in popular literature of the nineteenth century, as the American scholar Seymour Becker found, was that Russia's cultural superiority was "so obvious that her Muslim subjects could not help but perceive it, given time, and voluntarily assimilate into the Russian nation." With exceptions, the same condescension tainted the Communist approach.

The Islamic question originated in 1552, when Ivan the Terrible's armies conquered Kazan and for the first time brought large numbers of Muslims under Muscovy's direct rule. Annexing Kazan and its sister khanate Astrakhan ensured Russia mastery of the serpentine Volga, opening the way to Russia's commercial and military penetration of Tatar and Turkic lands to the east and southeast. Toeholds in the Caucasus were secured under Peter the Great (1682–1725). Russians then charged southward during the reign of Catherine II (1762–1796), defeating the Turks in two wars, conquering southern Ukraine and the Crimea, and extending protection to the Christian kingdom of Georgia. This was chiefly the work of Catherine the Great's longtime favorite and likely secret husband, Prince Grigory Potemkin, the tireless founder and principal architect of "New Russia."

A one-eyed giant, strongly beaked, with leonine locks, known across Russia as Serenissimus, Potemkin was a young courtier when he first caught Catherine's eye. Their affair evolved into a durable partnership, enabling Serenissimus to vastly enlarge Catherine's empire, create Russia's Black Sea fleet and found the cities of Sevastopol and Odessa—not just the sham villages universally and unjustly affixed to his name. He was that rare creature: a visionary with a sure instinct for the realities of power. In the words of his diligent British biographer, Simon Sebag Montefiore, "Russia had not possessed an imperial statesman of such success in both dreams and deeds since Peter the Great."

His dreams and deeds are worth reexamining in light of the prevalent Western notion that Russia's autocratic character reflects the negligible influence of the European Enlightenment. Not entirely so; the luminaries of the Enlightenment found an eager and responsive audience in Catherine's Russia. Nearly all of Voltaire's sixty-odd works were rendered into Russian, along with prompt translations of Diderot's mighty *Encyclopedia* and of Montesquieu's monumental *Spirit of the Laws*. "Francomania" was the fashion of the hour. The empress herself not only corresponded devotedly with Voltaire but also sent scholars to Scotland to study political economy with Adam Smith. Her court so lionized Jeremy Bentham during his visit that Russian translations of his utilitarian essays outsold the original editions in English.

Especially popular under Catherine "was the vague idea that newly conquered regions to the south could provide virgin soil on which to raise out of nothing a new civilization. Voltaire told Catherine he would come to Russia if Kiev were made the capital rather than St. Petersburg," writes James H. Billington in his appraisal of Russian culture, *The Icon and the Axe*. Certainly no one outdid Potemkin in his infectious optimism about the utopian promise of the new territories in Ukraine and then in Crimea, where in 1783 the prince himself administered loyalty oaths (sworn on the Koran) to Tatar nobles and mullahs of the now humbled Crimean khanate. It seemed wondrous to Russians that these heirs of Jenghiz Khan now vowed fidelity to an Orthodox empress.

"Imagine the Crimea is yours, and the wart on your nose is no more!" an exultant Potemkin wrote to Catherine, alluding to the submission of a once hostile stronghold on the obtrusive Crimean peninsula. "Gracious Lady . . . You are obliged to raise Russian glory! See who has gained what: France took Corsica, Austria took more in Moldavia without a war than we did. There is no power in Europe that has not participated in the carving-up of Asia, Africa, America. Believe me, that doing this will win you immortal glory greater than any other Russian Sovereign ever. This glory will force its way to an even greater one: with the Crimea, dominance over the Black Sea will be achieved." The prince closed with his customary panache, "Russia needs paradise."

To populate paradise, Potemkin resettled New Russia with ecumenical zeal, inviting persecuted German Mennonites, industrious Swedish Protestants, Orthodox Romanians fleeing Ottoman rule and Jews seeking an exit from Polish ghettoes. His policies increased the estimated male population of Crimea from 52,000 in 1782 to 130,000 by 1795, with a comparable jump for the same period in all New Russia from 339,000 to 554,000. He befriended a French grandee, Armand-Emanuel, duc de Richelieu, the great-nephew of the cardinal, who later became the first governor of New Russia. He recruited Samuel Bentham, a brother of the philosopher, to build ships for Russia's budding navy at newly founded Sevastopol. Of particular concern to Potemkin was the protection of Muslim Tatars from the bullying intolerance of Russian soldiers. He ordered his commanders to set an example of scrupulous conduct and to report any boisterous slights by other ranks. He gave money to maintain mosques and accorded Tatar *murzas* the rank of Russian nobility, with the vital right to own land. "It was traditional Russian imperialism to co-opt the Moslem hierarchies," notes the prince's biographer, "but Potemkin's sensitive care for them is unusual in a Russian soldier of any epoch."

STILL, THIS WAS NOT the whole story. Serpents too lurked in paradise. Having annexed Crimea, the prince sensed an opportunity to eliminate finally the dangers posed by another remnant of Jenghiz Khan's Golden Horde—the Nogai, warlike nomads on the Kuban steppe east of Crimea. Potemkin wished to resettle the Nogai Horde between the Volga and the Urals, and he turned to a legendary Russian general, Alexander Suvorov, to enforce his plan. The diminutive and wiry Suvorov, charming in manner but ruthless in battle, made no secret of his "bayonets before bullets" credo: "The head of the army does not wait for the tail. The bullet is a fool, the bayonet is a sportsman; fortune goes past like a flash of lightning; seize her by the hair: she will never come back to you." Steel was Suvorov's favored medium: "Cold steel—bayonets and sabres! Push the enemy over, hammer them down, don't lose a moment." He attacked by storm, he did not trust the musket ("that crazy bitch") and his greatest battles, even admirers acknowledged, were bloodbaths.

General Suvorov summoned the Nogai by the thousands to meet him on the shores of the Sea of Azov, where he read the declaration in which the last Tatar khan of the Crimea abdicated in favor of Catherine II, yielding to her all his rights and privileges, including suzerainty over the Nogai. What followed is related by British author John F. Baddeley, whose *The Russian Conquest of the Caucasus* (1908) remains the authoritative account by a foreigner:

> The assembled clans listened in silence, and took without demur the oath of allegiance to their new ruler. A mighty feast at which 100 beeves and 800 sheep furnished two items in the bill of fare, followed by horse races and *djighitova* [feats of horsemanship], marked the close of the ceremony, and the popular contentment seemed to give promise of peace and happiness in their new relationship for Russians and Nogais alike. But when, a little later, Souvóroff, having won over some of the more influential chieftains, allowed Potemkin's plan to be known, the disillusionment was great. The evil news ran like wildfire through the vast encampment; murmured discontent rapidly grew into loud-voiced protest, and from word to deed with the semi-savage Tartars was but a single step. . . . A little later blood flowed in torrents. The first victims were those mourzas and sultans who had been seduced by Russian promises and probably by Russian gold; and so swift was the deed of vengeance, that before the Russians could interfere, one and all had paid for their treachery with their lives. But Souvóroff, with a sagacity which wins him the commendation of his countrymen, had foreseen some such turn of affairs and had taken his measures accordingly. When the infuriated Nogais proceeded to attack the nearest of the Russian detachments, regiment after regiment closed in upon them, and in a short time it was all over. Driven into a boggy ground and seeing no possibility of escape, the miserable nomads in a mad access of despair destroyed their valuables, slaughtered their women, and threw their little children into the neighbouring stream.

A remnant of the Nogai fought on vainly, only to be routed by Suvorov's regiments, reinforced ferociously by Cossacks now settling on the steppe. A minority of survivors fled to the Caucasus. Most of the rest were transferred to Crimea, whence, "panic-stricken at Russian methods of government," many Tatars fled to Turkey so that "to this day the peninsula has never recovered its former population" (Baddeley). For his action, Suvorov received the Order of St. Vladimir (first class), and all other combatants, down to lowly Cossacks, were generously rewarded by Catherine. The rich black soil of the steppe was opened to Russian settlers, whose number swelled rapidly, with the intended result that the Circassians (the generic term for mountaineers of the North Caucasus) henceforth found few Islamic allies north of the Kuban.

This strategic deportation anticipated the massive and brutal ethnic surgery perpetrated by Stalin during World War II. Confirming Communism's distrust of Islamic peoples, the Soviet dictator ordered the wholesale deportation from November 1943 to June 1944 of four Caucasian nationalities—Chechens, Ingush, Karachai and Balkars—together with Crimean Tatars, on the claim they had "collaborated massively with the Nazi occupier." In December 1944, Stalin followed up by expelling other nationalities whose loyalty was doubted: the Greeks, Bulgars and Armenians from the Crimea, the Meskhetian Turks, Kurds and Khemshins from the Caucasus. One can hardly overstate the suffering and bitterness resulting from these deportations, mostly to Central Asia and carried out with heavy casualties on suffocating freight trains or cattle trucks.

Especially pathetic is the plight of more than 70,000 Meskhetian Turks, shipped en masse in 1944 to Uzbekistan, subjected to pogroms as recently as 1989, and to this day barred from returning to their Georgian homeland or gaining citizenship rights in Azerbaijan. Even when the "right of return" is formally acknowledged, the results have been melancholy. This was the experience of 250,000 Crimean Tatars, forcibly expelled in 1944 and allowed to resettle in the Crimea only after Mikhail Gorbachev's advent in 1985. As visitors today can readily observe, returning Tatars live in cement-block villages, reportedly underwritten by Saudis, on the outskirts of bigger Crimean cities. They work as waiters in truck-stop cafés and belly dancers in roadside restaurants not far from the venerable Tatar capital of Bakhchisarai, now redolent of mothballs and tourism.

Most obdurate of all were the Chechens, who rebelled repeatedly against tsarist and Soviet authority. As early as 1828, General Alexei Yermolov tried to teach the Chechens a lesson once and for all. He dispatched six companies from his best regiment together with seven hundred Cossacks to wipe out a thriving and populous *aul* or village above the banks of the Terek, the river forming Caucasia's recognized boundary. As artillery and muskets poured shells point-blank into the village, the Chechens fought with a stubbornness the Russians had not experienced before. When it ended, only 14 men and 140 women and children of the *aul* still lived. The village was then totally demolished. "Such were Yermóloff's methods," relates Baddeley, "and it cannot be denied that, as in the present case, they were immediately effective. The remaining villages of the clan were deserted, the inhabitants seeking refuge in Tchetchnia proper. But they took a bloody revenge during the next thirty years, and it is strange that Russian writers, so far, fail to see any connection between the vaunted 'Yermóloff system' and the Murid war."

More than a century later, on February 24–28, 1944, 194 convoys of 64 trucks each deported 521,247 Chechens and Ingush, an operation carried out by 119,000 agents of the NKVD, the predecessor of the KGB. A detailed NKVD report noted with satisfaction (and with a precision Eichmann might have admired), "We now put 45 people into each cattle truck as opposed to the previous 40. By placing the people together with their possessions, we also cut down on the number of trucks required, thus saving 37,548 meters of planks, 11,834 buckets, and 3,400 stoves."

Many Chechens wound up in labor camps in Kazakhstan, where they especially impressed Aleksandr Solzhenitsyn. "I would say that of all the special settlers," he writes in the third volume of *The Gulag Archipelago* (1976), "the Chechens never sought to please, to ingratiate themselves with the bosses; their attitude was always haughty and openly hostile. . . . As far as they were concerned, the local inhabitants and those exiles who submitted so readily, belonged more or less to the same breed as the bosses. They respected only rebels. And here is the extraordinary thing—everyone was afraid of them. No one could stop them from living as they did. The regime which had ruled the land for thirty years could not force them to respect its laws."

Those who know this history find it easier to understand the implacability of Russia's recent wars with Chechnya (in 1994–1996 and from 1999 on). With hindsight, one can appreciate the pragmatic wisdom of imperial Britain's self-restraint after provoking two bad wars with Afghanistan, a comparable Islamic borderland inhabited by no less warlike mountaineers. Twice the British sought to impose their candidate as emir in Kabul (1839–1842; 1878–1881), and twice they were compelled to recognize a ruler acceptable to the Afghans. After the Second Afghan War, its acclaimed British hero, Major General Sir Frederick Roberts, supplied its best epitaph in a letter to a friend: "It may not be very flattering to our *amour propre,* but I feel sure I am right when I say that the less the Afghans see of us, the less they will dislike us. Should Russia, in future years, attempt to conquer Afghanistan, or invade India through it, we should have a better chance of attaching the Afghans to our interests if we avoid all interference with them in the meantime." This was the essence of British policy from the 1880s until 1919, a hands-off agreement mutually formalized in a 1907 pact with tsarist Russia. After it broke down, owing to renewed Anglo-Russian rivalry for Kabul's favor, the wars with and over Afghanistan recommenced. General Roberts's thesis was amply vindicated when the Soviet Union in 1979 finally and recklessly invaded Afghanistan.

In retrospect, Russia would have been far wiser to treat the Caucasus as a neutral buffer between its territories and those of the Turks and Persia. Militating against this self-denying strategy, however, was the existence of two Christian communities in the South Caucasus, whose leaders viewed Russia as an Orthodox ally, albeit not always trustworthy or easy to live with. It chanced that Prince Potemkin was again the vital interlocutor in securing Russia's connection with the ancient royal house of Georgia.

O N July 24, 1783, Kartli-Kakheti, the larger and more important of two Orthodox Georgian kingdoms, agreed by treaty to accept Russian protection. Signing for the empress was Count Pavel Potemkin, commander of the Caucasus corps and Prince Grigory's cousin. Signing for Georgia was King Hercules II (Erakle in Georgian). Hercules was renowned as a sword-wielding warrior, terror of the heathens and scion of the Bagratid dynasty almost reaching back to his kingdom's embrace of Christianity in A.D. 334. Potemkin, who engineered the accord, was ecstatic. He wrote to his empress:

> Lady Matushka, my foster-mother, the Georgia business is also
> brought to an end. Has any other Sovereign so illuminated an epoch
> as you have? But it is not just brilliance. You have attached the terri-

tories, which Alexander and Pompey just glanced at, to the baton of
Russia, and Kherson of Taurida [where Grand Prince Vladimir of
Kiev was said to have been baptized]—the source of our Christianity and thus of our humanity—is already in the hands of its daughter. There's something mystic about it. You have destroyed the Tartar
Horde—the tyrant of Russia in old times and its devastator in recent
ones. Today's new border promises peace to Europe and fear to the
Ottoman Porte. So write down this annexation, empurpled with
blood, and order your historians to prepare much ink and much
paper.

Viewed more prosaically, the Russo-Georgian linkage constituted a
triumph of hope over experience (to echo Dr. Johnson's oft quoted cau-
tion about second marriages). As early as the sixteenth century, the tsars of
Muscovy sent embassies to Tiflis (Tbilisi to Georgians) only to receive
head-scratching reports on Georgia's contentious relations with its ethnic
kin and neighbors, some Christian, some Muslim and some mixed—
Mingrelians, Ossetians, Abkhazians, Ingush and Chechens. The emissaries
found that successive invasions, the Black Death and a plunging economy
had enfeebled the Georgian state and emboldened its headstrong nobles.
For their part, Georgians found that Russian promises of military aid were
usually held hostage to the tsar's worries about matters elsewhere. Russia
had failed to provide the help it promised as recently as the 1770s, to the
exasperation of King Hercules and his regal brother in western Georgia,
King Solomon of Imereti. Nevertheless, Hercules signed the treaty with
high hopes and salutary intentions, brushing aside warnings that Russia
would again default and that becoming a protectorate was the prelude to
total annexation. Both warnings proved well-founded.

In 1784 the famous Georgian Military Highway was opened. A Russian fort rose on its northern end, and Russian troops bivouacked in Tbilisi—a promising start under the watchful eyes of Georgians. But
Catherine peremptorily withdrew her forces to fight in the Balkans when
the Second Russo-Turkish War broke out in 1787, leaving Georgia un-
protected as Persians opportunely invaded in 1795 and sacked Tbilisi. To
her credit, Catherine ordered the troops back to Georgia before her death
in 1796, but her son Paul rescinded her order as soon as he became tsar.
Abandoned and forced to flee his capital, Hercules died in exile. His heir,
George II, seeing no alternative, pleaded for the incorporation of his king-

dom into Russia. Paul obliged, issuing a decree in 1800 that formally annexed the kingdom and allowed Georgian nobles to retain their privileges
but left unresolved the fate of the venerable monarchy. Paul's brief reign
ended in 1801, when this maddest of modern tsars was murdered (he was
strangled during a melee with dismissed army officers demanding his abdication). His son and heir, Alexander I, decided cursorily to abolish eastern Georgia's kingship. "By unilaterally removing the Bagratids from the
throne," writes Ronald Grigor Suny, an American historian of Georgia,
"Alexander ended any pretense of Georgia's acquiescence in Russia's actions. Instead of signing a treaty of mutual consent, the tsar made the final
decision without even consulting the Georgian representatives in St. Petersburg. Prince Garsevan Chavchavadze wrote to his relatives in Tbilisi
that the Russians 'had not fulfilled [even] one of King Georgi's requirements. They have abolished our kingdom. . . . No country has ever been
so humiliated as Georgia.'"

I F SO, IT CAN BE ventured that Russia received its just deserts. The
decision permanently embroiled the tsars (and later the Soviets) in
the seemingly intractable ethnic conflicts of the Caucasus. Having chosen
to rule directly one Christian community, Russia soon became protector
of another, the Armenians. In 1829, tsarist forces wrested substantial portions of the historic Armenian homeland from Persia, including the capital, Yerevan. Armenia had been the first kingdom to convert to Christianity
(in A.D. 301), and at its height its territory extended from its highland
birthplace in Caucasia to the shores of the Black and the Caspian Seas.
This placed Armenia at the contested crossroads of four empires—Ottoman, Arab, Persian and Byzantine. The Armenian kingdom was sequen-
tially dismembered among them and then erased from maps altogether in
1375. Stateless and scattered, this stubborn and creative people nevertheless preserved their culture, distinctive alphabet and national church. After
the tsarist conquests of the nineteenth century, the Armenian homeland
was divided among Russia, Turkey and Persia. An independent Armenia
reemerged in the aftermath of World War I, only to be overwhelmed in
1920 by the Bolsheviks. In Soviet times, Armenia was nominally a union
republic, but, crucially, its borders were drawn to minimize Moscow's difficulties with newborn nationalist Turkey, the first important country to

sign a treaty with the Communist regime. Thus Nagorno-Karabakh—in Armenian eyes the cradle of their race—wound up within the new, predominantly Muslim Soviet Republic of Azerbaijan, thereby preparing the ground for today's ongoing war between independent post-Soviet neighbors.

Such are the perplexities of empire. Over and again, proconsuls who believe themselves instruments of Enlightenment or selfless servants of church, throne or history end up burying explosive caches, like so many land mines, that blow up ruinously in their descendants' faces. This pattern is illuminated in the eventful career of one of the most interesting, and beyond Russia least known, of the outsize figures who shaped the tsar's empire. He is Count (later Prince) Mikhail Semyonovich Vorontsov (1782–1856), an Anglophile by upbringing, a hero of the Napoleonic wars, and for thirty years governor-general, commander in chief and eventual viceroy of New Russia and the Caucasus. For much of that time, Vorontsov was second only to the tsar in the wide reach of his plenary authority. Yet in striving sedulously to bind Christian Georgians to Russia, while simultaneously assailing Imam Shamil's Islamic guerrillas, he anticipated the subsequent frustrations of the region's future Marxist masters.

Like the great Whig nobles he befriended as a youth in England, Vorontsov conceived of himself as a patrician liberal. Few Russian families, certainly, boasted bluer blood or greater wealth. His title was listed third in the empire's hierarchy of counts, and his inheritance included 27,000 serfs, a palace in St. Petersburg designed by the popular Italian architect Rastrelli and 750,000 acres on estates strewn across Russia. Young Mikhail came of age in England, where his father was Catherine the Great's ambassador. His sister married the eleventh earl of Pembroke, and his flamboyant portrait as a fashionable blade proved the year's sensation at the Royal Academy (winning the painter, Sir Thomas Lawrence, his seat as academician). Returning to Russia in 1801, shortly before the coronation of Alexander I, Count Mikhail was offered a lieutenant's commission. He eagerly accepted a posting in Georgia just as its eastern kingdom was being annexed. There, while a subaltern barely in his twenties, Mikhail Vorontsov coaxed a friendship treaty from the worried and wary last ruler of western Georgia, King Solomon of Imereti. On the battlefield, Vorontsov was decorated for heroism in campaigns against the Persians at Yerevan and against Ossetian guerrillas occupying the Daryal Pass, the key to control of the newly built military highway. As a major general a decade later, the count distinguished himself in the Napoleonic wars. He fought at Borodino and at Leipzig, then in France at Craonne in March 1814. Facing Bonaparte himself, he defended a critical plateau, retreating only under direct orders from his Prussian superior.

While quartered in Paris with the victorious allies, Tsar Alexander was impressed by Count Mikhail's tactful good sense as commander of Russia's occupation troops, and as a diplomat in the imperial entourage. Thus when Vorontsov, who turned forty in 1822, requested transfer to a civilian post, preferably in southern Russia, the emperor agreed with alacrity. A year later, as governor-general of New Russia, Vorontsov arrived in Odessa, accompanied by his Polish-born bride, née Elzbieta Branicka. Effervescent and beguiling, Elzbieta was the daughter of Potemkin's favorite niece, Alexandra, and gossips hinted that the prince himself was her father. She inherited Potemkin's vast estate, and her dowry amply increased her husband's fortune. A suitable official residence for the couple, in the neo-classic mode, soon rose on a crest overlooking Odessa's fine harbor. From the start, Vorontsov spurred a lethargic bureaucracy, promoted shipping lines, established vineyards (still producing champagne), imported English cattle and added, as Soviet-era historians rarely failed to note, to his already immense wealth through land speculation.

As the Vorontsovs settled in, Odessa was enlivened by a new arrival, Alexander Pushkin, recently exiled for his irreverent verse about serfdom and censorship. At the tsar's request, the poet was attached to Vorontsov's staff. Then twenty-four and an accomplished womanizer, Pushkin promptly courted Countess Vorontsova. What happened in the bowers of the count's gardens is conjectural. The governor-general's jealousy is a matter of record, as is this doggerel, familiar to generations of Russian students, that the poet purportedly scribbled about the stiff-necked count:

Half Milord, half shopkeeper,
Half erudite, half philistine,
Half criminal. Now there's a chance
For some integrity at last!

It suffices that Vorontsov secured Pushkin's transfer.

Indisputably, the count proved a superlative administrator. Schools, libraries, scientific institutes and botanical gardens bloomed in Odessa; elsewhere, roads and canals proliferated. He promoted experimental breeding of silkworms, Merino sheep and other plants and livestock. Like most pro-consuls, Count Mikhail spent lavishly on monumental architecture. A colonnaded archaeological museum (still functioning) and a splendid opera house formed part of a gleaming ensemble culminating in a great wide staircase descending to the sea wall, a city landmark immortalized in Eisenstein's film *Potemkin*. While building his official mansion in Odessa, Vorontsov began constructing a 150-room palace near Yalta in Crimea. "Alupka" took its name from an old Tatar village on its site, and its Tudor-Gothic-Moorish form was the work of England's Edward Blore, remembered for designing Sir Walter Scott's castle and completing Buckingham Palace. Alupka somehow survived three wars and a Nazi occupation, and today visitors still gape at the sleeping Britannic lions guarding its entrance and the richly appointed rooms where Winston Churchill resided during the Yalta Conference in 1945. At this temple to Anglophilia, twenty years in the making at colossal cost, the Vorontsovs never missed a weekly issue of *Punch,* not even during the Crimean War.

Vorontsov brought the same zeal and style to his next task, as Tsar Nicholas's viceroy and commander in chief in the Caucasus, the post he held for a decade following his arrival in Tbilisi in 1845. To win over the Georgian elite, the viceroy became impresario and host in the grand manner, bringing Italian operas to Georgia and cultivating the country's nobles at formal dinners served on Staffordshire ware while liveried footmen stood discreetly behind each guest. As at Odessa, he assumed that the superior tastes and high culture of the tsarist court would prove irresistible. He certainly dazzled the first American known to have visited Crimea and the Caucasus, the Boston lawyer George Leighton Ditson, whose *Circassia: Or, A Tour to the Caucasus* was published in two editions in the 1850s. Visiting the viceroy's palace in Tbilisi, Ditson marveled at Vorontsov's excellent English and was impressed by his up-to-date knowledge of America's Mexican War as reported by London dailies. During ten- or twelve-course dinners, he was also captivated by his courtiers and their ladies. Ditson led the way for other Americans overwhelmed and seduced by Russian hospitality. His book was effusively dedicated to "Prince Woronsoff," and a key passage shows how well he absorbed the viceroy's brief:

> The view I have taken of Russia's advance southward, I am conscious will neither in Great Britain nor on the Continent meet with

much favor. All Englishmen will condemn it instanter—condemn it for no other cause than that of mere habit; for they daily proclaim the infamy of the Czar as he leads his armies towards India from the north, while the vocabulary of laudatory words is exhausted on Britain's conquering hosts advancing on the same country from the south. The Americans, however, though they may recognize in it many of those shameless and cruel features which characterize our wars with the Red Men, as we drive tribe after tribe from their homes, lands and the sacred graves of their fathers, may see an analogous tendency in the Muscovite Progress, ultimately as beneficial—to be willing to assert to what all my observations bear me out in asserting, that Russia is doing much to civilize and Christianize the eastern world.

Ditson was too easily persuaded. As a critic remarked, Vorontsov was a liberal but no democrat. In the schools that he established, as in the honors he conferred, his focus was invariably on the privileged few. His aim was good government, not self-government. And in the end, by a dialectical process familiar elsewhere during the great age of imperialism, in appearing to patronize local languages and popular culture, he simply increased their allure among the less privileged as weapons of resistance. Nor was Vorontsov more successful in bridging the abyss between Christianity and Islam. His primary task as viceroy was to end the guerrilla rising in the North Caucasus. After a chastening early defeat resulting from an ill-conceived frontal assault, he initiated the forest razing, felling what was one of the world's largest oak forests. His village-by-village strategy eventually prevailed, the hard price being the enduring estrangement of his mountaineer adversaries.

Among the aristocratic officers flocking to Georgia was the young Leo Tolstoy, who fought in the Murid wars and was impressed by Vorontsov. He was also impressed by the stern and gallant Circassians. In his old age, even as he professed indifference to literary arts, Count Tolstoy returned to an episode so compelling that he obtained old military records to recapture essential details. The episode was the 1853 surrender of Imam Shamil's principal lieutenant, an incident that inspired Tolstoy's last major fiction, *Hadji Murad*, written between 1896 and 1904.

With his pen, Tolstoy laid bare the multiple deceits lurking in practiced military courtesies and the incurable distrust separating Russians and rebels. Claiming he now wishes to fight for the Russians because of a blood feud with Imam Shamil, Hadji Murad surrenders to Prince Sem-yon Vorontsov, commander of a frontier regiment and the viceroy's son. Semyon brings Hadji Murad to the viceregal palace to meet father Mikhail, an encounter finely engraved by Tolstoy. The viceroy is past the age of seventy, with a clean-shaven, foxlike face, moving briskly with soft, quick steps. He is gentle and kind with inferiors, and a finished courtier with superiors, but, adds Tolstoy, "he did not understand life without power and submission." Talking to Hadji Murad through an interpreter, Vorontsov listens politely as his prize captive offers to lead a Russian force against Shamil, explaining that he could only do so if the viceroy agreed to exchange prisoners for his vulnerable family. The viceroy promises to consider Hadji Murad's proposal and then takes him as his guest to an Ital-ian opera in a new theater decorated in the Oriental style. For weeks thereafter, Hadji Murad is paraded at receptions, balls and dinners, a caged eagle, the object of talk and curiosity. But there are no replies to his offers of help, and it becomes obvious to Hadji Murad that he is disbelieved and distrusted. He thus plots his escape, kills his guards, takes their arms and flees to the mountains, where Russians track and slay him. As he is dying, he imagines seeing Vorontsov, with his cunning white face and soft voice. Tolstoy's tale is both a lyrical testament to and an implicit exposé of im-perial vainglory. Tactfully unmentioned was the epilogue: Hadji Murad's corpse was decapitated and his head embalmed, exhibited in a Tbilisi gallery by Vorontsov and sent along as a *memento mori* to the tsar.

OUTWARDLY PRINCE VORONTSOV and the Soviet overlords of the Caucasus and Central Asia would seem to have little in common. But curiously and paradoxically, this was not the case. In an original and thoughtful historical comparison, *Empires: The Russian Empire and Its Ri-vals,* the British scholar Dominic Lieven maintains that the Georgian-born Stalin and his leading lieutenant, V. M. Molotov, were guided by traditional tsarist perspectives on territorial expansion and imperialism. As the long-time foreign minister tells us in his memoirs ("with a crudity which might even have made Nicholas II's ministers shiver," interpolates Lieven), Stalin understood better than anyone else "the great historical destiny and fate-ful mission of the Russian people—the destiny about which Dostoyevsky

wrote: the heart of Russia, more than that of any other nation, is predestined to be the universal, all-embracing humanitarian union of nations."
Stalin was convinced that when the Communist system triumphed, as it
assuredly would, "the world's main language, the language of international
communication, would be the language of Pushkin and Lenin." To this
end, Molotov candidly added, "my task as minister of foreign affairs was to
expand the borders of our fatherland." (One can almost hear Stalin saying,
"Take Czechoslovakia for me, Viacheslav Mikhailovich!")

To be sure, other leading Communists had different views on what
was called "the nationalities question." These differences help explain the
abrupt shifts in Soviet colonial policy as it veered between indulgence and
repression, especially of Islam. But the dominant view in the Stalin years
was that History with a capital *H* had nominated Moscow to propagate
the gospels of Marx and Lenin, whose ideology was an outgrowth—indeed the very fulfillment—of the Enlightenment. Strip away the ideological verbiage and *au fond* one can detect a striking kinship between Lenin's
heirs and the British colossi of empire they otherwise excoriated—the
Curzons, the Joe Chamberlains and Balfours. All sought to justify alien
rule morally by pointing at improvement in the lives of natives, Kipling's
"new-caught sullen peoples / Half devil and half child." Unresolved was
the dilemma of what to do when the goals of Russification and modernization conflicted, as they did time and again, with native beliefs and stubborn ethnicity.

In the Caucasus, the contradictions of Soviet policy were especially
evident in Azerbaijan, a republic of mixed and uncertain ancestry that
Russia annexed following its victory over Persia in 1806. A new border on
the Araxes River divided the majority of Turkic-speaking Muslims on the
Russian side from their ethnic kin in northern Persia, a source of con-
tention to this day. Moreover, Russia's new Islamic subjects were initially
divided between adherents of mainstream Sunni Islam and dissenting
Shias. Sunnis predominated in northwest Azerbaijan, close to Imam
Shamil's mountain citadel. When Sunnis in Azerbaijan rose up in sympa-
thetic rebellions, the Russians deliberately pitted Shia militias against
them, the result being mutual recriminations and a mass Sunni exodus to
Turkey. By the 1860s, according to a tsarist census, Shias outnumbered
Sunnis two to one.

Further compounding communal ill will was Muslim resentment
about Russia's real or imagined favoritism to Christian Armenians. Ten-

sions flamed into violence after Baku suddenly emerged in the 1890s as
the world's oil capital. This was an event nobody could have foreseen, the
world's developing thirst for petroleum, and the realization that around
Baku—the lair of the Zoroastrian fire gods—oil gushed like fountains on
the Caspian shoreline. Astonished drillers gave their gushers nicknames
like "Kormilitsa" (Wet Nurse) and "Druzhba" (Friendship).

The population of what had been a walled fortress-town on the
Caspian ballooned from 15,000 in 1874 to 112,000 in 1897. Workers
flocked to Baku's forest of oil rigs, many still visible on today's seafront, as
the world's first pipelines, tanker ships and railway tankers carried petroleum to distant markets, yielding windfall fortunes to a new breed of oil
barons, Sweden's Nobel family and the French Rothschilds among them.
In peak years, from 1885 to 1915, as much as half the world's oil came from
Baku. Scores of luxurious mansions rose on handsome boulevards around
the labyrinthine Old City with its creamy white mosques, palaces and
Maiden Tower. So also rose a philharmonic hall, a ballet and opera theater,
the latter witnessing the gala first night in 1908 of the first opera composed in the Islamic East, *Layla and Majnun* by Uzeir Hadjibekov, followed
by other novel cultural hybrids, *Nargiz* by Muslim Magomayev and *Sevil*
by Fikret Amirov (its story centering on a Muslim wife's refusal to wear
her prescribed veil).

Unfortunately, during this golden windfall, the Armenians, comprising a third of Baku's population, were perceived as benefiting from it inordinately. Rising above their lowly status of groveling underlings to
Muslim chieftains, some Armenians became merchants, bankers, manufacturers, lawyers, doctors, teachers and engineers. They rose even in the
army. An Armenian general, Loris Melikov, commanded the Russian
forces in the campaign of 1877 against Turkey. Later, as chief minister to
Alexander II, he reputedly drafted the constitution that would have been
promulgated had the tsar not been assassinated in 1881. "The affection of
the Armenian people for Russia is thus easy to understand," reported a
discerning Italian traveler, Luigi Villari, in 1906. "Under Russian rule, although subject to all the disabilities of an autocratic Empire, and to those
entailed by a corrupt and inefficient bureaucracy, they were at least not liable to periodical massacres; no bar was placed on their advancement in
any profession; their property was comparatively secure; and if the conditions of public safety in Transcaucasia left much to be desired, they were
incomparably better than those prevailing in Turkey or Persia."

To resentful Muslims, all this was inexplicable and infuriating, and following Russia's humiliating defeat in the 1905 war with Japan, this anger flowed into the political and ethnic violence that spread through the empire. In 1905–1907, Baku was shaken by a "Tatar-Armenian war," riots fomented by Shia clergy that often culminated in a frenzy of mass self-flagellation. Among those in Baku impressed by this passion was the young Josif Djugashvili, then a labor organizer and not yet Joseph Stalin, who helped turn the funeral of a local Social Democratic leader in 1907 into a comparably turbulent demonstration.

After a parenthesis during World War I, communal riots resumed in clashes known in Baku as the "March days" of 1918. But within months local disputes were subsumed and overwhelmed by the Bolshevik seizure of power. Startled secular reformers in Georgia, Armenia and Azerbaijan, seeing empires dissolve around them, heartened by Woodrow Wilson's Fourteen Points, grasping for the once unthinkable and acting separately, proclaimed their countries independent. Conservative Islamic mullahs, also caught by surprise, inveighed against secularism, so heatedly that one hard-line faction, miscalled Unity, actually welcomed the Soviet conquest of Azerbaijan in 1920.

This unpredictable hiatus between tsardom and Communism left as its literary legacy an enigmatic novel, first published in Vienna in 1937. Written in German, purportedly by one Kurban Said, *Ali and Nino* is set in Baku, circa 1917, and recounts the courting of a beautiful Georgian Christian girl by the son of an old and honored Muslim family. The world of the oil barons and a collapsing tsarist empire is recaptured in photographic detail. At one point, Ali comes upon a rally promoting national independence. "And what do you think of it, Ali Khan?" a friend demands. Without waiting for an answer, the friend whispers: "Wouldn't it be wonderful to kill all Russians in our country. And not only the Russians—kill all these foreigners who talk and pray and think differently from us. We all want to do that, really, but I'm the only one who dares say it aloud. . . . We must exterminate all foreigners." He spoke the word "exterminate" with tender longing, the author adds, "as if it meant 'love.'" In the novel, the Muslim-Christian blood feud eventually claims the lovers.

Building slowly, *Ali and Nino* acquired classic status, and in Azerbaijan today it almost has the status of a national novel. But who wrote it? It now appears that Kurban Said was born Lev Nussbaum in Baku and grew up in a Russified Jewish household. He may have converted to Islam, and he wrote a dozen or so other books under the name Essad Bey. He lived under a false identity in Nazi Germany and, when exposed, fled to Italy, where he died, possibly by his own hand, in 1942. These facts were established in a feat of literary detection by Tom Reiss writing in the *New Yorker*. Not only does the novel preserve in amber language a time and place where unreason was the norm and subterfuge the key to survival, but the very circumstances of its creation distill what Virgil called the tears of things in the past century.

WHEN THE EXUBERANT Bolsheviks defeated White armies and beat back British expeditionary armies in the Caucasus, it was their turn, in 1920, to cope with the nettle of Islam. Yielding to euphoria and believing that the fire of revolution was about to sweep through Asia, the Council of People's Commissars in Moscow convened "the First Congress of the Peoples of the East" in Baku. By precise Communist count, 1,891 delegates gathered there, a true rainbow coalition—Hindus, Armenians, Turks, Bokharans, Uzbeks, Georgians, Ingush, Turkomans, Chechens, Persians, Tajiks, Chinese and others—to hear this peculiar summons on September 1, 1920, by Gregory Zinoviev: "The Communist International turns to you today and says, 'Brothers, we summon you to a holy war first of all against British imperialism!'" As described by the American journalist and scholar Louis Fischer, the delegates, or at least the Muslims among them, "sprang to their feet, lifted aloft studded daggers and naked swords, and shouted 'Jehad, Jehad! We swear, we swear!'" Also on hand was the American writer and rebel John Reed, who dutifully denounced his own country's imperial sins. But Reed had come to Baku reluctantly and was already pondering the darker side of the revolution. On his return to Moscow he contracted typhus and died at age thirty-three.

The dreams of "setting the East ablaze" never materialized; there would never be a Second Congress. Instead, the Bolsheviks took to heart the icy reality that their survival required propitiating Turkey, Persia and even imperial Britain as the price for diplomatic recognition. For the Caucasus, the effects were profound. In 1920 officials from still independent Armenia negotiated at agonizing length with the Bolsheviks on the terms of their republic's survival within the Soviet Union. According to evolving Communist theories of nationality (shaped in great measure by Stalin), a distinctive cultural community living in a defined "homeland" constituted a legitimate "nation." Then what about Karabakh, with its predominantly Armenian population? The Stalinist thesis was brushed aside. Through a diplomatic variant of open-heart surgery, in order to placate Turkey especially and also Muslims in general, the Bolsheviks sliced Nagorno-Karabakh from Armenia and designated it an "autonomous" enclave within Azerbaijan. In the careful words of two ranking American authorities on the Caucasus, David D. Laitin and Ronald Grigor Suny, "Autonomous Karabakh was separated from Armenia proper by a six-mile swath of land—the Lachin corridor—that was primarily settled by Muslim Kurds. . . . Though Armenia had nominal political control over the regional Karabakh soviet, the pseudo-federal structure of the Soviet Union's autonomy meant little, and Karabakh remained subservient to Baku and its Azerbaijani Communist party." These were the seeds for the revolt that erupted in Karabakh in 1988, during the Gorbachev era, and precipitated a new round of Azeri-Armenian riots in Baku, resulting within a few years in 30,000 battle casualties, almost 1 million displaced persons (most of them Azeris) and an ongoing undeclared war between post-Soviet Armenia and Azerbaijan.

Sadly, seven decades of scientific socialism failed to narrow the abyss of distrust between Muslims and Christians. Nor did the Soviets ever manage, with all their sacred texts by Marx and Lenin, to master the mysteries of Islam. It would be tedious to chronicle all the back-and-forth shifts in Azerbaijan, the three changes of alphabet, the closing of mosques (from fourteen hundred in 1928 to a scant seventeen five years later), the ill-thought-out campaigns to emancipate Muslim women and the serio-comic creation of the Godless Society (to which Muslims flocked, under the doctrine of *taqiya*, justifying apostasy under threat, so that the society's rolls increased as *soi disant* atheists enrolled, from a mere three thousand in 1930 to twenty times that figure a year later). Concealment, in short, became a high art, secrets guarded by a fortress-like family system. Today, despite official assurances that Islamic extremism has few adherents in Azerbaijan, nobody can really be sure. Throughout the Soviet period, all officials, from bottom to top, ritually called each other "Comrade." This practice only reinforced the cynicism about social usages, whose hollowness in tsarist days was laid bare by Tolstoy in *Hadji Murad*.

To visit the Caucasus today is to inspect the dust of empire, tsarist and Marxist. The Israeli writer Yo'av Karny has devoted years to exploring its jumble of peoples and cultures, and his compendious *Highlanders* (2000) is the nearest thing to a Baedeker. Its pages are filled with interesting facts, for example, that Caucasian mountaineers feel a kinship to the Scots and that the American film *Braveheart* (about William Wallace) was a sellout in 1995. Chechen nationalists triumphantly destroyed a huge statue of the murderous tsarist General Yermolov in Grozny, the city he founded, and Stalin once derided Imam Shamil as "an English and Turkish agent." What I found to be most interesting and telling is that no fewer than four former Soviet generals returned to their mountain homeland, on horseback. The best known is General Jokar Dudayev, the dapper extremist who provoked the Chechen rebellion in 1994 and proved implacable as Yermolov to his former employers. ("They're beasts of prey who don't know when to stop," he said of the Russians.) Dudayev was killed in 1996 when a Russian rocket locked onto the telephone frequency he was using. The second ex-general is Mukhuddin Kakhrimanov, a veteran of the Afghan war and once head of the Soviet military mission to Angola, who returned to Daghestan after the Soviet implosion. "There," writes Karny, "like many Soviet veterans, he found that what he once stood for was no longer an object of admiration. His advice and expertise were no longer of any use. . . . And so the ultimate paradox resulted: the proponent of what the Soviets called 'proletarian internationalism' became a nationalist agitator." Kakhrimanov took up the separatist cause of his own minuscule nationality, the Laks, explaining to Karny, "To me, the most important capital city in the world is Ghazo-Ghumuq."

The third ex-general, Ruslan Aushev (said to be the youngest officer in the Soviet army to reach that rank), returned to become the first president of Ingushetia, a small autonomous republic in the North Caucasus. Finally, Sufyan Beppayev, formerly deputy commander of the Caucasus military district, returned home to lead an attempt to create a Balkar republic for a minuscule ethnic minority. And not only generals returned. It is not hard to picture shocked officers, accustomed to sleek limousines and motorcades, to welcoming brass bands and toadying underlings, suddenly reduced to the status of ordinary mortals in a dusty Caucasus village. Thus Caucasia is the repository, even the boneyard, for the failures of two empires and for their servants, who were left out in the cold when the rickety structures collapsed. Yet there is another legacy, the reflexive resistance to, and distrust of, official authority, even when the imperial systems have vanished. This is a chronic affliction in the five Central Asian republics to which we now turn, where the ex-Communist leadership has moved from Marxism to regime survival, with a vengeance.

VII
CENTRAL ASIA
Invented States, Real Godfathers

Central Asia's leaders on recent stamps. Top, Kazakh President Nazar-bayev; middle, Tajik President Rahkmanov; bottom left, Turkmen President Niyazov, with Bill Clinton; and bottom right, Uzbek President Karimov, also with Clinton. Missing: Kyrgyz President Akayev, who alone has declined philatelic immortality. *Author's collection.*

THE SETTING IS THE airport serving Ashkhabad, capital of the Soviet Republic of Turkmenistan, its tarmac blending into a pancake-flat desert dotted with tufts of foliage and whirling sand devils. The date is December 12, 1991. Shivering on the tarmac are honor guards and a military band, on hand to welcome the Communist chieftains of Central Asia's other Soviet republics, Kazakhstan, Uzbekistan, Tajikistan and Kyrgyzstan. These worried men in their dark business suits have come to Ashkhabad to preside at a grand assembly known variously in the region as a *jirga, majlis* or *ulus*—but only after a private and tense discussion about their shared and unexpected disaster. Unthinkably, unbelievably, independence is being thrust upon them. They are like dazed understudies summoned on an hour's notice to perform the title role in *Don Carlos* or, more appositely, *Boris Godunov.*

Witnessing this remarkable *tableau vivant* is the Pakistani journalist Ahmed Rashid, reporting for the *Far Eastern Economic Review.* Here, he marveled, were the heirs of Central Asia's earth-shaking conquerors, Jenghiz Khan, Tamerlane and Babar, and yet their hands seemed to tremble at the prospect of actual sovereignty. As Rashid related, it was as if they had been suddenly orphaned, since all they had known of the previous seventy-four years seemed to vanish before their eyes. Four days earlier, at a dacha near Brest, some two thousand miles westward, Russian President Boris Yeltsin and his counterparts from Ukraine and Belarus formally uncoupled the Soviet Union and created a new Commonwealth of Independent States (CIS). Yet as Rashid discovered, in so abruptly disposing of Lenin's legacy, "these Slavic leaders had not bothered to inform or consult with their fellow republican presidents in Central Asia."

Thus in its demise, the Union of Soviet Socialist Republics confirmed its underlying imperial character. "Why should we bail out these strife-torn regions of Central Asia, who share nothing with us—least of all our religion?" Rashid was briskly informed in Moscow by an aide to Deputy Prime Minister Yegor Gaidar. "We would be much better off on our own, for then Russia could become a great power again." Trooping before the press in Ashkhabad, the five presidents smiled bravely, said nothing of their humiliation and offered to become founding members of the CIS, but only on the basis of equality. Their offer was taken up, and a week later the CIS was ceremoniously launched at Almaty, then the capital of Kazakhstan. Eleven of the fifteen Soviet republics became members of the amorphous new body (a wary Georgia later signed on, but the three Baltic republics, fearing a recrudescence of Russian influence, stayed out). Still, gloom rather than jubilation marked Central Asia's rebirth of freedom. "We are not celebrating, we are mourning," a Foreign Ministry official candidly admitted to reporters in Ashkhabad. Soviet Russia had been the region's protector, its dominant trading partner, its colonizer and its ideological tutor. Under Stalin's direction, boundaries had been demarcated to parcel out bigger ethnic groups and thus deter fictive republics from becoming the real thing. And yet here they were, in 1991, adding five new flags to the United Nations esplanade, their rulers scrambling to make the best of necessity, beginning with a decision to treat existing frontiers as fixed and final, whatever their anomalies.

To the world beyond, the Soviet implosion confounded both ordinary mortals and the foreign policy elite. Central Asia in particular was terra incognita. It had been generally out of bounds for Western travelers, save for visits to dollar-earning tourist destinations like Bokhara and Samarkand, and then nearly always in the company of Intourist minders. Indeed, all the West's academic and strategic experts on the region could, circa 1991, barely fill a single lecture hall. Post–1991, this shortage vanished with surprising rapidity as specialists in Soviet affairs repositioned themselves as analysts of Central Asia and the Caucasus, the two regions often being grouped together. Still, as one can deduce from the carefully hedged conclusions in the handbooks and policy studies that soon proliferated, Western observers were as uncertain about the region's future as were its five bewildered presidents.

WAS IT ALL a charade? Would Moscow's new rulers seek renewed dominion of Russia's "Near Abroad" by other means? After all, almost 40 percent of Kazakhstan's 36 million inhabitants were ethnic Russians, and since the republic contained a hundred other ethnic groups, Kazakhs had become a minority in their own titular nation. Add to that the overnight popularity within Russia for the nationalist politician Vladimir Zhirinovsky, born in Kazakhstan and rabidly anti-Muslim. The largest of the region's five republics, its arid steppe extending from Europe's Urals to western China, Kazakhstan was believed to possess 60 percent of the Soviet Union's known mineral resources, notably including oil. Might not Russia covertly instigate a separatist revolt, then hive off northern Kazakhstan, with its petroleum reserves? Compounding these initial concerns was Kazakhstan's inheritance of 104 Satan rockets, 40 bombers, a nuclear test site and around 1,000 Soviet-made nuclear warheads—making Kazakhstan the first predominantly Muslim nation to acknowledge its possession of atomic weapons. Sober voices wondered what might happen if Islamic radicals gained control of even part of that arsenal.

Or consider Uzbekistan, the second most populous of the five republics, with its 22 million or so people, two-thirds of them Uzbek, making it one of the more homogeneous of Central Asian republics. Another 2 million Uzbeks inhabited neighboring Afghanistan, and Uzbeks dominated the Ferghana valley, the region's volatile heartland, which by Soviet design was split into three, the other thirds falling into Tajikistan and Kyrgyzstan. Hence the nervousness when Uzbek President Islam Karimov aggressively spoke of a "Greater Uzbekistan." Given his country's chronic water crisis, exacerbated by Uzbekistan's dependence on cotton as an export crop, and a linked ecological disaster that devastated the Aral Sea, the ingredients for trouble were grimly apparent.

Additionally, there was the matter of Central Asia's neighbors and kinfolk in Afghanistan, Iran, Pakistan, China and Turkey, each with its own interests and its potentially interventionist agenda. All had, so to speak, an insider advantage in a region that had been effectively closed to Western political and economic penetration (we tend to forget) since Alexander the Great's conquests in the fourth century B.C. Afghanistan was directly embroiled, given its frontiers with Turkmenistan, Uzbekistan and Tajikistan, each of which championed kindred dissidents within Afghanistan (this cross-border aid would be the lifeblood of the yet unborn Northern Alliance). Iran, for its part, had once dominated all of Central Asia. For centuries its traders plied caravan routes to Bokhara and Samarkand. It shared a common language with the Tajiks, and its ruling ayatollahs were eager to propagate their vision of Islam. Similarly, Pakistan provided the springboard for the militant Islamist movement that later prevailed in Kabul, where its scouts immediately began foraging for allies in Central

Asia. This mattered to China, whose leaders persistently worried about separatist rumblings among their own repressed Muslim subjects in Xinjiang province: tribal nomads who roamed freely back and forth into newly independent Kazakhstan, Kyrgyzstan and Tajikistan. For Turkey, the opening of the region offered a different and unexpected opportunity— to reassert ancestral ethnic ties with Central Asia, whose indigenous inhabitants (Tajiks excepted) all spoke a Turkic language. Moreover, as Ankara was quick to point out, the secular Turkish Republic provided an attractive and compatible model for the region's new nations—a point emphasized by the Anatolian entrepreneurs who now streamed into Central Asia on newly established Turkish Air routes.

What, finally, was the right and wise course for the United States to follow? Not an easy question, since Washington was betting heavily on the success of Boris Yeltsin, the founding president of the Russian Federation. Anything that appeared to be a crude American power grab in Central Asia—Moscow's "backyard"—would undermine Yeltsin to the advantage of his paleo-nationalist rivals. "I grew up in Central Asia," wrote Vladimir Zhirinovsky in his best-selling autobiography. "We considered it Russia, not Central Asia. At first, only Russians lived there. Russians brought in civilization while the Kazakhs were living in mud huts without electricity, without anything, just raising animals, sheep, just like the primitive communities of tribes, where there were no states."

For potential nationalist voters, as the *New Yorker*'s David Remnick commented, "passages like that one had an attractive resonance, even if they seemed like bigotry to non-Russians. In the most vulgar way, Zhirinovsky played to the Russian sense of betrayal, the sense that Russians brought everything from nuclear weapons to decent roads to the lowly Asians and now, in the wake of the 1991 crack-up the ungrateful Asians had merely expropriated these resources. In his autobiography, he also signaled an affinity for one of the most important of all nationalist issues: the diaspora of over twenty-five million ethnic Russians who suddenly found themselves living outside of Russia in places like Estonia, Latvia, Kazakhstan, Ukraine, and Uzbekistan."

With these imponderables in mind, one has to be impressed by the diplomatic agility with which the first Bush administration addressed what was plainly the most explosive issue, defusing Kazakhstan's huge nuclear arsenal. Building on the START agreement that President George H.W. Bush had propitiously signed in early 1991 with Mikhail Gorbachev,

Secretary of State James A. Baker III dealt serially with three new members of the nuclear club, Kazakhstan, Belarus and Ukraine. He coaxed,
coddled and prodded the three presidents to secure their assent to the dis-
mantling of their inherited Soviet stockpiles, notwithstanding their credible fears of Russian recidivism. This half-forgotten episode is detailed in
the memoirs of Secretary Baker, President Bush, National Security Adviser Brent Scowcroft and Jack Matlock Jr., then the U.S. ambassador in
Moscow. Their collective cajoling resulted in what became known as the
Lisbon Protocol to the Strategic Arms Limitation Treaty, which converted
the three republics into nonnuclear states, consistent with the Nonprolif-
eration Treaty (NPT). The Bush team lubricated the protocol with necessary incentives. When all its missiles were finally dismantled by 1995, for
example, Kazakhstan gained $400 million in total compensatory pay-
ments, a bargain by any reckoning.

The difficulties involved in forging this agreement can be sensed in
Baker's account of a telephone dialogue in April 1992 with President
Nursultan Nazarbayev of Kazakhstan:

> In a letter to President Bush a few days earlier, Nazarbayev had tried
> to find a "third way" with regard to the NPT. He wanted Kazakh-
> stan to become a "temporary" nuclear power for purposes of the
> non-proliferation pact. He had linked the length of time it would
> take Kazakhstan to join the NPT as a full non-nuclear state to secu-
> rity guarantees from nuclear weapons states, notably the United
> States. I told him that security guarantees had been addressed in the
> original NPT negotiations, and that the United States had formally
> declared its intent in 1968 to seek U.N. Security Council assistance
> if any non-nuclear state were threatened by a nuclear power. I told
> Nazarbayev that we stood by this commitment, and would reiterate
> it in terms of Kazakhstan. Nazarbayev was rather cagey, thanking me
> and noting that he hoped our "special relationship" would con-
> tinue—but he also elliptically said that he felt certain I recognized
> Kazakhstan's special geopolitical role. He ended by urging me to use
> American diplomacy to influence the Russian leadership. "If Rus-
> sian chauvinism is not checked, blood may be shed, civil war might
> erupt, all the reforms could go up in smoke, and Kazakhstan might
> get involved," he concluded.

In so plucking safety from the nettle danger, the Bush team in a single stroke confirmed the worth of arms control treaties, of the Security Council as a perceived guarantor against aggression, of carrots to encourage responsible nuclear policies, of preparation and teamwork to ensure coherence, as well as the human importance of striving empathetically to see events through another's eyes. One cannot but be struck by the contrast with the second Bush administration, most especially with the regrettable tendency among its senior officials to sneer at arms control or at any multilateral agreement perceived as limiting America's freedom. Insufficiently appreciated at the time, the first Bush administration made the planet measurably safer by shrinking four nuclear republics into one, Russia. Its focused, professional performance provided an unheeded model for its successors.

WITH A DECADE's hindsight, we can remark with some relief that the direst scenarios attending the rebirth of Central Asia failed to materialize. Russia did not incite rebellion among its diaspora, though there has been a heavy, not always voluntary exodus from the region by ethnic Russians. Aside from a devastating civil war in Tajikistan and episodic outbreaks in Uzbekistan, violence in Central Asia proved negligible. The contrast is with the Caucasus, where wars in newly independent Georgia, Azerbaijan and Armenia displaced nearly 1.4 million people. With the exception of Tajikistan, Central Asia's republics have avoided civil wars. Short-term stability has been the rule in Central Asia. Of the five presidents who had sovereignty thrust upon them in 1991, four were still in office a decade later: Islam Karimov (Uzbekistan), Nursultan Nazarbayev (Kazakhstan), Askar Akayev (Kyrgyzstan) and Saparmurad Niyazov (Turkmenistan).

What accounts for the comparative calm of the region and the survival of its leaders? An insufficiently appreciated factor is geographic. Central Asia is like a huge flat saucer bounded on the south and east by the Hindu Kush and the Pamirs, and on the west by the Caspian Sea. To the north, no natural boundaries separate the grassy Kazakh steppe and Uzbekistan's parched Kyzlkum ("Red Sand") from Russia and Siberia. Two long rivers flank Central Asia's historical core, once known as Transoxiana. The Oxus, now called Amu Darya, flows from the Hindu Kush, and over a course of 1,578 miles its banks form the historic frontiers with Afghanistan as it heads into the sequestered Aral Sea. The Jaxartes, now called Syr Darya, originates in the Tian Shan, flows through the fertile Ferghana valley and the less fertile Kyzlkum, pressing northward until it also terminates in the Aral Sea, a course of 1,370 miles. Hence to medieval Arabs, Central Asia was "the land between two rivers."

It is an environment ideally suited to the great steppe empires, horse-borne warriors, nomadic pastoralists, and in some areas cotton growing. It is also a setting favorable to camels and caravans, thriving oasis cities like Bokhara and Khiva, and the musings of poets and philosophers. Not co-incidentally, Sufi mysticism and Islamic learning both took hardy root in Central Asia, especially Bokhara, where the scholar Bukhari (died A.D. 869) compiled and classified some seventy-three hundred hadith, or say-ings of the Prophet, deemed second in authority only to the Koran. Less well-known, in 1070 the eminent Persian poet Omar Khayyam settled in Samarkand, where he wrote (in Arabic) his seminal *Treatise on Demonstra-* *tions of Problems of Algebra.* There he also computed the length of the year as 365.24219858156 days—"a computation of time," wrote Gibbon, "which surpasses the Julian and approaches the accuracy of the Gregorian style."

It is also an environment conducive to tyranny and megalomania. In a fascinating magnum opus, *Oriental Despotism*, the historian and Sinolo-gist Karl Wittfogel singled out control of water as the means by which Chinese emperors assumed absolute dominion over their subjects. Doubt-less Wittfogel's grand theory is severely reductionist, reflecting his own history as a former Marxist who fled Nazi Germany for a college campus in the American Midwest. Yet one can scarcely find a sadder illustration of "hydraulic tyranny" (Wittfogel's phrase) than the Soviet-era scheme to di-vert river waters into Uzbekistan's cotton fields. In the name of socialism, ironically, Moscow imposed a scheme of exploitation as ruthless, mindless and destructive as any of the greedy imperial projects Lenin decried.

The project's socialist genesis was anticipated in a 1953 tract declar-ing that the Communist Party and Soviet government "are doing every-thing possible to transform nature, to do away with deserts, to attain a further big rise in agricultural productivity. . . . The grand projects out-lined by Stalin's genius . . . will make it possible to master the forces of na-ture in the U.S.S.R." To that end, Moscow ordained that water from Central Asia's two great rivers would be diverted to expand arable land de-

voted to growing cotton, mainly in Uzbekistan, though this could doom
that republic to even greater dependence on a single export crop—the
commonest reproach of Third World nations against First World ex-
ploiters. In *Imperium* (1994), the Polish writer Ryszard Kapuscinski describes how this came to pass:

> The catastrophe began in the sixties. Two more decades were then
> needed to turn half of the fertile oases of Uzbekistan into desert.
> First, bulldozers were brought in from all over the Imperium. The
> hot metal cockroaches crawled over the sandy plains. Starting from
> the banks of the Syr Darya and the Amu Darya, the steel rams began
> to carve deep ditches and fissures in the sand, into which the water
> from the rivers was then channeled. They had to dig an endless num-
> ber of these ditches (and they are still digging them now), consider-
> ing that the combined lengths of the Syr Darya and the Amu Darya
> is 3,662 kilometers! Then along these canals, the kolkhoz workers
> had to plant cotton. At first they planted upon desert barrens, but be-
> cause there was still not enough of the white fibers, the authorities
> ordered that arable fields, gardens, and orchards be given over to cot-
> ton. It is easy to imagine the despair and terror of the peasants from
> whom one takes the only thing they have—the currant bush, the
> apricot tree, the scrap of shade. In villages, cotton was now planted
> right up against the cottage windows, in former flower beds, in
> courtyards, near fences. It was planted instead of tomatoes and
> onions, instead of olives and watermelons. Over these villages
> drowning in cotton, planes and helicopters flew, dumping on them
> avalanches of artificial fertilizers, and clouds of poisonous pesticides.
> People choked, they had nothing to breathe, went blind.

Before Leonid Brezhnev began turning Uzbekistan into a land of
cotton, the Aral Sea was the world's fourth largest inland body of water,
its surface area of 66,000 kilometers surpassed only by the Caspian Sea,
Lake Superior and Lake Victoria. After two decades, as irrigated areas in
Uzbekistan and neighboring Turkmenistan ballooned from 2.9 million
hectares to 7.2 million hectares, the Aral Sea imploded. Its surface area
halved and its volume shrank by two-thirds as a result of water being diverted from its replenishing rivers. In a chain of disasters, fish stocks dwindled, killing a once vibrant commerce; salt-laden storms turned the

immediate area into a dust bowl, toxic to plants and humans; and all the while cotton's appetite for virulent chemicals proved insatiable. On attaining independence, Uzbekistan inherited this environmental disaster, forfeiting even the benefit of greater revenues since, despite the irrigation canals, cotton production steadily declined. Experts differed on what might be done, their dispute compounded by a further twist. Basic statistics had been routinely faked for years, enabling a "cotton mafia" to pocket huge sums for nonexistent tons of cotton, known as "white gold," so that those principally concerned, the people of Uzbekistan, did not know who or what to believe.

Assuming sovereign power in Tashkent, the Uzbek capital, was Islam Karimov, the wintry, unsmiling first secretary of the Uzbekistan Party who had been elected president in 1990. Born in Samarkand in 1938, the son of an Uzbek father and a Tajik mother, young Islam grew up in a state orphanage, a traditional breeding ground (as in the Ottoman empire) for loyal servants of the state. Thoroughly Russified, Karimov spoke Uzbek badly, provoking discreet titters when he delivered his coached and scripted speeches. His political outlook was foreshadowed by his remarks welcoming the August 1991 attempted coup against Mikhail Gorbachev. "We have always been supporters of firm order and discipline," he averred. "A leadership that abandons order and discipline can never return to power."

It would be superfluous to detail the many ways that President Karimov has honored his credo. It suffices that Uzbekistan is matched in its region only by Turkmenistan in the variety and harshness of its crackdowns on all modes of nonconformity—political, cultural and religious; that it has played a spoiler role in vain attempts at forming regional trading markets; that its draconian suppression of Islam (save in its housebroken official guise) has helped promote the Islamic Movement of Uzbekistan (IMU), whose sporadic violence is then invoked to justify further repression. Even so, President Karimov has been indulged by Washington, first by the Clinton administration and then more assiduously by the Bush administration following September 11, on the grounds that he is a vital partner in the struggle against terrorism. (There is now a major U.S. air base in Uzbekistan.) Yet when faulted by human rights groups for indefinitely detaining those accused of abetting terrorism, his officials retort that Uzbekistan is following America's example, a rebuttal that unfortunately has a measure of validity. BULLSHIT

Nonetheless, an outsider pondering Uzbekistan's privations might sensibly wonder why Uzbeks don't rise in a general strike or a massive rebellion. With seemingly fewer grievances in the Caucasus, to cite one example, Abkhazians have sustained a decade-long uprising against far less repressive Georgia. Again, topography plays its part. Political scientists James D. Fearon and David D. Laitin, drawing on a database of 161 post–World War II civil conflicts, found that empirical evidence does not support conventional wisdom about "ancient hatreds" or "clashes of civilization" as fuel for these conflicts. Instead, poverty and distribution of population seemed more closely associated with civil war; more unexpectedly, so was mountainous terrain. What is interpreted as a recrudescence of "ancient hatreds" may therefore owe more to altitude.

This conclusion has been elaborated by another American scholar, S. Frederick Starr, who was struck by the many conflicts erupting during the 1990s in the Peruvian Andes, the Balkans, the Afghan Hindu Kush, the Nepalese Himalayas, southeastern Turkey, Karabakh and Chechnya in the Caucasus, the Colombian highlands, the Atlas Mountains of Algeria and the High Pamirs of Tajikistan. "Until recently, few were prepared to acknowledge the existence of a 'mountain problem' as such," he writes. "Even today it is convenient to treat each instance of armed combat in mountain areas as unique. Those who take this course often trace the roots of each instance of conflict to age-old local ethnic or religious tensions. It is true that such factors frequently play a role. Yet in almost every case where they are invoked, the same warring parties and groups managed to coexist with one another for decades or even centuries prior to the recent outbreaks." AUTHORITARIAN GOVERNMENT MAY HAVE KEPT THE LID ON

Starr noted the common factors of relative poverty and an absence of basic services in highland areas as compared with conditions in the lowlands. Not only are distant urbanized metropolitan centers better off, but their inhabitants rely freely on streams of mountain water that are the highland equivalent of oil as a natural resource. These disparities nurture a sense of victimhood among highlanders, so Starr speculates, a resentment reinforced by radio and television broadcasts that inform even illiterate farmers of their backwardness. And even the dullest mountaineers realize that their territory has natural advantages of inaccessibility and more open frontiers. Very sensibly the stateless Kurds affirm that their only friends are the mountains, a sentiment echoed down the ages by Scottish highlanders and all their aggrieved counterparts across the planet.

On the Central Asian steppe, by contrast, stability is favored by another factor. Not only are the founders of its five republics veterans of the Soviet party machine (the exception being Kyrgyzstan's Askar Akayev, formerly a scientist), but they are also legatees of the tsarist imperial tradition. Kremlin infighting tutored them in the disciplines of survival, the necessary arts of flattery and deception, and the fatiguing power of interminable speeches. In dealing with rivals and critics at home, they have become as adept in ferreting out hidden crevices dividing their opponents. And they are steeped in Central Asian history. They know how the tsar's armies in the nineteenth century picked off the squabbling independent khanates in what was called Turkestan. They know as well that the tsarist justification for conquest relied on claims of benefits for the ruled: the abolition of the slave trade (which had flourished in Bokhara, Khiva and other khanates), the building of railroads to link Central Asia to Russia (whose strategic value alarmed geopoliticians like Halford Mackinder) and the establishment of schools, hospitals and Orthodox missions.

Yet there was another code of mastery, seldom put in words with the rare exception of a memorandum penned in 1816 by a tsarist officer, Philippe Paulucci. His advice was unearthed in an obscure archive by the Polish-born scholar Tadeusz Swietochowski, a leading authority on Azerbaijan. Here was Paulucci's code for dealing with newly conquered lands beyond the Caucasus: "1. Refrain from anything that could weaken their perception of our power, the principal source of our strength in these regions. 2. Establish commercial relations so as to generate among them needs that they still do not feel. 3. Maintain a continuous state of dissension among their diverse nations and never forget their unity would be fatal for us. 4. Introduce among them the light of Christianity. 5. Absolutely prevent them from the possibility of links with Turkey and Persia."

Substitute "scientific Marxism" for "Christianity" and one has a shrewd forecast of Soviet policies in Central Asia. In the first years after the Bolshevik takeover in 1917, an Islamic guerrilla resistance sprang up in Central Asia, assisted by the British but caught in the crossfire of civil war. Known as the Basmachis and based in the Ferghana valley, they were warriors of a brave if anarchic spirit, whose uprising endured for more than a decade until its extinction in 1929. To contain the rebellion, Stalin redrew the map of Turkestan, creating five socialist republics with borders designed to suppress likely ethnic uprisings. The Ferghana valley was parceled among three republics, and frontiers were drawn to separate villages and clans. A new Tajik republic was stripped of its cultural and economic centers, Bokhara and Samarkand, both of which went to Uzbekistan. "Far from ending dissent," remarks Ahmed Rashid, "these artificial divisions became the source of many of the ethnic conflicts, border and water disputes, and infrastructure problems that plague Central Asia today."

While combating the clan-based Basmachis, Stalin's security chiefs also turned their guns on a very different group, the Jadids, an Islamic movement whose supporters sought to reconcile the Koran with Western modernism. Founded by reform-minded Tatars in the 1880s, Jadidism was taken up in Central Asia, where its disciples established schools, promoted science and the arts, staged plays, performed operas and celebrated the Turkic language and culture, to the dour disapproval of Muslim traditionalists. Some leading Jadids welcomed the Bolshevik Revolution, but when Central Asia was reconquered by Russians, they were branded as bourgeois reformers. With Stalin's accession, the massacres began, and the last Jadid was executed in 1937, by which time most mosques and *madrassas,* the citadels of the traditionalists, had also been shuttered. At the same time, the new Soviet rulers severed links between Central Asians and the wider world of Islam, notably Turkey and Iran. One method of severance was alphabet reform. "Here the trajectory was particularly chaotic," writes Olivier Roy in *The New Central Asia.* "The changes went from a reformed Arabic alphabet (1923–29), still to be found today in Chinese Sinkiang, to Latin (1929–40), then to Cyrillic (1940), and finally, today, back to Latin (Azerbaijan, Turkmenistan and Uzbekistan), or to Arabic-Persian (Tajikistan)." These abrupt changes not only distanced Central Asia from Turkey and Iran but also raised a wall between generations as the written record of the past became less accessible to the young.

A LL THESE FACTORS—altitude, poverty, ethnic gerrymandering and repression—coalesced lethally in newly independent Tajikistan. The southernmost territory in both tsarist and Soviet empires, Tajikistan is a classic borderland. It entered European history in or around 329 B.C., when the armies of Alexander the Great forded the Oxus, struck north for Maracanda (Samarkand) and the Jaxartes, encountered and treated with the Scythians, fell back and established a riverside military settlement "both as an excellent base for a future possible invasion of Scythia and as a defensive position against raiding tribes from across the river." As Peter Green's biography goes on to relate, the settlement was named "Alexander-the-Furthest," becoming today's Khodjent, formerly Soviet Leninabad (an immense statue of Lenin still broods over the Syr Darya). Centuries later, Tajikistan became an eastern outpost of the neo-Persian empire, served as a link in the Silk Road and was conquered in the fourteenth century by Tamerlane, a Turkicized Mongol who founded the Timurid empire with its seat in Samarkand.

Some 93 percent of Tajikistan's 143,100 square kilometers is mountainous, and even its valleys can rise a mile above sea level. Tajikistan was the most impoverished of the fifteen Soviet republics, and according to a United Nations study it remains among the world's twenty poorest countries, with an average per capita yearly income of $330. Typical monthly salaries have been reckoned at $4.70 for teachers and $3.80 for health workers. Its people have the highest infant mortality rate in the Soviet Union: 115 deaths per 1,000 births. Not surprisingly, Tajikistan has become a breeding ground for narcotics traffickers, and profits from drugs provide local warlords with the cash essential for developing their armed networks.

Adding to its plight is Tajikistan's physical vulnerability. It shares a mountainous 650-mile border with Afghanistan, the homeland of 4 million ethnic Tajiks, among them the renowned leader of the Northern Alliance, Ahmad Shah Masoud, who was assassinated by gunmen posing as journalists shortly before September 11, 2001. Tajikistan is separated on its east from Pakistan by the sliver of Afghanistan known as the Wakhan corridor, devised in the imperial era to ensure that the tsar's empire nowhere directly touched British India. Further east lies its frontier with China's Xinjiang province, where 200,000 Tajiks also live. To the west lies Uzbekistan, the cultural motherland of a fourth of Tajikistan's population, while a million ethnic Tajiks inhabit Uzbekistan. Within their own titular homeland, Tajiks comprised 62 percent of the 5.1 million inhabitants in the 1989 census, along with a dozen ethnic groups, an important one being the Ismailis, a sect best known for its leader, the Aga Khan.

Soon after independence in 1991 all came to a boil. Mingling with the groups mentioned above, there was also (as in the Caucasus) a host of valley-based clans headed by petty warlords. Always there were Russians, both settlers and military personnel, since Tajikistan became the staging area for the Soviet assault on Afghanistan—a protracted conflict that rad-

icalized young Tajiks and promoted Islamic fundamentalism. The end result was a civil war in 1992–1993 that claimed some 60,000 lives, displaced
as many as 600,000 people, caused 100,000 Tajiks to flee into Afghanistan
and spurred the exodus of another 100,000. War damage is estimated at $7
billion; the cost in Tajikistan's pride, incalculable.

The conflict ignited in Dushanbe, formerly a dusty market town of
six thousand souls (its name means "Monday" in Persian) that the Soviets
designated as the capital despite the possibility of earthquakes (in 1909,
1911 and 1949). As Dushanbe evolved into an industrial center (textiles,
shoes, knitwear, light manufactures) its population grew to 600,000, many
of its people living in the concrete warrens that were the hallmark of the
Brezhnev era. The spark was the rioting that attended the 1990 founding
of the Islamic Renaissance Party (IRP), the first legal group of its type in
Soviet Central Asia. Local Communists responded to the disorders by
banning all opposition candidates from a March 1990 election to the republic's Supreme Soviet. The party followed up by naming a new and
tougher chief, Rakhmon Nabiev, who imposed a state of emergency. As
the Soviet Union began to dissolve, local leaders in Central Asia, like survivors on a raft, turned on one another and threw the weaker overboard.
Nabiev wavered between crackdowns and conciliation as demonstrations
persisted. He then allowed contested elections, which resulted in a strong
opposition showing that dismayed his comrades even as the IRP cried
foul, leading to more clashes and mass arrests, then to forays by firebrands
like the Afghan warlord Gulbuddin Hekmatyar. The initial phase of the
conflict culminated in September 1992 with Nabiev's ouster at gunpoint,
"the worst possible nightmare for Central Asian leaders," writes Ahmed
 Rashid in his early account, *The Resurgence of Central Asia*.

By this time, weapons were flooding into Tajikistan from Afghanistan.
An airlift evacuated panicky ethnic Russians from Dushanbe, while *soi disant* diplomats from Iran with bags of cash arrived. Russian troops began
guarding airports and took over strategic centers in the capital but played
no part in the fighting. "Anarchy was now rampant and the crisis had
reached such proportions that a few hundred armed men could attempt
to take over the entire country," Rashid relates. "The government, riven
by factionalism, had now lost all credibility and was forced to accept the
demand for a meeting of Parliament in Khodjent, where its pro-commu-
nist members could dominate the proceeding." Parliament named Imam
Ali Rakhmanov, an avowed pragmatist, as president. He appealed for

peace but offered no concessions even as killings spread and Uzbekistan's forces entered the war. In a climactic assault on rebel-held areas in Dushanbe in December 1992, Uzbeks fought alongside Tajiks while Uzbek gunships blasted nearby towns still controlled by insurgents. As Dushanbe fell to pro-government forces, a Tajik commander permitted a convicted killer named Sanjak Safarov to lead a squadron in flushing out surviving rebels. Here is Rashid's account:

> People were dragged out of their beds at night and shot in the street, hundreds of women were raped and children saw their parents being shot before their eyes. . . . Perhaps as many as five thousand people were killed in this Tajik-style ethnic cleansing to which neighbors like Russia and Uzbekistan turned a blind eye. . . . Six months after coming to power the government had made no attempt to reconcile the warring factions inside Tajikistan. Instead it had gone on the offensive against Islamic fundamentalism and the opposition as it tried to consolidate the former Soviet-style nomenklatura in power. The government was only able to carry out such pogroms because of unconditional support from Moscow and Tashkent. With the tacit approval of all the Central Asian states, Uzbekistan had now become the gendarme of the region and dictated strategy to the Rakhmanov government.

THIS MOSTLY FORGOTTEN episode gives some sense of what another meltdown in Central Asia might look like, its facade of stability notwithstanding. In the case of Tajikistan, the sequel to its mountain war was positive. With the support of Russia, Iran and other Central Asian states, U.N. mediators turned a thirty-six-month cease-fire into a transitional peace agreement. At the same time, the U.N. coaxed $350 million in gifts, loans and pledges from foreign donors and multilateral banks to jump-start reconstruction. Propitiously, the peace agreement signed in February 1997 called for a general amnesty and the legalization of opposition parties. Despite difficulties and defaults, notwithstanding Tajikistan's shattered economy and fragmented politics, the pact has held. This was the first time Central Asia's former Communist politicians agreed to share power with the Islamic opposition. To promote compliance, the United

Nations posted a mission of observers (UNMOT) to Tajikistan, whose seventy-odd officers and fifty-odd civilians also kept watch on Russian forces still deployed along Tajikistan's international borders. In an unusual arrangement, by mutual agreement, Russia's 201st Motorized Rifle Division not only guards frontiers but also protects the Nurek hydroelectric facility, which provides power to all of Central Asia. Regrettably, this significant positive compromise failed to catch the media's eye and has received only token international support.

In truth, so many variables affect life in Central Asia—the winds of war, vicissitudes of nature, health of the global economy, capricious regional leaders—that nobody can guess its future. Its nomadic character has made Central Asia the more mutable. When tsarist and then Soviet rulers became its masters, they found a vast, sparsely populated flatland bordered by mountains, with few urban centers besides the famous Silk Road cities. Almaty (population 1.5 million), the former and longtime capital of Kazakhstan, originated as a Russian fort in 1854. Tashkent (population 2.3 million), the Uzbek capital and the largest city in Central Asia, was a caravan crossroads with eleven gates when the tsar's armies overwhelmed it in 1865. Bishkek (population 670,000), the capital of Kyrgyzstan, was a camel-and-horse stopover through the Tian Shan mountains when first garrisoned by the Russians in 1862. After the Bolsheviks captured Bishkek in 1926, they named it Frunze, after the Russian commander Mikhail Vasilievich Frunze, who had crushed the indigenous Basmachi insurgents, rather as if the British—had they prevailed in the American Revolution—renamed Albany for Benedict Arnold. Bishkek resumed its homely former name when Kyrgyzstan gained its independence in 1991. (In Kyrgyz, a *bishkek* or *pishpek* is a churn for making *koumiss*, or fermented mare's milk.)

A Westerner visiting either Almaty or Bishkek nowadays will hear mostly Russian on the streets and in the city center will encounter tree-lined boulevards swarming with honking cars, new Mercedes-Benzes as well as rusting Soviet-era Ladas. Clustered around spacious open markets, the cities are laid out in squares, low lying and horizontal. Except for the poplar trees and channels carrying runoff to adjacent canals, they are not all that different from American cities in the Great Plains states. Bustling shops and eclectic restaurants—Italian, Georgian, French, Azeri, Chinese and Tex-Mex bars and grills—catering mostly to an expatriate clientele intermingle with prerevolutionary Orthodox churches, Soviet war memorials and a few sleek, recently built international hotels. Aside from the multicultural markets featuring Korean kimchi vendors and Uighurs selling cheap Chinese luggage, there seems little that connotes Central Asia, save for displays in ethnographic museums.

The erstwhile tsarist Turkestan has long been the blank slate on which successive conquerors have inscribed alien visions, a region where radically different ideologies have been taken to extremes. The most egregious was Stalin's use of Central Asia as a dumping ground for luckless Soviet minorities, and for prisoners in his Gulag Archipelago. Their descendants survive. On weekends, at a hilltop café overlooking Almaty, one can see members of Kazakhstan's ethnic German minority, trucked here during World War II, taking snapshots of one another in what has become a farewell ritual for those emigrating elsewhere.

Central Asia remains a laboratory for Big Ideas. Current examples are Kyrgyzstan, whose president has tried to bypass centuries of economic development by moving directly from a nomadic culture to a free market economy based on the doctrines of the International Monetary Fund, and Turkmenistan, whose president has pushed the cult of personality to extravagant limits.

THE RISE OF Askar Akayev in Kyrgyzstan is an anomaly in the region's post-Soviet era. He is the intellectual, the liberal, the putative democrat, the convert to free market ideology, or so he has struck his Western admirers. In 1990 Akayev was elected president by the republic's Supreme Soviet thanks to a factional deadlock in which he emerged as a novel compromise choice. At the time he headed the Kyrgyz Academy of Sciences, having earned his first engineering degree in Leningrad and his doctorate in 1980 at the Moscow Institute of Physical Engineering. That he was of a different political color was apparent from the start. He was the only Central Asian president who condemned the aborted August 1991 coup against Mikhail Gorbachev on the crucial first day. Akayev boldly deployed troops in Bishkek to frustrate any would-be local conspirators, spoke out warmly for Boris Yeltsin and, when the Moscow cabal collapsed, dissolved the Kyrgyz Communist Party.

Could Akayev, as he promised, turn his country into the "Switzerland of Central Asia"? It seemed possible. Cradled in the Tien Shan and Pamir mountains, Kyrgyzstan boasts the crystal lake Issyk-Kul, where Jenghiz Khan once camped and where the greatest of Russian explorers, Nikolai Przhevalsky, lies buried. Mountains cover 93 percent of Kyrgyzstan's 125,000 square miles, and its glaciers are so immense that someone has calculated that if all the country's ice melted, its terrain would be under nine feet of water. The descendants of nomadic pastoralists predominate among its 4.8 million people, of whom 52 percent are Kyrgyz, some 13 percent Uzbek and up to 20 percent Russian. Yet dwarfing the country's human population are 10 million sheep and goats, 2 million horses and yaks, and a half million pigs. More marvelously, many of the shepherds tending these herds continue to inhabit portable yurts, with their carpeted floors, very like the ones their ancestors knew a millennium ago.

From the moment of independence, President Akayev sought to break irrevocably with the Soviet system. He decreed the privatization of state farms whose profits fell below 15 percent, he welcomed foreign investors, he gave tenants title to their apartments, he named Westerners to key economic jobs, and he invited the International Monetary Fund to outline an economic plan, which he put into effect in 1993. Five years later, Kyrgyzstan became the first Central Asian state to join the World Trade Organization. Akayev also opened the political system, permitted multiparty elections, met regularly with opposition leaders, lifted the more onerous curbs on the press and invited local representation on Western nongovernmental organizations. And he ended restraints on Islamic institutions, leading to an influx of Saudi Arabian businessmen who arrived, cash in hand, to promote the construction of an estimated three thousand mosques.

Akayev's economic hopes failed to materialize. Foreign investors were more generous with applause than with money, partly owing to the logistical difficulties of doing business in landlocked Kyrgyzstan. Moreover, his country proved too vulnerably dependent on Uzbekistan and Kazakhstan for essential supplies of oil and gas. Appalled by his disruptive reforms, Akayev's neighboring leaders periodically shut the tap, claiming bills were unpaid, further disabling a floundering economy. As the numbers of jobless grew, so did political opposition. To this was added ferment among ethnic Uzbeks concentrated in the south of Kyrgyzstan. Their major city is Osh, the country's second most populous and the scene of communal riots in 1990. Grumbling became louder in 2002 when the police imprisoned an ethnic Uzbek parliamentary leader, Azimbek Beknazarov, stirring protests in Aksy, his home town. In March 2002, police fired on marchers proceeding from Aksy, killing five demonstrators, the first such bloodshed in independent Kyrgyzstan.

Beknazarov was ostensibly charged with abusing power as a local prosecutor seven years earlier, but his real offense evidently was his outspoken attack on a treaty that Akayev had pushed through parliament to resolve a long-standing border dispute with China. At issue was a barren mountainous region claimed by Beijing; in a propitiatory gesture, Akayev agreed to cede 30 percent of the contested territory. Beknazarov opposed any compromise with China and deplored the secret diplomacy that hatched the deal. Still, it is hard not to sympathize with Akayev. China's goodwill is vital to Kyrgyzstan, and there is less injury to principle in surrendering uninhabited territory than in submitting to Beijing's relentless pressure for a crackdown on nomadic Muslims who cross the same frontier. The charges against Beknazarov were eventually dropped and an inquiry ordered into police killings at Aksy. When its report faulted government actions, Akayev dismissed his prime minister—an unheardof sequence in neighboring states.

The bigger clouds over the Switzerland of Central Asia are America's military involvement and the perennial questions of nepotism and succession. Overnight, following September 11, Washington turned to Bishkek for assistance in the looming Afghan campaign. Akayev agreed to provide an air base for two thousand U.S. and allied troops, and in return he became an honored guest at the White House. The fear among Kyrgyz democrats is that if the base becomes permanent (as also seems likely in Uzbekistan), the host government may view it as an immunizing shield. They worry that Washington will brush aside allegations of corruption, presidential nepotism and the muzzling of what has been a relatively free press. The New York–based Committee to Protect Journalists has already listed Kyrgyzstan as one of the ten worst countries to work in as a journalist. And as visitors to Bishkek quickly discover, the prime focus for political gossip is the affluence of the president's family.

Outwardly, the Akayev children exemplify cultural globalization. Daughter Bermet, the eldest, won a gold medal in Russia for her work as a mathematician and then earned a master's degree in Switzerland; another daughter, Sadaat, also studied in Switzerland and at Tufts University near Boston. The eldest son, Aidar, is a graduate of the University of Maryland, and a younger son, Ilim, is currently studying abroad. On returning to Bishkek, Aidar was awarded a post in the Finance Ministry and reportedly owns a restaurant called Manchester and a nightclub called Soho. A son-in-law, Adil Toigonbayev, is believed to covertly own the country's most popular newspaper, *Vecherny Bishkek* (Evening Bishkek) and to control a substantial broadcasting empire, a vodka business, a sugar refinery, a cement factory and latterly a jet fuel business now reaping millions in sales to coalition air forces using Manas Air Base (named after Manas, hero of the Kyrgyz national epic).

On a recent visit to Bishkek, Robert G. Kaiser, an associate editor and former Moscow correspondent of the *Washington Post*, asked Akayev about his family's business dealings. "In our family, there is one businessman, my son-in-law," the president replied. "My oldest son works as a humble official in the Ministry of Finance. I have forbidden my children from getting into business. But the son-in-law I couldn't forbid; he's been a businessman all his life. But his business isn't connected to Kyrgyzstan. He delivers aviation fuel from Turkmenistan, from Kazakhstan." Asked if that was all, he replied, "That's his basic business. There's nothing more."

One suspects that President Akayev is being equally candid when he denies having any interest in continuing his rule under a new constitutional arrangement after his second presidential term expires in 2005. Critics fear that the region's only quasi-democrat has turned quasi-authoritarian, fears quickened by his eldest son Aidar's dynastic marriage in 1998 to Aliya Nazarbayev, the youngest daughter of the Kazakh president (though the couple later separated). It would be a pity if Central Asia's most promising leader should dwindle into yet another decrepit liberator-for-life.

To turn from Kyrgyzstan to Turkmenistan is to pass through a mirror from a predominantly mountainous country to one that is nine-tenths steppe and desert, from a country that welcomes curious Westerners to one that shuns them. Turkmenistan belongs to a special political category, the hermit state. Like North Korea under Kim Il Sung or Albania under Enver Hoxha, Turkmenistan is in the smothering shadow of its president and former Communist Party boss, Saparmurad Niyazov, self-anointed as Akbar Turkembashi, "The Great Leader of All Turkmen." He has recreated the extravagances of Joseph Stalin's cult of personality, although (to echo Karl Marx's shopworn but apt remark about Louis Napoleon) history has repeated itself, first as tragedy, then as farce.

Item: By unanimous vote, a Turkmen national assembly in 2002 changed the names of the months, turning January into "Turkembashi." It also decided to rename October "Rukhname," or "Spiritual Revival," after a compilation of the president's musings that was published a year earlier and was already required school reading (two more volumes are promised).

Item: A golden statue of Turkembashi roosts on a 246-foot arch in the capital, Ashkhabad (now Ashgabat), where it rotates slowly, so that its extended arm always points to the sun.

Item: To ensure that all benefited from their leader's three-hour speech in March 2001 setting forth a new code of "spiritual conduct," the address was televised in full every Monday. For six months.

Item: Acting on an oral order from the president, the government in August 2002 banned all vehicles with left-hand drives from using Turkmen motorways, where driving on the left remains the rule. According to news accounts, this unusual order was prompted by the president's dislike of a rival Turkmen clan, the Tekins, centered in Mary, a city better known to history as Merv. The order's real targets, it appeared, were Mary's taxi drivers and their foreign cars, whose high earnings reportedly irritated Turkembashi.

What led to these extravagances? Niyazov's career provides some clues. Born in 1940 to working-class parents who died while he was a child, Niyazov was raised in an orphanage, as was Uzbekistan's Karimov. The Communist Party figuratively became Niyazov's foster parent. Trained as an engineer, he was first secretary of the Ashkhabad City Council. He impressed higher-ups in Moscow with his party loyalty and malleable convictions as the Soviets moved from Brezhnev-era torpor to Gorbachev's perestroika. Named Turkmenistan party chief in 1985, Niyazov became president five years later, just before the Soviet dissolution. He again shifted with the wind. The Communists became the Democratic Party of Turkmenistan, and Niyazov turned from Marxism to nationalism. Street names were changed, old traditions revived and the country's pre-Soviet past glorified.

In truth, Turkmenistan's setting abets hyperbole. Most of its 305,000 square miles consists of barren steppes whose punishing character Anton Chekhov graphically captured: "Sultry heat in summer, in winter frost and terrible snowstorms, terrible nights in autumn when nothing is to be seen but darkness and nothing is to be heard but the senseless, angry howling wind, and, worst of all, alone, alone for the whole of life." It is also chronically subject to earthquakes; Niyazov's mother perished in a 1948 disaster that razed Ashkhabad, a catastrophe that wiped out most of the country's educated middle class. The country is also renowned for its caves and a vast underground lake, Bakharden, its forty-four hundred dinosaur footprints and the ferocity of its warriors. In the mid-nineteenth century, Teke tribesmen fended off Russian armies until their climactic defeat in 1881, making Turkmenistan the last portion of Russian Central Asia to be folded into the tsarist empire.

Above all, Turkmenistan is the land of the "good Turcoman horses" that Marco Polo saw or heard about on the ancient Silk Road. "The Eurasian steppes are almost indisputably the place where humans first domesticated, bred, and eventually mounted horses," writes Jonathan Maslow in *Sacred Horses: The Memoirs of a Turkmen Cowboy*. "Everything learned from paleontology and archaeology tends to confirm the idea that a wild blood horse continued to exist in Central Asia long after domestication." What appears to be the modern kin of this ancient breed is the Akhal-Teke, a long-necked desert purebred capable of extraordinary feats of endurance. So fascinated was Maslow, a writer and naturalist from Cape May, New Jersey, that he studied Russian and with considerable difficulty journeyed twice to Turkmenistan, in 1988 and 1992, to see and ride the imperiled Akhal-Teke in its own habitat. His book is doubly interesting. It is a rare and sympathetic account of an attractive people and a little-known country. Instead of welcoming his interest, however, Turkmen authorities treated Maslow as a spy and did what they could to frustrate any sustained contact by local people with this quirky, good-humored American. To draw the curtain even tighter, Niyazov has since curtailed the teaching of English, notified foreigners that all their mail and telephone calls would be monitored and stripped Internet providers of their licenses.

Not surprisingly, Turkembashi's reign has further impoverished his hardworking nation of 4.7 million people, of whom 72 percent are Turk-

men and 13 percent Uzbek. When his country became independent, the
president predicted it would develop into "another Kuwait." Turkmenistan sits on proven oil reserves of 546 million barrels, and its gas reserves of 250 trillion cubic feet are reckoned the seventh largest in the
world. The problem is getting the oil and gas to market. In a decade of negotiations, every major scheme for building pipelines has collapsed, due
partly to Russian obstruction and partly to nearly unanimous complaints
among would-be partners about the difficulty of dealing with Niyazov.
Ambitious pipeline proposals involving Turkey, Pakistan, Iran and India
have yet to be realized, while Russia—anxious to favor and protect its
own sales from Siberia—has insisted that Turkmenistan pump gas at prices
below international levels and use the existing inadequate pipeline system. The result, according to industry analysts, is that Turkmenistan's natural gas production in 2001 fell 40 percent below its output in 1991 and
met only half of the modest targets that the government had set for itself.

So dismal is the country's economic performance that were Turkmenistan a democracy, its people would have ousted their president years
ago. But in the sober words of the U.S. Commission on International Religious Freedom, in its report to President Bush in March 2002:

> Though a facade of democratic governance has been created by the
> establishment of three separate branches of government, in fact, the
> country's parliament, or *Mejlis*, rubber-stamps Niyazov's decisions
> and the judiciary is not independent of his whim. Criticism of Niya-
> zov or his government is not tolerated and there is no legal organ-
> ized opposition. Major opposition figures have been imprisoned,
> institutionalized, deported, or have fled the country, and their fam-
> ily members are routinely harassed by the authorities. As the gov-
> ernment completely controls all media, there is no press freedom
> and foreign media is not permitted.

There is no likelihood that these conditions will improve in the near
future, since in December 1999 parliament voted to enthrone Niyazov as
president for life. Even so, with a weather eye to past earthquakes, he has
reportedly parked substantial government funds in foreign banks.

COMPARED TO Turkmenistan, Kazakhstan is a pluralist oasis with a fair chance of becoming the wealthiest Central Asian republic. In June 2001, a State Department authority informed Congress that within a decade Kazakhstan could be one of the top five oil producers in the world. It was then producing some 800,000 barrels of oil daily, and its estimated reserves as of autumn 2002 totaled at least 16.4 billion barrels, and new finds are continually reported. Additionally, the country harbors some 7.52 *trillion* cubic feet of gas reserves.

Kazakhstan readily survived immediate postindependence fears of civil strife, economic disarray and Islamic insurgency. It had every appearance of stability under Nursultan Nazarbayev, its president since 1990. In the informed view of Martha Brill Olcott, Nazarbayev "was probably the only Soviet party leader simultaneously to enjoy the strong support of his population, the respect of his fellow leaders, and the trust of Mikhail Gorbachev." Still, when Olcott published her book, *Kazakhstan* (2002)— the most comprehensive analytic study of any Central Asian republic available in English—its subtitle was *Unfulfilled Promise.* A political scientist at Colgate University, codirector of the Carnegie Moscow Center Project on Ethnicity and Politics in the Former Soviet Union, Olcott summed up the bleaker auguries: "The process of democratic institution building has all but halted in Kazakhstan after an initial phase in which Kazakh leaders had resigned themselves to taking such steps as the price of good relations with the West in general and the United States in particular. Over time the region's leaders have become more adept at rebuffing the implied conditionality of the early U.S. policy in the region, and U.S. pressure has also become less sustained, making these men less apologetic about their behavior."

Little of this concerned Westerners attending KIOGE 2001: The Ninth Kazakhstan International Oil and Gas Conference, held at Almaty's new and resplendent Regent Hotel in early October 2001. Most speakers painted a glowing picture of future prospects, post–9/11 uncertainties notwithstanding. Display tables in the lobby featured upbeat booklets and brochures with titles like *Doing Business in Kazakhstan* or glossy almanacs touting Caspian oil and gas. Delegates heard fresh reports on Atyrau, dubbed by the *Wall Street Journal* as "the world's newest oil boomtown," serving the Tengiz oil fields on the Caspian coastline. Atyrau is the staging point for a 948-mile, $2.6 billion pipeline to Russia's Black Sea port at Novorossisk, where Tengiz oil can flow west via tankers through the straits.

But at free-flowing bars, oilmen gossiped more unguardedly about doing business locally. After four years of negotiation, Chevron in 1992 entered a joint venture with Nazarbayev to develop Tengiz and build the essential pipeline, the first such contract with a foreign oil giant in Central Asia. Few in the American-based firm anticipated it would take so long to complete the pipeline, owing to bureaucratic stasis, shortages of skilled labor and persistent difficulties with Russian energy companies, which have demanded and won a stake in all joint ventures. Once Chevron signed, other foreign entrepreneurs—American, European, Asian—flocked to Almaty. On the positive side, they encountered the region's best banking system and an expanding infrastructure of highways and telecommunications. But they also encountered a culture of kickbacks, payoffs and crony capitalism downplayed in law firm brochures. Corruption is omnipresent, writes Olcott: "Kazakhstan is said to have lost $500 million in 1996 alone in a transaction in the oil sector. Stories of bribes and insider deals involving Nazarbayev and his family abound, giving an element of farce to President Nazarbayev's very public anticorruption campaign and his claims that corruption 'threatens the existence of the state.'"

Moreover, say oilmen, Kazakhs and other Central Asians do not share the common understanding about costly searches for new fields. If oil is discovered, it may not advantage the finder, who is likely to be asked to bid competitively in a fresh auction against rivals who played no part in the find. Certainly (they add) the Tengiz field is productive, and the new Kashagan fields offshore may be as vast as excited reports claim. But Kazakh oil has a high sulfur content and requires special refinery techniques, thereby giving a premium to the greatest feasible volume. Instead of shipping to the Black Sea or the Mediterranean, it would make more sense to send tankers across the Caspian to a short pipeline linkup with Iran, where oil is needed in the north. Iran could refine and sell Kazakh oil locally and then "swap" a matching amount of its own crude in the Persian Gulf. Oilmen complain that for political reasons Washington officials won't discuss anything that might benefit Iran. Instead, it is committed to the less practical $3 billion Baku-Tbilisi-Ceyhan pipeline, a 1,091-mile engineering nightmare meant to carry oil from Azerbaijan via unstable Georgia, over difficult mountains to Turkey's Mediterranean port of Ceyhan by 2005. Drilling rigs and offshore platforms are yet another problem—and before that can be faced, there is the interminable, unresolved dispute over the legal status of the Caspian Sea among its five littoral states—Russia, Iran, Azerbaijan, Turkmenistan and Kazakhstan.

The Caspian, the world's largest inland sea, has not been subject to international maritime laws. Instead, its legal status was defined in treaties of 1921 and 1940 between the former Soviet Union and Iran. With the dissolution of the Soviet Union, Iran proposed an equal division of the Caspian, meaning each state would control 20 percent of the sea's surface and seabed—a clear gain for Iran, which controls only 13 percent under existing treaties. Russia, which controls 19 percent, has proposed a "modified median line" that would split the seabed while keeping waters in common, a view more or less shared by Kazakhstan (29 percent) and Azerbaijan (21 percent) but not Turkmenistan (18 percent). However, all the principals have switched sides and arguments in a frustrating, inconclusive and complicated dispute that turned violent in July 2001, when an Iranian gunboat forced a British Petroleum exploration ship from waters also claimed by Azerbaijan.

Listening to all this, the nonoilman may reflect on petroleum's dubious blessing for poorer countries that its discovery supposedly favors. For nations as well as people, great expectations of inherited wealth can corrupt and paralyze. Its perils are pungently expressed by Ryszard Kapuscinski in *Shah of Shahs*: "Oil kindles extraordinary emotions and hopes, since oil is above all a great temptation of ease, wealth, strength, fortune, power. It is a filthy, foul-smelling liquid that squirts obligingly up into the air and falls back to the earth as a rustling shower of money. To discover and possess the sources of oil is to feel as if, after wandering long underground, you have stumbled on a royal treasure. Not only do you become rich, but you are also visited by the mystical conviction that some higher power has looked upon you with the eye of grace and magnanimously elevated you above the others. . . . In this sense, oil is a fairy tale and like every fairy tale, a bit of a lie."

HOW THE TALE ENDS depends greatly on Nursultan Nazarbayev, Kazakhstan's former party chief and its president since 1990, who on the whole has presided with moderation in leading a diverse people scattered through a sprawling country into novel terrain. The early years were not easy. Under Boris Yeltsin, Russia could often be an intrusive and bullying neighbor, ostensibly to defend the rights of its "Near

Abroad" diaspora but also to undercut an energy competitor and shut out Westerners. In so interfering, Russia worked with or had the support of Uzbekistan's President Karimov, sullenly envious of Kazakhstan's oil riches and the foreign attention bestowed on its president. Here again, one can sympathize with Nazarbayev. Why shouldn't he relish the royal treatment he has received? For generations, proud Kazakhs, descendants of the Golden Horde, had to kowtow to overbearing Russians. In Soviet times, Kazakhs, like all other Central Asians, were so distrusted that key security posts in their republics were invariably reserved for Slavs. Now foreign potentates bestow gifts on Nazarbayev in such quantities that they fill a large gallery in Almaty's historical and natural history museum.

The contrary consideration, carefully detailed by Martha Brill Olcott, is that after experimenting with political pluralism, the president has retreated into the secretive politics of family and clan, the petty harassment of critics and an obsession with vast and wasteful projects. His moving the Kazakh capital from cosmopolitan Almaty northwestward to Astana, whatever its merits, proved an unmixed blessing for the Kazakh construction industry. "For better or for worse," writes Olcott, "Kazakhstan will probably move toward further consolidation of the present system, which appears to lie somewhere between autocracy and oligarchy. . . . Following the lead of the region's other presidents, Nazarbayev has extended his own term of office into the new millennium and has rewritten the constitution to reduce parliament to little more than a cheering section, which he can suspend at will if the cheering fades."

In doing so, as elsewhere in Central Asia, Nazarbayev has given fresh life and importance to family, clan and tribal loyalties. By tradition, Kazakhs are divided into the Great Horde, the Middle Horde and the Small Horde, with each horde subdivided into tribes and clans. An old proverb expresses the spirit: "He is a fool who has forgotten what became of his ancestry seven generations before him and who does not care what will become of his progeny seven generations after him." The president, born humbly in a peasant community in southeastern Kazakhstan, moved up a notch by marrying into a politically influential Middle Horde family, even though his bride, Sara Alpysovna, was a cafeteria worker in a metallurgical plant. Such family networks have reestablished themselves through most of Central Asia. After six decades of scientific socialism, the oldest of all political units, the family, is once again the building block of political influence.

Nazarbayev's daughter Dariga heads the country's only independent national television channel. A son-in-law, Rakhat Aliev, was deputy head of Kazakhstan's national security forces until scandals forced his resignation. His methods were described by a businessman: "First they come to you and say, 'Pay 30 percent, and don't bother to pay your taxes.' Then they come and demand 60 percent, and then 90 percent." Another son-in-law, Timur Kalibayev, has extensive links to the oil industry and has headed one of the country's largest banks. Olcott writes:

> In addition to his daughters and sons-in-law, who control most of Kazakhstan's media, dominate Kazakhstan's security forces, are involved in the trade of alcohol, tobacco, and sugar, and have a growing role in the oil industry and the various mining and metallurgy sectors, Nazarbayev has made good use of his wife's relatives as well as more distant kin. . . . More recently, Kairat Saltybaldy Nazarbayev, the son of the president's younger brother, has come into official prominence. Saltybaldy (he has now legally dropped the name Nazarbayev), who was born in 1970, spent several years working as the deputy head of Astana and then worked as the first vice president of Kazakhoil. Before that he spent several years working for the National Security Committee (KNB), as deputy head of the fight against corruption among high-ranking officials. Presumably he had the job of protecting Nazarbayev family interests.

These hard-won facts, one suspects, are little known to ordinary citizens in Kazakhstan. It would be refreshing if President Nazarbayev confounded his critics by allowing the translation of Martha Brill Olcott's book into Kazakh and Russian; refreshing, but hardly likely. The task facing Washington is to deal fairly and effectively with Central Asia's new rulers without becoming their accessories in abusing human rights, creating dynastic oligarchies and funneling unearned increments into Swiss bank accounts.

"What Is to Be Done?"

I F A SPECTER HAUNTS the preceding pages, it is that of history, the awareness that the United States risks following a well trod path into the Asian heartland, a path littered with the dust of empire. Does it matter? Americans tend to live in a perpetual present, viewing the past as at best a diverting idyll, suitable for theme parks. In what other society is the word "history" used as an epithet, as in "You're history!" This prevailing allergy to things past is especially evident in network television programming, whose gatekeepers are locked in a frantic quest for the demographically coveted audience of viewers between eighteen and thirty-four. How revealing that in the year 2000, the threshold of a new millennium, out of 107 weekly series offered on six networks, only one was set in the past, Fox's *That '70s Show*, the remote epoch in question being the 1970s.

The year 2000 also yielded a real-life American melodrama, a deadlocked presidential vote so fiercely contested that for twenty-two consecutive days, beginning November 7, the *New York Times* greeted its readers with banner headlines spanning a full six columns—a peacetime record, according to the paper's editors. Yet as the arguments ground on, commentators typically seemed as baffled as ordinary voters by the existence of the Electoral College, whose indirect apportioning of votes lay at the heart of the controversy. Forgotten was the fact that when the Constitution was drafted in 1787, there was little support for the direct election of a president. The alternative favored by key delegations at the Philadelphia Convention was election by the U.S. Congress, with victory in that event probably going (as the authors of *The Federalist* cautioned) to a politician "with talents for low intrigue and the little arts of popularity." What the Framers devised instead was a republican means of choosing a chief executive who would be neither the tool nor the master of Congress. The president was to have moral and political authority rooted in a national election using an electoral system that encouraged rivals to seek support in less populous states as well as bigger ones. If not perfect, according to *The Federalist*, the resulting method is "at least excellent," with its three exceptional breakdowns over more than two centuries proving the rule. And since no model existed for the federal system the Framers fashioned, their achievement was the more astonishing.

To an American traveling through post-Soviet lands, the merits of federalism are readily apparent. Consider, for example, the South Caucasus, a comparatively tiny area with around 15 million inhabitants whose three states—Armenia, Azerbaijan and Georgia—have a combined gross domestic product of $10 billion, less than the annual budget of the New York City Board of Education ($11 billion). Few foreigners have crossed these frontiers more frequently than the British correspondent Thomas de Waal. "Objectively speaking," he told a NATO Parliamentary Assembly in Tbilisi, "what we have in this part of the world is a tangle of closed borders, dead ends and roadblocks, the different parts of which do not communicate with each other. Armenia's two longest borders are closed. . . . From Yerevan it is easier to fly to Los Angeles than to Tbilisi. Abkhazia and South Ossetia are no-go zones for Georgians. And even if a normal trader wants to cross the border between Azerbaijan and Georgia, the two friendliest states in the region, he or she has to spend hours and go through about ten different checks."

For the post-Soviet South Caucasus, one may fairly remark, Woodrow Wilson's exaltation of self-determination has proved a calamity, while the principles of James Madison, Alexander Hamilton and John Jay have scarcely been discussed. It needs recalling that the most fruitful act of American diplomacy in memory was President Harry S. Truman's offer to help rebuild postwar Europe through the Marshall Plan, *provided* that the Europeans came up with a matching plan for integrating their economy. This was not just an idea but "a practical necessity," in the view of the plan's administrator, Paul Hoffman, the president of the Studebaker auto corporation. As Hoffman explained in October 1949 to the European council formed to carry out the plan, "The substance of such integration would be the formation of a single large market within which quantitative restrictions on the movements of goods, monetary barriers to the flow of payments, and eventually all tariffs are swept away. The fact that we have in the U.S. a single market of 150 million consumers has been indispensable to the strength and efficiency of our economy. The creation of a permanent freely trading area comprising 270 million consumers in Western Europe, would have a multitude of helpful consequences."

Which indeed happened. The Marshall Plan opened the way to the Treaty of Rome, to the European Common Market and today's European Union. Concerning the South Caucasus and Central Asia or any other fragmented region, a reasonable question arises: Why shouldn't U.S. assistance be conditioned on a prior but firm agreement to open borders, lower tariffs and nurture common political and cultural institutions? Why not build on the principles of *The Federalist*, the one inspired work of political theory native to the United States? The answer is usually a weary shrug and an allusion to "ancient hatreds," sometimes illustrated by a folk tale said to define the deep-rooted malaise of Central Asia. The "Eye Tale" goes like this:

One day while plowing his field, a peasant named Ahmed came upon a beautiful jar and pried it open, freeing a genie who rubbed her eyes and turned gratefully to her liberator. "Ahmed," she said, "you deserve a reward, but I must explain that the rules in my particular order are that if you wish for something, all your neighbors will receive twice as much of the same thing." Ahmed sat down. He thought and thought and thought, and finally said: "Genie, here is my wish. Take out my right eye."

WHAT IS THE MORAL of the story? Obviously culture matters, and reciprocal detestation can turn every negotiation into a zero-sum game, in which one party's benefit has to be matched by another's loss. It would be foolish, indeed purblind, to deny there is a problem. Yet let us look again at the initial question about history. Isn't Ahmed's churlish decision rooted in immutable ancient hatreds? Or as a Marxist might argue, doesn't his alienation reflect the commodity obsessions of an acquisitive society meanly wedded to beggar-thy-neighbor economics? Doesn't history signify that attitudes like Ahmed's will persist so long as peasants own their land, and that Ahmed won't be truly liberated until capitalist inequalities are abolished under the dedicated leadership of an enlightened vanguard? Such was the core outlook vehemently articulated by V. I. Lenin in *What Is to Be Done?*, a manifesto published in 1902 shortly after his release from Siberian exile. Its pages contain the germ of the "audacious conception that inspired the Bolshevik revolution of 1917, and the founding of the Communist International," in the words of

Bertram D. Wolfe, in his pioneering and still valuable *Three Who Made a Revolution* (1948).

Here let us digress to look critically at Leninism and the supposed "lessons of history" before circling back to Central Asia and the Caucasus. The first part of Lenin's tract is a sustained attack on the very notion of "freedom of criticism," which he invariably brackets within derisory quotation marks, as if the term itself were a fraud. For Lenin, the issue was settled, the answers known: "freedom" was a bourgeois illusion and true democracy lay in the abolition of class domination. "Freedom is a great word," he asserts with blistering sarcasm. "Under the banner of industrial freedom the most predatory wars have been waged, and under the banner of freedom to work, the workers have been plundered." What is needed, he argues, is a revolutionary vanguard, a disciplined cadre of professional agitators, to awaken the slumbering proletariat to its beckoning destiny. Moreover, history has singled out Russia to lead the way. In his impassioned words: "History has set before us a task to be accomplished in the near future which is far more revolutionary than all the immediate tasks of the proletariat of any other country. The fulfillment of this task, the destruction of the most powerful bulwark of European and (we may even say) of Asiatic reaction, would surely make the Russian proletariat the vanguard of the international proletarian revolution."

Lenin here draws confidently on a theory of history whose Western origins can be traced to Giovanni Battista Vico, an obscure scholar in Naples who in 1725 published *Principles of a New Science Dealing with the Nature of Nations*. Vico's essay was rediscovered in 1824 by a French savant named Jules Michelet, who enthusiastically applied its concepts to his own detailed history of the French Revolution. In Michelet's recounting, "I was seized by a frenzy caught from Vico, an incredible intoxication with his great historical principles." The intoxication spread through Europe and America, inspiring oracles of every persuasion, most contagiously in the case of Karl Marx and Friedrich Engels, who borrowed Hegel's dialectic to pronounce the doom of capitalism. Theirs was the ideological scalpel that fell into the zealous fingers of Lenin, of whom Maxim Gorky said, "His words always give one the impression of an irresistible truth," for he seemed to speak "not of his own will, but by the will of history."

The quotations are from Edmund Wilson, who traced the above progression in *To the Finland Station*. "We find Lenin identifying history with his will," Wilson writes, "as when he writes to the Central Committee on

the eve of the October Revolution:'History will not forgive delay by rev-
olutionists who could at once be victorious.'" History thus took on an an-
thropomorphic cast, becoming an Olympian divinity handing out prizes
to winners and punishing losers. Yet Lenin and his disciples also perceived
history as a science, so grounded in the impersonal forces of social evolution that Marx wished to dedicate *Das Kapital* to Charles Darwin (who
politely declined the honor). Armed with this science, so Lenin deeply believed, the vanguard of the proletariat would ignite a global revolution
with petrol supplied by the Third (Communist) International.

From the beginning, however, the victorious Bolsheviks found that
the Marxist-Leninist divining rod was fallible. The revolutions they confidently expected to break out across Europe and Asia failed to materialize, and in the end the fate of Soviet Communism itself provided the most
deflating refutation of Marxism as a prognosticator. But Lenin's heirs were
not the only ones to be dumbfounded by the Soviet unraveling; it also
came as a shock to non-Marxists. In *The Book of Predictions* (1980), Andrew
Greeley, a Catholic priest and novelist, suggested that the Soviet Union
would be overthrown internally in 1990. His was a wholly solitary voice.
In the same collection, David Sullivan, a Soviet foreign policy analyst for
the CIA, spoke for the agency's despairing realists when he guessed that
by the 1990s, "the U.S. will have ceased to be a great power and will be
struggling to hold itself together as a viable nation. The Soviet Union will
be approaching hegemony over most of the world."

The past century should have chastened those who trade in historical certitude. An example relevant to post-Soviet Asia is the democratic
transition in Spain. While Generalissimo Francisco Franco lived, many experts viewed Spain as the prisoner of an extremist history—an isolated
labyrinth sealed off by mountains, a priest-ridden country that somehow
had not benefited from the Enlightenment. In *Spain in the Modern World*
(1953), the British author James Cleugh saw tyranny as the norm: "Spanish 'liberalism' always has, and always will, represent only a strangely mixed
minority of cosmopolitan intellectuals and illiterate opportunists. Spain is
not, and never will be, a 'democratic' country." Even well-wishing American liberals like James Michener wrote guardedly about Spain's future. In
Iberia, his encyclopedic 1967 travel essay, Michener recorded a prevalent
view: "We have what you might call an ipso facto oligarchy to which the
only alternative is anarchy. . . . What we will have when Franco goes is
something roughly like the present form of government."

These forecasts reflected more than memories of the civil war that brought Franco to power. In the preceding century, Spain experienced 3 major civil wars, 26 revolutions, and 109 changes of government. A popular adage held that one half of Spain would never be content until the other half was dead. Carlists fought against Bourbons, Basques and Catalans rebelled against Castille, and during their war against Franco, Communists engaged in bloody vendettas against rival Marxists and anarcho-syndicalists. Anarchists insisted that Spain would never be free until the last priest was strangled with the entrails of the last capitalist.

In fact, no such excitement followed Franco's passing in 1975. With orderly dispatch, and with but a single seriocomic coup attempt, Spain instituted a democracy, witnessed a peaceful transfer of power from right-of-center conservatives to a Socialist prime minister and joined the European Community in 1985. Granted, Spain's smooth transition occurred with the help of a popular king and strong democratic parties, and a flourishing market economy was already in place. But what ensured success was the rise and influence of a new middle class and a new generation vibrantly liberated from old orthodoxies. As we shall see, some of these voices can also be heard in Central Asia and the Caucasus.

HISTORY IS NOT A blueprint but a cautionary tale. It is replete with warnings to those who believe that they can outguess the future, or that their country has a mandate from providence, or that alliances are a nuisance, or that a brusque arrogance is preferable to simulated humility. "The hardest strokes of heaven," the British historian Herbert Butterfield has warned, "fall in history on those who imagine they can control things in a sovereign manner, playing providence not only for themselves but for the far future—reaching out into the future with the wrong kind of far-sightedness, and gambling on a lot of risky calculations in which there must never be a single mistake."

Butterfield might have cited Britain's secret encouragement of the Jameson Raid into the Transvaal in 1896, the botched operation that Churchill viewed as the first downward step for imperial Britain. The raid's covert patron was the colonial secretary, Joseph Chamberlain, who believed that a regime change in the Transvaal would solidify British dominion over southern Africa, together with its gold and diamond riches, then as important as oil is today. When the raid failed ignobly, Chamberlain advised his prime minister, Lord Salisbury, that "an act of vigour" was needed "to soothe the wounded vanity of the nation," adding "it does not matter which of our numerous foes we defy but we ought to defy someone."

This happened amid growing concern over Britain's "splendid isolation," a phrase concocted by a Canadian politician but snapped up by the *Times*, then the voice of the elite and thereafter indelibly associated with Lord Salisbury. Though Britain did have a number of treaty agreements, it remained proudly aloof from ties with other major powers, France, Germany, Russia, the Austro-Hungarians and the United States. In 1896 Victoria herself wrote to her prime minister, "The Queen cannot help but feel that our *isolation* is dangerous." For his part, Salisbury did not like the word "isolation," but nonetheless in his deeds saw to it that Britain would not be hampered by Lilliputian treaties that could in any way conflict with British national interest, as he construed it.

History does not repeat itself, but leadership attitudes certainly do. Speaking for the Bush administration during a television interview in 2001, National Security Adviser Condoleezza Rice frankly declared, "The President of the United States was not elected to sign treaties that are not in America's interest." As she elaborated, "We are going to be honest with our allies about which treaties are in our interest and our dealing with problems with which they purport to deal. And those that are not, we are not prepared to be a party to." Still, it seems pertinent to recall that when the Boer War broke out, Britain found itself truly isolated. The war divided Britons as well as Americans, many of whom rooted for the Boers, and during "Black Week" in December 1899, when whiskered farmers mowed down invincible regiments such as the Black Watch, surprise and cheers spread around the world.

As this is written, it is not known whether the United States will forcibly impose a new leadership on Iraq, whatever the effect such a move might have on the ongoing war against terrorism. But to those familiar with history, there is a clear echo of times past in the vehement preference expressed in Washington for independent U.S. military action, "unfettered" being the telltale word. "This is a fundamental misjudgment," rejoins General Wesley K. Clark, the supreme allied commander in Europe from 1997 to 2000. "The longer this war goes on—and by all accounts it will go on for years—the more our success will depend on the willing cooperation and active cooperation of our allies to root out terrorist cells in

Europe and Asia, to cut off funding and support of terrorists and to deal with Saddam Hussein and other threats."

Not only does acting jointly lend legitimacy to the use of force, but alliances are a key to military victory, according to General Clark, who commanded the seventy-eight-day NATO war against Serbia in the spring of 1999. "NATO itself," he writes, "acted as a consensus engine for its members. Because it acts on the basis of such broad agreement, every decision is an opportunity for members to dissent—therefore every decision generates pressure to agree. . . . This process evokes leadership from the stronger states and pulls the others along." Thus collective action was not an obstacle to victory but an asset. "NATO worked. It held political leaders accountable to their electorate. It made an American-dominated effort essentially their effort. It made an American success their success. And because an American-led failure would have been their failure, these leaders became determined to prevail. NATO not only generated consensus, it also generated an incredible capacity to alter public perceptions, enabling countries with even minimal capacities to participate collectively in the war."

What General Clark asserts is the simple common sense inscribed on every American coin: E Pluribus Unum. Arrayed against President Slobodan Milosevic, moreover, was not only NATO but the significantly underestimated force of international law, as was also the case in the first Bush administration's campaign to liberate Kuwait. If NATO had taken part in the Afghan campaign, Clark goes on, "We could have simply phased the operation and turned over what had begun as a U.S.-only operation to a NATO mission, under U.S. leadership." He might have added that his point is as old as the Trojan War. It was the joint appeal of the allied Greek commanders that finally coaxed the sulking Achilles from his tent and back into the field, thereby opening the way to victory in the ten-year war (albeit gained through a covert trick).

A LL THE FOREGOING applies with particular force to Washington's relations with the region geopoliticians now call "Central Eurasia," the five republics of Central Asia and the three republics of the South Caucasus. This is an area to which Americans are newcomers, inhabited by proud peoples with difficult governments, and the challenge is to deal correctly with the latter without estranging the former. Americans have already plunged headlong into Central Eurasia, the way led before 9/11 by high-minded nongovernmental organizations and profit-minded energy executives, followed after 9/11 by convoys of Pentagon officials, special White House emissaries and eager members of Congress.

The resulting messages have been mixed, as evidenced by a Reuters dispatch datelined Bishkek on January 23, 2002, headed "Franks Sees No Permanent U.S. Bases in Central Asia," quoting General Tommy Franks as declaring, "We don't intend to have permanent bases in the region." But on February 6, an Associated Press story from Washington was headed "U.S. May Remain in Asia." The report noted that two days after a January referendum in Uzbekistan that human rights groups faulted, a State Department official visiting Tashkent promised to triple U.S. assistance to $160 million. The report went on: "The scene was reminiscent of the Cold War era when the United States routinely set up alliances with regimes which, while not democratic, at least were anti-Communist: Zaire, Somalia and a slew of erstwhile autocracies in Latin America come to mind. A similar pattern is now developing as the United States seeks allies in the war on terrorism."

The AP version has a dismayingly plausible ring. With scant attention and perfunctory debate, Washington has headed down a familiar path, negotiating security arrangements with authoritarian clients eager for a partnership that offers them the life insurance conferred by U.S. bases and promises less pressure on such irritants as human rights, corruption and nepotism. Not least, host governments are sure to view a permanent U.S. presence as a shield against undue interference from Russia. For America, the immediate benefits are obvious: basing rights in the war against terror, access to intelligence on militant Islamic movements and the promise of enhanced security for U.S. investments in oil and gas pipelines.

Yet following this path amounts to abandoning Central Eurasians who have taken seriously America's oft repeated pledges to promote human rights and genuine elections, as well as to succor freedom of speech and worship. It is already happening.

Item: In May 2002, Irina Petrushka, the editor of an independent newspaper in Kazakhstan, found the headless body of a dog tied to her office door, with a note saying this was her last warning. She found the dog's head near her home. "Shortly afterwards her paper's office was burnt down," relates a Reuters dispatch. "Over lunch with Reuters a few days later—when she arrived with a bodyguard—she spoke of her fears, both for herself and her country. And now she has had enough. 'Irina has left Kazakhstan for an undisclosed destination,' said an opposition spokesman, adding she was tired of constant police surveillance."

DOES US HAVE BASES IN THAT COUNTRY? ?

Item: On August 28, 2002, the Kazakh journalist Sergei Duvanov was attacked outside his home in Almaty by unknown assailants who reportedly said, "You know why we are doing this" and "Next time we'll make you a cripple." Duvanov had been invited to a meeting in Warsaw of the Organization for Security and Cooperation in Europe (OSCE) to discuss human rights abuses in Kazakhstan. Security agents had already seized two computers owned by Duvanov and told him he would face criminal charges for an article he wrote for an Internet site (which few Kazakhs can read) that criticized President Nazarbayev for opening a secret account in Switzerland and asserted that Kazakhs were afraid to tell the truth about their country's personality cult.

I have singled out Kazakhstan because it was once deemed a less oppressive Central Eurasian state, yet post–9/11 it has plunged downhill. "Tragedies are occurring every second in this country," said Murat Auezov, a writer who served as Kazakhstan's first ambassador to China, in a July 2002 interview by Robert G. Kaiser of the *Washington Post*. Now a critic of the government, Auezov described his country's leaders as "temporaries" who "never thought about the past, are afraid to think about the future, and use the present to grab all they can." Variations of the same despair can be heard, though seldom on the record, from pro-democracy dissidents throughout Central Eurasia. Evidence of their harassment is amply documented in the 670-page *World Report 2002* published by Human Rights Watch.

What is to be done? If ever a region called out for a multilateral approach, in which America's presence would be one among many, it is Central Eurasia. If military bases are needed, let them be NATO bases, thereby making good use of an alliance whose nineteen members, for the first time ever in 2001, evoked the one-for-all mutual defense clause in the founding charter. Yet mystifyingly, Washington all but brushed off the NATO initiative while at same time senior officials complained sourly and inconsistently about alleged European pusillanimity. As it happens, five of Central Eurasia's eight countries have signed up for NATO's Partnership for Peace program, so that links already exist with the alliance. For Americans, a NATO presence offers a prudent means of securing military facilities in the region, while diluting Washington's identification with repressive regimes. For an alliance unsure of its mission even as it enlarges, a security role in the global fight against terrorism would be a source of new purpose and direction.

Similarly, it makes sense to seek influence through numbers in promoting freer institutions in Central Asia. As in the case of NATO, an instrument already exists: the badly named Organization for Security and Cooperation in Europe, which actually is global in scope. An offshoot of the 1975 Helsinki Final Act, the OSCE played an important catalytic role in the democratic evolution of the former Soviet and Warsaw Pact states. Now comprising fifty-five participating members, the Stockholm-based OSCE has centers in Kyrgyzstan, Uzbekistan, Kazakhstan and Turkmenistan, as well as in the South Caucasus. Lacking funds, energy and leadership, however, OSCE has been mainly a paper presence, "with few carrots and even fewer sticks," in the words of a thoughtful International Crisis Group report in September 2002. Because of its important past history and its relevant ongoing mission, OSCE deserves support from a White House wary of "nation building." Supporting OSCE not only would make policy sense but would give President Bush a laudable chance to see the jaws of his critics drop—should he genuinely try to make this neglected organization effective. WHY DOESN'T EUROPE SUPPORT IT MORE?

Cultural programs, finally, are the most benign, least appreciated and most financially challenged of American diplomatic implements. Fortunately, there is an existing program that works—the Muskie Scholarship Program. In the last decade, some twenty-six hundred citizens from the five Central Asian republics have studied in America at places like Cloudcroft, New Mexico; Bozeman, Montana; and Columbia, South Carolina. Some exchange students attend high school; others are teachers or graduate students, but all have benefited from this program, named for the late Senator Edmund Muskie of Maine. To meet a beneficiary (in Almaty I met a teenager who had spent six months in El Paso) is to talk with someone who has been to the moon and back, and now sees her own society from a more critical distance. Robert Kaiser, in his swing through Central Asia, wrote one of the few articles describing this mostly unknown program. Among his interviewees was Janybek Omorov, thirty-nine, a Kyrgyz

banker with a master's degree from the University of Illinois. He noted
that there were already two hundred graduates of various American programs in Kyrgyzstan. One day, they will form a "critical mass," he predicted, "to change the country." A vanguard, one is tempted to add, more
likely than Lenin's to foment permanent and democratic change in Central Eurasia.

I F AMERICA HAS A crippling disadvantage in its encounter with the
inner Asian world of ancient silk routes, modern pipelines and imperial debris, it is something worse than lack of knowledge. It is lack of
curiosity. This was evident in the inch-deep U.S. media coverage of the
Afghanistan campaign. Correspondents on the scene seemed unaware of
or unwilling to address Washington's complicity in the rise of the Taliban.
With the exception of the *New Yorker*'s Isabel Hilton (who is British),
hardly anybody seemed to know about, or ask about, Ghaffar Khan, the
"frontier Gandhi," whose rise and fall was central to the modern tragedy
of the Pashtuns. As for Iran, even as the fiftieth anniversary of the 1953
coup approaches, most Americans seem unaware of Washington's role in
deposing a constitutional leader, a "regime change" whose reverberations
are felt to this day. ALSO UNAWARE OF OUR ROLE KEEPING SOVIETS OUT OF THE AREA
                        OR OTHER POSITIVE THINGS - WHY NOT MENTION THAT? ONLY NEG-
   History and geography are indifferently taught in American second-
ary schools. By contrast, how startling to scan this passage in the opening
scene of Christopher Marlowe's *Tamburlaine the Great* (1590), in which a
Persian emperor is enthroned:

> We do crown thee monarch of the East,
> Emperor of Asia and Persia;
> Great Lord of Media and Armenia;
> Duke of Africa and Albania;
> Mesopotamia and of Parthia,
> East India and the late-discovered isles;
> Chief Lord of the wide, vast Euxine Sea,
> And of the ever-raging Caspian lake.

Elsewhere in the play, Marlowe refers to "the fifty-headed Volga," to
the Scythians and the Tatars, to Barbary and Fez, to Buda and Bohemia,

to Trebizond and Zanzibar, and to the Tigris and Euphrates. His extensive and generally accurate knowledge doubtless reflects the spirit of the age, when every month seemed to bring back to Britain exciting news of unmapped lands. Even so, he and his audience seemingly possessed a voracious curiosity lacking in our own era of instant access to CNN and the Internet, when familiarity too often breeds boredom. *SEE "THE CLOSING OF THE AMERICAN MIND" BY BLOOM*   *DUE TO CULTURAL RELITVISM*

Americans could pay no higher compliment to Central Asia and the Caucasus than to learn about its peoples, their problems and their past. Some of the New World figures who adventured among the non-Russians in the tsar's empire lend themselves to celebration in biography, historical fiction and, indeed, television programming. Leading the procession is Virginia's Captain John Smith, of Pocahontas fame, whose *True Travels and Adventures* (1630) relates his ordeals as an Ottoman slave and goes on to provide a favorable portrait of the Islamic Crimean Tatars: "They are Mahometans, as are the Turks, from whom they also have their Lawes, but no Lawyers, nor Attournies, onely Judges, and Justices in every Village. . . . Justice is with such integrity and expedition executed, without covetousnesse, bribery, partiality, and brawling, that in six months they have sometimes scarce six cases to heare." *B. S. !*

Next is John Ledyard, who at twenty-two sailed from New England and then joined up with James Cook on the great captain's last voyage in quest of the North-West Passage (1776–1779). Ledyard published a lively account of Cook's explorations but regrettably left unpublished his diary of an even bolder journey across Siberia (1787–1788), which had the patronage of Thomas Jefferson. He was probably the first American to see Lake Baikal and the cities of Omsk, Irkutsk and Kazan. His diary, finally published by the University of Wisconsin Press in 1966, is notable for its hostility to Russian officialdom and its sympathy for indigenous Siberians and Tatars: "The Tartar is a Man of Nature—not of Art—his Philosophy is therefore very simple, but sometimes very sublime—Let us enumerate some of his virtues—he is a lover of Peace—no Helen & no System of Religion has ever yet disturbed it. He is contented to be what he is, never did a Tartar speak ill of the Diety, or envy his Fellow Creatures . . . They do not prostitute even a Smile or a Frown any more than an European Monarch." Ledyard died at thirty-seven in Cairo and today is unremembered. *MORE ROMANTICIZING*

Better known is John Lloyd Stephens, the first notable American travel writer, famed among archaeologists for his early accounts of the colossal Mayan ruins in Central America and the Yucatan. Less familiar is his *Incidents of Travel in Greece, Turkey, Russia and Poland* (1838), written with his customary brio, as in this description of arriving at Odessa, where he smuggled in a proscribed copy of Byron's verse after being stripped, fumigated and examined by the port doctor: "I could not help but calling him back to ask him whether he held the same inquisition of the fair sex; to which he replied with a melancholy upturning of the eyes that in the good old days of Russian barbarism this had been part of his duties, but that the march of improvements had invaded his rights and given this portion of his professional duties to a *sage femme*."

In Odessa, Stephens attended a performance of *The Barber of Seville*. "I should as soon thought of an opera-house at Chicago as here," the visitor from New York remarks, "but I already found what impressed itself more forcibly upon me at every step, that Russia is a country of anomalies. . . . There is no country where cities have sprung up so fast and increased so rapidly as in ours." He pursued: "We are both young, and both marching with gigantic strides to greatness, yet we move by different roads, and the whole face of the country, from the new city Odessa, on the borders of the Black Sea, to the steppes of Siberia, shows a different order of government and a different constitution of Society. With us a few individuals cut down the trees of the forest, or settle themselves on the banks of a stream, where they happen to find some local advantages, and build houses suitable to their necessities; others come and join them, and by degrees, the settlement becomes a large city. But here a gigantic government, endowed almost with creative power, says '*Let there be a city!*'"

In our volume *Tournament of Shadows*, my wife and I tried to revive the memory of Josiah Harlan, the fighting Quaker who led an Afghan army over the Hindu Kush, as well as the two young Americans who together made their way into Central Asia and detailed its conquest and governance: the war correspondent Januarius MacGahan of New Lexington, Ohio, and the diplomat Eugene Schuyler, a New Yorker who went on to initiate Russian studies at Yale University. But among pioneers, none stands higher than the forgotten George Kennan—not the twentieth-century diplomat but his great-uncle, the traveler, author and popular lecturer, born in Norwalk, Ohio, in 1845. He lived until 1924, just before his great-nephew joined the newly formed Foreign Service. Kennan's first book, *Tent Life in Siberia* (1871), described his encounters as a surveyor mapping the route for a telegraph line meant to cross Alaska and then pass under the Bering Strait overland through Siberia to European Russia. He followed with an extended trip in 1870 to the Caucasus, where he became the first American to travel through Daghestan. (His journal was published for the first time in 2003 by the University of Washington Press.)

Kennan began as an enthusiast for Russian rule, firmly believing that accounts of the horrors of the tsar's penal colonies had been exaggerated. With the approval of tsarist authorities, in 1885 he undertook a journey through Siberia. His devastating two-volume account, *Siberia and the Exile System* (1891), was the spark for the first sustained American human rights assault on Russia's autocracy. He distinguished carefully between political prisoners—liberals, revolutionaries and terrorists—and condemned unreservedly political violence perpetrated by the latter. Kennan, who had covered the U.S. Supreme Court as a reporter for the Associated Press, went on to say:

> The Government first set the example of lawlessness in Russia by arresting without warrant; by punishing without trial; by cynically disregarding the judgment of its own courts when such judgments were in favor of politicals; by confiscating the money and property of private citizens whom it merely suspected of sympathy with the revolutionary movement; by sending fourteen-year-old boys and girls to Siberia; by kidnapping the children of "politically untrustworthy" people and exiles, and putting them into state asylums; by driving men and women into insanity and suicide in rigorous solitary confinement without giving them a trial; by burying secretly at night the bodies of people whom it had thus done to death in dungeons; and by treating as a criminal, *in posse* if not *in esse*, every citizen who dared to ask why or wherefore.

Through articles and a cross-country speaking tour, Kennan followed with a successful campaign to attach human rights conditions to legislation pertaining to Russia. Yet he is almost wholly forgotten. My point is that Americans have long since earned the right to speak out as friends of liberty in Russia and for the human rights of non-Slavic peoples in Central Eurasia. George Kennan and other friends of freedom bear witness to American bona fides, and it would be splendid if they were restored to their rightful pedestals. Yet I strongly believe that Washington's voice carries farthest when it is less loud, that few benefits result from endless self-advertisement, and that Communism's fate argues strongly against assuming that history has decreed the universal triumph of America's political and economic system.

A good model is a little cited speech by John F. Kennedy, delivered at the University of Washington on November 16, 1961. The president began by saying that the United States could not compete with its adversaries in the tactics of terror or assassination, or abandon the slow process of consulting with allies whose leaders are not satellites, or control international organizations, since America casts 1 percent of the votes in the U.N. General Assembly. He noted that while the United States possesses weapons of tremendous power, they are least effective when used against the weapons of freedom's foes: infiltration, guerrilla warfare and civil disorder. He concluded:

> In short, we must face problems which do not lend themselves to easy or quick or permanent solutions. And we must face the fact that the United States is neither omnipotent nor omniscient—that we are only 6 percent of the world's population—that we cannot impose our will upon the other 94 percent of mankind—that we cannot right every wrong or reverse each adversity—and that therefore there cannot be an American solution to every world problem.

It was an address that showed the decent respect for the opinion of mankind promised in America's birth certificate.

NOTES ON SOURCES

The Dust of Empire could not have been attempted if not for the outpour-
ing of books, papers and articles on Central Eurasia by a prolific host of
scholars and journalists on whose work I have drawn extensively, and
gratefully. An ongoing caravan of conferences dealing with Central Asia,
the Caucasus, the Silk Road and Islam yielded a trove of specialized papers and personal contacts, as have many special seminars and panel discussions in New York, notably those sponsored by the World Policy
Institute, the Open Society Institute and the Carnegie Council on Ethics
and International Affairs (the last also hosting the invaluable Foreign Policy Roundtable, moderated by Nicholas X. Rizopoulos).

The richest seam of day-to-day information about the region is to be
found on the Internet and its scores of relevant Web sites. Most mornings
for several years my wife, Shareen, trawled key sites on the Caspian Sea,
Central Asia and Russia. In partial recompense, The Century Foundation
and PublicAffairs have agreed to post a Web site for this book, www.
dustofempire.com. It will carry reviews, page-by-page sources for quoted
matter and bibliographic notes on new works, with links to related sites.

In this chapter-by-chapter overview of sources, I have used short note
form for books and authors listed in the select bibliography.

PROLOGUE

PAX BRITANNICA, SQUARED

Professor Kennedy's remarks on American hyperpower, "The Eagle
Has Landed: The New U.S. Global Military Position," appeared in the *Financial Times* on February 1, 2002. Regarding the ubiquity of English, see

McCrum, Cran and MacNeil, *The Story of English*. Baron de Coubertin's
concerns are recorded in Burama, *Anglomania*. The Crossman quotation
is from Hitchens, *Blood, Class and Nostalgia*.

I

PATTERNS OF MASTERY, BRITISH AND AMERICAN

The literature on Pax Britannica is exceptionally rich. An invaluable
resource is the five-volume *Oxford History of the British Empire,* edited by
a University of Texas scholar, William Roger Louis. I have consulted volume 3, *The Nineteenth Century,* edited by Porter; volume 4, *The Twentieth
Century,* edited by Brown and Louis; and volume 5, *Historiography,* edited
by Winks. For a panorama replete with scents and sounds, nothing excels
James (later Jan) Morris's imperial trilogy; I have drawn especially on *Pax
Britannica: The Climax of Empire*. A distillation of contemporary scholarship can be found in Hyam, *Britain's Imperial Century*. For a comparison of
British and American forms of dominion, see Smith, *Pattern of Imperialism*.
For a diplomatic overview, the still unsurpassed work is Langer's *Diplomacy
of Imperialism*. Hobsbawm's *Age of Empire* provides a learned view from the
left, as does Williams's too schematic but deeply felt *Roots of the Modern
American Empire*. Ronald Steel's *Pax Americana* has survived the decades
with exemplary freshness.

On Lansing v. Wilson, see Moynihan. Lansing's associations with the
Dulles brothers are noted in Peter Grose, *Gentleman Spy*. Langer is the
richest source on imperial euphoria. My account of Omdurman is based
on Pakenham, *Scramble for Africa*; Manchester, *Last Lion*; Churchill, *River
War;* Farwell, *Prisoners of the Mahdi*; and Randolph Churchill in his filial
biography, *Winston S. Churchill: Youth*. For an iconoclastic corrective, see
Ellis, *Social History of the Machine Gun*; and Twain, *Collected Tales, Sketches,*
etc. On imperial massacres, the reader is referred to Pakenham's *Scramble*;
Farwell's *Queen Victoria's Little Wars* and (for Tibet) French's *Younghusband*
and Fleming's *Bayonets to Lhasa*. On Marchand, see Lewis's *The Race to
Fashoda*. The Lugar theory of indirect rule is detailed in Margery Parham's
Lugard: The Years of Authority.

Of the many histories of America's 1898 plunge into imperialism, I
have turned to O'Toole, *The Spanish War;* Karnow, *In Our Image;* and Bain,
Sitting in Darkness. On Mr. Dooley, see my own anthology of newspaper

columns, *Pundits, Poets and Wits* (New York: Oxford University Press, 1990). Justice to Belgium's Congolese adventure is rendered in Hochschild's *King Leopold's Ghost;* on Morel, see the fine sketch by A. J. P. Taylor in *The Troublemakers* (but Morel deserves a fuller portrait). Two outstanding accounts of the Boer War are by Farwell and Pakenham. The ironies of World War I are astringently recalled by Ferguson in *The Pity of War.* Keynes's verdict on Versailles is amplified in Macmillan's *Paris 1919.* Angell tells his own story in his autobiography, *After All.* Morris portrays Baring, Lugard and other imperial grandees in *Pax Britannica.* What Versailles meant for the Middle East is provocatively retold in Fromkin's *Peace to End All Peace.*

America's "informal empire" is perceptively limned in an outstanding chapter on imperialism in Schlesinger's *Cycles of American History.* On the ample literature about Olney, Panama and dollar diplomacy, I drew especially on Herring's long-standard history of Latin America; Thomas's huge and detailed *Cuba*; Szulc's *Twilight of the Tyrants;* the Heinls' *Written in Blood*; and Riding's *Distant Neighbors.* On America's own violent past, see *American Violence,* edited by Hofstadter and Wallace.

II

RUSSIA: THE LONG TALONS OF MEMORY

On the Russian past, I have benefited from an older work, once judged by some as too Russophile, Pares's *History of Russia,* as well as from Seton-Watson's *The Russian Empire,* another vintage work. Billington's *Icon and the Axe* remains high on any basic list. Among many books on Russia's expansion, I commend *Empire: The Russian Empire and Its Rivals* by Dominic Lieven; *The Russian Empire and the World,* by LeDonne; and *Russian Imperialism from Ivan the Great to the Revolution,* edited by Taras Hunczac.

Mackinder's theories are set forth in his *Democratic Ideals and Reality.* Grousset's *Empire of the Steppes* can be supplemented by Morgan's *Mongols,* McGovern's *Early Empires of Central Asia,* and *They Rode into Europe* by Jankovich, with its learned insights by a Hungarian equestrian. Of the biographies of Ivan the Terrible, I profited from Payne and Romanoff's and Benson Bobrick's. The ambiguous interplay between Mongols and Muscovy is described in Halperin's *Russia and the Golden Horde.* A fluent account of Ukraine history can be found in Reid's *Borderland*. Muscovy's dramatic expansion northeast is narrated by W. Bruce Lincoln in *The Conquest of a Continent*. Eisenstein's director's notes turned up in an obscure Soviet-era book of that title. Blok's famous poem is from an anthology of Russian poetry translated and edited by Carlisle and Styron. Ascherson's *Black Sea* provides a literate introduction to a region too little known in the West. Rolle's *World of the Scythians* offers an overview of a little-known civilization, its memory kept alive by Herodotus. I have relied on Aubrey de Sélincourt's translation of Herodotus, in the Penguin Classics series. On nomadic empires, also see Toynbee's now unfashionable and too neglected *Study of History*. On Soviet oil, see Yergin, *The Prize;* and Kotkin, *Armageddon Averted*. For a Russian insider's contemporary assessment of an imperial past, consult Trenin's *End of Eurasia*.

III

IRAN: THE AGONIES OF NONSOVEREIGNTY

A good starting point on Iran is Ghani's annotated bibliography, *Iran and the West*, regrettably available only in major libraries. A traditional British view of Persia can be found in Sykes's *History* and Curzon's voluminous and still impressive *Persia and the Persian Question*. Frye's *Heritage of Persia* provides an authoritative historical pageant. Britain and Russia's nineteenth-century rivalry in Iran is finely rendered in Kazemzadeh's *Russia and Britain in Persia,* anecdotally supplemented by Wright, *The English Amongst the Persians.* A wider time span is covered in *The Foreign Policy of Iran* by Ramazini. On the constitutional revolution, see Kazemzadeh and the firsthand account by Shuster. For the rise of the oil industry, I have profited from Yergin's *The Prize*, which can be fortified by Sampson's *Seven Sisters* and a basic document, *The International Petroleum Cartel,* mainly the work of a brilliant and unsung petroleum economist, John Blair, for the U.S. Senate Subcommittee on Monopoly.

On the rise of the Pahlavis, see *Britain and the Russian Civil War* by Richard Ullman, who opened the way to the ampler reconstruction; *Iran and the Rise of Reza Shah* by Ghani, who mined the British archives; and Abrahamian, *Iran Between Two Revolutions*, who synthesizes a complex history. Interested views from the well-born within are offered by Farman Farmaian, *Daughter of Persia,* and Manucher and Roxane Farmanfarmaian,

Blood and Oil. Shah Mohammad Reza Pahlavi gives his version in *Answer to History*, which requires as counterpoint Kapuscinski, *Shah of Shahs,* and Shawcross, *The Shah's Last Ride.* Kermit Roosevelt's *Countercoup* is revealing in its careless indiscretions about the overthrow of Mossadeq, and Wilber offers his own account in a privately published memoir, *Adventures in the Middle East.* For a synthesis, I am in debt to Stephen Dorril's exhaustively detailed *MI6.*

The emergence of Khomeini is carefully related in Mottahedeh's *Mantle of the Prophet* and in Bakhash's *Reign of the Ayatollahs*; I have relied on the former for translations of key sermons by the ayatollah. Sick's *All Fall Down* is by a former National Security Council officer who describes the hostage crisis as seen from the West Wing. Sciolino's *Persian Mirrors* is a fine study by a *New York Times* correspondent who has covered the Iranian Revolution from its beginning. Sandra Mackey's *The Iranians* is a lively portrayal by a prolific Middle East hand. Dorman and Fahrang's *The U.S. Press and Iran* is an essential case study in flawed reportage. Special mention is owed to the many books and articles by the Iranian-born scholar Sharin Hunter, notably *Iran After Khomeini* and *Iran and the World*. Finally, a *plus ça change* curiosity turned up as these pages were written: Kelly's *Diplomacy and Murder in Tehran,* recounting the killing of a gifted Russian writer and diplomat, Alexander Gribiyedov, by a Tehran mob in 1829.

IV

PAKISTAN: SINS OF PARTITION

On the broad issue of partition, I am happy to note the prescient work of Robert Schaeffer in *Warpaths: The Politics of Partition,* whose forebodings in 1990 were vindicated by events in former Yugoslavia and elsewhere. On the synthetic nature of nationhood, see Anderson, *Imagined Communities*; Geary, *The Myth of Nations;* Pfaff, *The Wrath of Nations;* and Hobsbawm and Ranger, *The Invention of Tradition.* The quotation from Tocqueville apropos Gobineau is from Lukacs's paperback edition of the former's letters. Amos Elon in *Herzl* unearthed the great Zionist's comments on flags.

To the present writer's prior bibliography of books on the British Raj in *Tournament of Shadows*, three important histories can be added: Shashi Tharoor's *India*, Lawrence James's *Raj* and John Keay's *India: A History.* On the partition of Bengal, I have drawn on Chaudhuri, *Autobiography;* Dilkes, *Curzon in India: The Achievement;* and Wolpert, *Jinnah.* In the continuing debate over the 1947 partition, basic texts include Hodson, *The Great Divide;* Menon, *The Transfer of Power;* Ziegler, *Mountbatten;* and Moon, *Divide and Quit;* all are variations of Mountbatten-did-his-best; for contrary views, see Rajmohan Gandhi, *The Good Boatman;* Chaudhuri, *Thy Hand, Great Anarch!;* and Hamid, *Disastrous Twilight* (the last, in its revised edition, contains a new preface detailing Radcliffe's role in shifting boundaries to favor India). More generally, on the conundrums of nationhood, see Khilnani's *The Idea of India.*

On Ghaffar Khan and the North-West Frontier, the most extensive work on the noble Pashtun is by Gandhi's biographer Tendulkar, which is exceedingly hard to find; more accessible recent works include Banerjee, *The Pathan Unarmed;* Easwaran, *Nonviolent Soldier of Islam;* and Korejo, *The Frontier Gandhi.* An important new entry on the North-West Frontier is Allen, *Soldier Sahibs,* by a veteran chronicler of the Raj. Caroe's *The Pathans* remains a standard authority; for a sympathetic American view of the same people, see Spain, *Way of the Pathans.* On the province's critical run-up to independence, see Mehra's *North-West Frontier Drama.* One of the few American studies of Baluchistan is Harrison's *In Afghanistan's Shadow.* Concerning Washington's strategic tilt to Pakistan, see McMahon, *Cold War on the Periphery.* On Pakistan itself, Bennett-Jones's recent *Pakistan* can be commended, supplemented by Weaver's *Pakistan: In the Shadow of Jihad and Afghanistan.* The two halves of divided India remain united in their devotion to cricket; why this should be is explored by Ramachandra Guha, while the Pakistani cricket star and politician Imran Khan describes his own Pashtun people in *Warrior Race.*

v

AFGHANISTAN: IN A DARK DEFILE

There is a rich literature in English on Afghanistan, with too little by Afghans themselves. British accounts begin with Elphinstone's *Kingdom of Caubul* (1815) and continue with military and personal memoirs of two Afghan wars (works itemized in *Tournament of Shadows*), continuing with Sykes's two-volume *History of Afghanistan* (hard to come by, since a bomb destroyed all warehoused copies during the Nazi blitz). Sirdar Ikbal Ali

Shah's *Afghanistan of the Afghans,* published in the 1930s, is the more valuable, given its Afghan authorship, notably for its chapter on Afghan Sufism. More recently, a standard history has been Dupree's *Afghanistan*, written by an American who was for many years a teacher, entrepreneur and U.S. government adviser in Kabul. (His widow, Nancy Dupree, now leads a valiant campaign to save Afghan antiquities from predatory dealers and unprincipled museums.)

There is by now a whole library of works by foreigners. Some are lyrical, like Elliot's *An Unexpected Light;* others are impassioned memoirs by Westerners who reported the war against the Soviets, like Lohbeck's *Holy War, Unholy Victory.* Still others are by an earlier generation of young Americans fresh from the Midwest, who taught or served in Afghanistan, like Roseanne Klass, born in Cedar Rapids, Iowa, in *Land of the High Flags.* Among American pilgrims was James Michener, resulting in a generally forgotten novel, *Caravans,* to which he appended a note explaining his fascination with Afghans.

Thus books about Afghanistan have tended to be long on feeling, short on analysis. Stewart's *Fire in Afghanistan,* to cite an example, implausibly ennobles Kabul's failed reforming king, Amanullah, and seeks to blame all that went wrong on the British. A more balanced note was struck in 1969 by Gregorian in *The Emergence of Modern Afghanistan.* Following in this tradition are Rubin's *Fragmentation of Afghanistan* and *Search for Peace in Afghanistan;* Harrison and Cordovez's *Out of Afghanistan;* and Rashid's deservedly popular *Taliban.*

I have drawn as well on Cooley, Archie Roosevelt and Kermit Roosevelt's *Arabs, Oil and History.* Two convoluted Pakistani accounts, Khan's *Untying the Afghan Knot* and Yousaf and Adkin's *The Bear Trap,* only underscore the mistake in letting Islamabad dictate the terms of covert U.S. aid to the Afghan resistance. Yet to this day, those responsible for that policy are unwilling to acknowledge the scale of their mistake, as evidenced in former Texas Congressman Charlie Wilson's remarks in his *Sixty Minutes* interview on August 25, 2002.

Other references are to Weaver's *Portrait of Egypt,* detailing the link between Egyptian Islamicists and the Afghan resistance; Strachey's *End of Empire*; and Anatoly Dobrynin's *In Confidence,* on the Kremlin decision to invade Afghanistan.

VI

THE CAUCASUS: A BEDLAM OF IDENTITY

Hauner's *What Is Asia to Us?* is a good starting point for examining
Russia's southward push into the Caucasus and Central Asia. No tsarist
prince did more to expand the empire than Potemkin, the subject of an
excellent biography by Simon Shebag Montefiore, a volume as outsize as
the prince himself. By contrast, Prince Vorontsov's biographer, Anthony
Rhinelander, does not quite fill his canvas. Special mention is deserved for
Laurence Kelly's graceful biography of Lermontov. The key work on the
Murid wars matching Vorontsov against Imam Shamil is Baddeley's *Russian Conquest of the Caucasus*, a theme elaborated with romantic panache
by Lesley Blanch in *The Sabres of Paradise*. The first American visitor was
Ditson, whose *Circassia* was notably sympathetic to the Russians, as was
George Kennan, the nineteenth-century traveler whose Caucasus diary
was published in 2003 by the University of Washington Press. The tangled
conflict following the Bolshevik Revolution is chronicled by Kazemzadeh
in *The Struggle for the Caucasus* (and see the same scholar's essay on the brutal last phase of the Murid wars in *Russian Imperialism,* edited by Hunczak).
A reconsideration of tsarist policies in the area can be found in Brower
and Lazzerini, *Russia's Orient*. See also Jersild, *Orientalism and Empire:
North Caucasus Mountain Peoples and the Georgian Frontier, 1848–1917*. A
devastating accounting of Soviet nationalities policies in the region can be
found in *The Black Book of Communism,* edited by Stephane Courtois
et al.

Karny's *Highlanders* offers a guided tour of the present-day Caucasus
in an account with details, including a comprehensive listing of dozens of
Web sites about and from the region. Ronald Grigor Suny ranks high
among specialists on the region; his *Making of the Georgian Nation* fills a
void. Nasmyth's *Georgia in the Mountains of Poetry* is part travel guide, part
history, part compilation of curiosities. The Hakluyt Society has enter-
prisingly translated and republished two volumes of reports of *Russian
Embassies to the Georgian Kings, 1589–1605* (edited by W. E. D. Allen).
Koestler describes his visit to Soviet Georgia in *The Invisible Writing,*
which also covers his forays into Central Asia.

Christopher Walker's *Armenia: The Survival of a Nation* covers the period until 1980, and Arlen's *Passage to Ararat* memorably evokes Soviet Armenia. I have relied on Tadeusz Swietochowski's extensive learning about

Azerbaijan, as evidenced in *Russia and Azerbaijan* (1995) and a forthcoming new history, of which a chapter has appeared in *World Policy Journal*. The mystery of *Ali and Nino* was unraveled by Tom Reiss in "The Man from the East" in the October 4, 1998, *New Yorker.*

VII

CENTRAL ASIA: INVENTED STATES, REAL GODFATHERS

Portmanteau volumes about Central Asia abound. A short list would include *Central Asia* (1994), edited by Malik (16 contributions); *Civil Society in Central Asia* (1999), edited by Ruffin and Waugh (12 contributions); *The Nationalities Question in Post-Soviet States* (1990), edited by Smith (24 contributions); *Central Asia* (3d ed., 1994), edited by Allworth (18 contributions); *Central Asia and the World* (1994), edited by Mandelbaum (8 contributions); *The New Geopolitics of Central Asia* (1994), edited by Banuazizi and Weiner (11 contributions); and *Central Asian Security* (2001), edited by Allison and Jonson (11 contributions). Works by individual authors tend to be more accessible, as, for example, Rashid's *Resurgence of Central Asia;* Roy's *New Central Asia,* which centers on nation invention; Soucek's *Inner Asia,* a cultural overview from medieval to modern times; Frye's *The Heritage of Central Asia,* a learned survey from antiquity to the Turkish expansion; and Knobloch's *Monuments of Central Asia,* by a Czech scholar who has traveled widely through the area since 1959.

What is missing is a synthesis addressed to nonspecialists, as well as full-scale studies of individual countries. In the latter category, Martha Brill Olcott's *Kazakhstan,* its tone empathetic but critical, is an exemplary model. I have as yet come upon no comparable studies in English of Uzbekistan, Turkmenistan, Kyrgyzstan and Tajikistan. As compensation, there is a miscellany of special works, such as Levin's *Hundred Thousand Fools of God,* a musical and ethnographic travelogue, complete with a compact disc. Or as beguiling, Maslow's *Sacred Horses: The Memoirs of a Turkmen Cowboy,* plus a score or so of travelers' tales, as in Malcomson's *Empire's Edge.*

For the record, other works cited in this chapter include Bush and Scowcroft, *A World Transformed;* Baker, *The Politics of Diplomacy;* Matlock, *Autopsy on an Empire;* Remnick, *Resurrection;* Kapuscinski, *Imperium;* and Wittfogel, *Oriental Despotism.*

"What Is to Be Done?"

The discussion of federalism benefited from *Saving the Revolution,* essays on *The Federalist,* edited by Charles Kesler. Paul Hoffman's comments can be found in Walker, *The Cold War.* Thomas de Waal's remarks were from a September 27, 2002, keynote speech to the NATO Parliamentary Assembly in Tbilisi. Of the many biographies of Lenin, Robert Service's is the most recent. I have also relied on Bertram Wolfe's classic *Three Who Made a Revolution* and Wilson's *To the Finland Station.* Butterfield's quotation is from his book *Christianity and History* (London: Fontana, 1957). Bob Kaiser's *Washington Post* articles appeared on July 1, July 8, July 13, July 14, July 22, August 1, August 5, August 27, 2002. I have drawn from Eugene Anschel, editor, *The American Image of Russia* (New York: Ungar, 1974), for American travelers' accounts and, for John Lloyd Stephens's Crimean forays, on Von Hagen's *Maya Explorer.* On the elder George Kennan, see his *Siberia and the Exile System* and the biographical essay in the forthcoming Caucasus diaries. The full text of John F. Kennedy's November 16, 1961, address at the University of Washington can be found in *Public Papers of the President* for 1961 (Washington, D.C.: Government Printing Office, 1962). And General Wesley Clark's remarks on NATO are from "An Army of One?" in *Washington Monthly,* September 2002, pp. 19–23.

SELECT BIBLIOGRAPHY

Author's Note: Listed here are books cited or consulted for The Dust of Empire. *I have omitted periodicals; selected key articles are cited in full in the chapter on sources that precedes this list. I have restricted the bibliography to books published in the English language that for the most part are readily available in academic libraries.*

Allen, Charles. *Soldier Sahibs: The Men Who Made the North-West Frontier*. London: John Murray, 2000.

Allen, W. E. D., ed. *Russian Embassies to the Georgian Kings, 1589–1605*. 2 vols. Cambridge, U.K.: Hakluyt Society, 1970.

Allison, Roy, ed. *Challenges for the Former Soviet South*. London: Royal Institute of International Affairs, 1996.

Allison, Roy, and Lena Jonson, eds. *Central Asian Security: The New International Context*. London: Royal Institute of International Affairs, 2001.

Allworth, Edward, ed. *Central Asia*. Durham, N.C.: Duke University Press, 1994.

———. *The Tatars of Crimea: Return to the Homeland*. Durham, N.C.: Duke University Press, 1998.

Anderson, Benedict. *Imagined Communities*. Rev. ed. New York: Verso, 1991.

Angell, Sir Norman. *After All*. London: Hamish Hamilton, 1951.

Arlen, Michael. *Passage to Ararat*. New York: Farrar, Straus & Giroux, 1975.

Armstrong, Terence, ed. *Yermak's Campaign in Siberia*. Cambridge, U.K.: Hakluyt Society, 1975.

Ascherson, Neal. *Black Sea*. New York: Hill & Wang, 1995.

Bain, David Haward. *Sitting in Darkness: Americans in the Philippines*. Boston: Houghton Mifflin, 1984.

Baker, James A., III. *The Politics of Diplomacy*. New York: Putnam, 1995.

Banerjee, Mukulika. *The Pathan Unarmed*. Karachi: Oxford University Press, 2000.

Banuazizi, Ali, and Myron Weiner, eds. *The New Geopolitics of Central Asia and Its Borderlands.* Bloomington: Indiana University Press, 1994.

Billington, James H. *The Icon and the Axe: An Interpretive History of Russian Culture.* New York: Knopf, 1968.

Blanch, Lesley. *The Sabres of Paradise.* London: John Murray, 1960.

Blank, Stephen, and Alvin Z. Rubinstein, eds. *Imperial Decline: Russia's Changing Role in Asia.* Durham, N.C.: Duke University Press, 1997.

Bobrick, Benson. *Fearful Majesty: The Life and Reign of Ivan the Terrible.* New York: Putnam, 1987.

Brower, Daniel R., and Edward J. Lazzerini, eds. *Russia's Orient: Imperial Borderlands and Peoples, 1700–1917.* Bloomington: Indiana University Press, 1997.

Brown, Judith, and William Roger Louis, eds. *The Oxford History of the British Empire: The Twentieth Century.* Oxford: University Press, 1999.

Buruma, Ian. *Anglomania.* New York: Random House, 1998.

Bush, George, and Brent Scowcroft. *A World Transformed.* New York: Knopf, 1998.

Carlisle, Olga Andreyev, and Rose Styron, eds. *Modern Russian Poetry.* New York: Viking, 1972.

Caroe, Olaf. *The Pathans: 550 B.C.–A.D. 1957.* London: Macmillan, 1965.

Chaudhuri, Nirad C. *The Autobiography of an Unknown Indian.* Reading, Mass.: Addison Wesley, 1989.

———. *Thy Hand, Great Anarch! India 1921–1952.* London: Chatto & Windus, 1987.

Chekhov, Anton. *Letters.* Edited by Louis S. Friedland. New York: Dover, 1966.

Cooley, John K. *Unholy Wars: Afghanistan, America and International Terrorism.* London: Pluto, 1999.

Dixit, J. N. *India-Pakistan in War and Peace.* London: Routledge, 2002.

Dobrynin, Anatoly. *In Confidence.* New York: Times Books, 1995.

Dorman, William A., and Mansour Fahrang. *The U.S. Press and Iran.* Berkeley: University of California Press, 1987.

Doyle, Michael W. *Empires.* Ithaca: Cornell University Press, 1986.

Dupree, Louis. *Afghanistan.* Princeton: Princeton University Press, 1980.

Easwaran, Eknath. *Nonviolent Soldier of Islam: Badshah Khan.* Tomales, CA: Nilgiri, 1999.

Eickelman, Dale F., ed. *Russia's Muslim Frontiers: New Directions in Cross-Cultural Analysis.* Bloomington: Indiana University Press, 1993.

Eisenstein, Sergei. *Notes of a Film Director.* Moscow: Arts Library, n.d.

Elliot, Jason. *An Unexpected Light: Travels in Afghanistan.* New York: Picador, 1999.

Ellis, John. *The Social History of the Machine Gun.* New York: Pantheon, 1975.

Elon, Amos. *Herzl.* New York: Holt, Rinehart & Winston, 1973.

Elphinstone, Mountstuart. *Kingdom of Caubul.* Karachi: Oxford University Press, 1972. New edition with introduction by Olaf Caroe.

Farman Farmaian, Sattareh, with Dona Munker. *Daughter of Persia.* New York: Doubleday, 1993.

Farmanfarmaian, Manucher, and Roxane Farmanfarmaian. *Blood and Oil: Memoirs of a Persian Prince.* New York: Random House, 1997.

Farwell, Byron. *The Great Anglo-Boer War.* New York: Harper & Row, 1976.

Felix, Chuev. *Molotov Remembers: Conversations with V. M. Molotov.* Chicago: Ivan R. Dee, 1993.

Ferguson, Niall. *The Pity of War.* New York: Basic, 1999.

Fischer, Louis. *The Soviets in World Affairs.* 2 vols. London: Jonathan Cape, 1930.

French, Patrick. *Younghusband: The Last Great Imperial Adventurer.* London: HarperCollins, 1994.

Frye, Richard N. *The Heritage of Central Asia.* Princeton: Markus Wiener, 1998.
———. *The Heritage of Persia.* Cleveland: World, 1963.

Gandhi, Rajmohan. *The Good Boatman: A Portrait of Gandhi.* New Delhi: Viking, 1995.
———. *Understanding the Muslim Mind.* New Delhi: Penguin, 1986.

Garnett, Sherman M., Alexander Rahr and Koji Watanabe. *The New Central Asia: In Search of Stability.* New York: Trilateral Commission, 2000.

Geary, Patrick J. *The Myth of Nations: The Medieval Origins of Europe.* Princeton: Princeton University Press, 2002.

Ghani, Cyrus. *Iran and the Rise of Reza Shah: From Qajar Collapse to Pahlavi Rule.* London: Tauris, 1998.
———. *Iran and the West: A Critical Bibliography.* London: Kegan Paul International, 1987.

Gregorian, Vartan. *The Emergence of Modern Afghanistan: Politics of Reform and Modernization, 1880–1946.* Stanford: Stanford University Press, 1969.

Griffin, Michael. *Reaping the Whirlwind: The Taliban Movement in Afghanistan.* London: Pluto, 2001.

Grose, Peter. *Gentleman Spy: The Life of Allen Dulles.* Boston: Houghton Mifflin, 1984.

Grousset, Rene. *The Empire of the Steppes: A History of Central Asia.* New Brunswick, N.J.: Rutgers University Press, 1970.

Guha, Ramachandra. *A Corner of a Foreign Field: The Indian History of a British Sport*. London: Picador, 2002.

Gunther, John. *Inside Russia Today*. New York: Harper, 1957.

Halperin, Charles J. *Russia and the Golden Horde: The Mongol Impact on Medieval Russian History*. Bloomington: Indiana University Press, 1987.

Hamid, Shahid. *Disastrous Twilight: A Personal Record of the Partition of India*. London: Leo Cooper, 1992.

Harrison, Selig S. *In Afghanistan's Shadow: Baluch Nationalism and Soviet Temptation*. Washington, D.C.: Carnegie Endowment for International Peace, 1981.

Harrison, Selig, and Diego Cordovez. *Out of Afghanistan*. New York: Oxford University Press, 1995.

Hauner, Milan. *What Is Asia to Us? Russia's Asian Heartland Yesterday and Today*. Boston: Unwin Hyman, 1990.

Heinl, Robert Debs, and Nancy Gordon Heinl. *Written in Blood: The Story of the Haitian People, 1492–1971*. Boston: Houghton Mifflin, 1978.

Herodotus. *The Histories*. Translated by Aubrey de Sélincourt. New York: Penguin Classics, 1996.

Herring, Hubert. *A History of Latin America*. New York: Knopf, 1959.

Hitchens, Christopher. *Blood, Class and Nostalgia: Anglo-American Ironies*. New York: Farrar, Straus & Giroux, 1990.

Hobsbawm, E. J. *Nations and Nationalism Since 1780*. Cambridge: Cambridge University Press, 1990.

Hobsbawm, Eric. *The Age of Empire, 1875–1914*. New York: Pantheon, 1987.

Hobsbawm, Eric, and Terence Ranger, eds. *The Invention of Tradition*. Cambridge: Cambridge University Press, 1983.

Hochschild, Adam. *King Leopold's Ghost*. Boston: Houghton Mifflin, 1998.

Hodson, H.V. *The Great Divide: Britain, India, Pakistan*. London: Hutchinson, 1969.

Hofstadter, Richard, and Michael Wallace. *American Violence: A Documentary History*. New York: Knopf, 1970.

Hunter, Shireen. *Central Asia Since Independence*. Westport, Conn.: Praeger, 1996.

———. *The Future of Islam in the West: Clash of Civilizations or Peaceful Coexistence?* Westport, Conn.: Praeger, 1998.

———. *Iran After Khomeini*. New York: Praeger, 1992.

———. *Iran and the World: Continuity in a Revolutionary Decade*. Bloomington: Indiana University Press, 1990.

————. *The Transcaucasia in Transition.* Washington, D.C.: Center for Strategic and International Studies, 1994.

Hunczak, Taras, ed. *Russian Imperialism: From Ivan the Great to the Revolution.* New Brunswick, N.J.: Rutgers University Press, 1974.

Hyam, Ronald. *Britain's Imperial Century, 1815–1914.* Lanham, Md.: Barnes & Noble Books, 1993.

Jankovich, Miklos. *They Rode into Europe.* London: George Harrap, 1971.

Jersild, Austin. *Orientalism and Empire: North Caucasus Mountain Peoples and the Georgian Frontier.* Montreal: McGill-Queens University Press, 2002.

Jones, Owen Bennett. *Pakistan: Eye of the Storm.* New Haven: Yale University Press, 2002.

Jones, Scott A., ed. *Crossroads and Conflict: Security and Foreign Policy in the Caucasus and Central Asia.* New York: Routledge, 2000.

Kaplan, Robert D. *The Arabists.* New York: Free Press, 1993.

Kapuscinski, Ryszard. *Imperium.* New York: Knopf, 1994.

————. *Shah of Shahs.* San Diego: Harcourt Brace Jovanovich, 1982.

Karnow, Stanley. *In Our Image: America's Empire in the Philippines.* New York: Random House, 1989.

Karny, Yo'av. *Highlander: A Journey in the Caucasus.* Farrar, Straus & Giroux, 2000.

Kazemzadeh, Firuz. *Russia and Britain in Persia, 1864–1914.* New Haven: Yale University Press, 1968.

————. *The Struggle for Transcaucasia, 1917–1921.* New York: Philosophical Library, 1957.

Keegan, John. *A History of Warfare.* New York: Knopf, 1993.

Kelly, Laurence. *Diplomacy and Murder in Tehran.* London: Tauris, 2002.

————. *Lermontov: Tragedy in the Caucasus.* New York: Braziller, 1978.

Kennan, George. *Siberia and the Exile System.* New York: Century, 1890.

————. *Vagabond Life: The Caucasus Journals of George Kennan.* Edited by Frith Maier, with contributions by Daniel C. Waugh. Seattle: University of Washington Press, 2003.

Kesler, Charles R., ed. *Saving the Revolution: The Federalist Papers and the American Founding.* New York: Free Press, 1987.

Khan, Imran. *Warrior Race.* London: Chatto & Windus, 1993.

Khan, Riaz M. *Untying the Afghan Knot: Negotiating Soviet Withdrawal.* Durham, N.C.: Duke University Press, 1991.

Khilnani, Sunil. *The Idea of India.* New York: Farrar, Straus & Giroux, 1998.

Klass, Roseanne. *Land of the High Flags.* New York: Random House, 1964.

Knobloch, Edgar. *Monuments of Central Asia*. London: Tauris, 2001.

Koestler, Arthur. *The Invisible Writing*. New York: Macmillan, 1954.

Korejo, M. S. *The Frontier Gandhi*. Karachi: Oxford University Press, 1993.

Kotkin, Stephen. *Armageddon Averted: The Soviet Collapse, 1970–2000*. New York: Oxford University Press, 2001.

Langer, William. *The Diplomacy of Imperialism*. Rev. ed. New York: Knopf, 1965.

LeDonne, John P. *The Russian Empire and the World, 1700–1917*. New York: Oxford University Press, 1997.

Levin, Theodore. *The Hundred Thousand Fools of God: Musical Travels in Central Asia*. Bloomington: Indiana University Press, 1996.

Lewis, David Levering. *The Race to Fashoda*. New York: Weidenfeld & Nicolson, 1987.

Lieven, Anatol. *Chechnya: Tombstone of Russian Power*. New Haven: Yale University Press, 1998.

Lieven, Dominic. *Empire: The Russian Empire and Its Rivals*. London: John Murray, 2000.

Lincoln, W. Bruce. *The Conquest of a Continent: Siberia and the Russians*. New York: Random House, 1994.

Lohbeck, Kurt. *Holy War, Unholy Victory*. Washington, D.C.: Regnery Gateway, 1993.

Lukacs, John, ed. *Tocqueville: The European Revolution and Correspondence with Gobineau*. New York: Anchor Books, 1959.

Maalouf, Amin. *In the Name of Identity*. New York: Arcade, 2001.

Macmillan, Margaret. *Paris 1919*. New York: Random House, 2002.

Malcomson, Scott. *Empire's Edge: Travels in South-Eastern Europe, Turkey and Central Asia*. London: Faber & Faber, 1994.

Malik, Hafeez, ed. *Central Asia: Its Strategic Importance and Future Prospects*. London: Macmillan, 1994.

Manchester, William. *The Last Lion: Visions of Glory, 1874–1932*. Boston: Little, Brown, 1983.

Mandelbaum, Michael, ed. *Central Asia and the World*. New York: Council on Foreign Relations, 1994.

Maslow, Jonathan. *Sacred Horses: The Memoirs of a Turkmen Cowboy*. New York: Random House, 1994.

Matlock, Jack F., Jr. *Autopsy on an Empire*. New York: Random House, 1995.

McCrum, Robert, William Cran and Robert MacNeil. *The Story of English*. New York: Viking, 1986.

McGovern, William Montgomery. *The Early Empires of Central Asia*. Chapel Hill: University of North Carolina Press, 1939.

McMahon, Robert J. *The Cold War on the Periphery: The United States, India and Pakistan*. New York: Columbia University Press, 1994.

Mehra, Parshotam. *The North-West Frontier Drama, 1945–1947: A Reassessment*. New Delhi: Manochar, 1998.

Menon, V. P. *The Transfer of Power in India*. Princeton: Princeton University Press, 1957.

Meyer, Karl E., and Shareen Blair Brysac. *Tournament of Shadows*. Washington, D.C.: Counterpoint, 1999.

Michener, James A. *Caravan: A Novel*. New York: Random House, 1963.

Montefiore, Simon Sebag. *The Life of Potemkin: Prince of Princes*. London: Weidenfeld & Nicolson, 2000.

Moon, Sir Penderel. *Divide and Quit*. Berkeley: University of California Press, 1962.

Morgan, David. *The Mongols*. Oxford: Blackwell, 1990.

Morris, James. *Pax Britannica: Climax of an Empire*. London: Faber & Faber, 1968.

Mottahedeh, Roy. *The Mantle of the Prophet*. Oxford: Oneworld Publications, 2000.

Moynihan, Daniel Patrick. *Pandemonium: Ethnicity*. New York: Oxford University Press, 1993.

Nasmyth, Peter. *Georgia: In the Mountains of Poetry*. Richmond, U.K.: Curzon, 1998.

Olcott, Martha Brill. *Kazakhstan: Unfulfilled Promise*. Washington, D.C.: Carnegie Endowment for International Peace, 2002.

O'Toole, G. J. A. *The Spanish War*. New York: Norton, 1984.

Pakenham, Thomas. *The Scramble for Africa, 1876–1912*. London: Weidenfeld & Nicolson, 1991.

Pares, Sir Bernard. *A History of Russia*. New York: Knopf, 1966.

Payne, Robert, and Nikita Romanoff. *Ivan the Terrible*. New York: Crowell, 1975.

Pfaff, William. *The Wrath of Nations: Civilization and the Furies of Nationalism*. New York: Simon & Schuster, 1993.

Porter, Andrew, ed. *Oxford History of the British Empire: The Nineteenth Century*. Oxford: University Press, 1999.

Power, Samantha. *"A Problem from Hell."* New York: Basic, 2002.

Raeff, Marc. *Understanding Imperial Russia*. New York: Columbia University Press, 1984.

Ramazani, Rouhollah K. *The Foreign Policy of Iran, 1500–1941*. Charlottesville: University of Virginia Press, 1966.

Rashid, Ahmed. *Jihad: The Rise of Militant Islam in Central Asia*. New Haven: Yale University Press, 2002.

———. *The Resurgence of Central Asia*. London: Zed, 1994.

———. *Taliban: Militant Islam, Oil and Fundamentalism in Central Asia*. New Haven: Yale University Press, 2000.

Reid, Anna. *Borderland: A Journey Through the History of Ukraine*. London: Phoenix, 1998.

———. *The Shaman's Coat: A Native History of Siberia*. New York: Walter, 2002.

Remnick, David. *Resurrection: The Struggle for a New Russia*. New York: Random House, 1997.

Reza Pahlavi, Mohammad. *Answer to History*. New York: Stein & Day, 1980.

Rhinelander, Anthony L. H. *Prince Michael Vorontsov: Viceroy to the Tsar*. Montreal: McGill-Queens University Press, 1990.

Riding, Alan. *Distant Neighbors: A Portrait of the Mexicans*. New York: Vintage, 1989.

Rolle, Renate. *The World of the Scythians*. Berkeley: University of California Press, 1989.

Roosevelt, Archie. *For Lust of Knowing: Memoirs of an Intelligence Officer*. Boston: Little, Brown, 1988.

Roy, Olivier. *The New Central Asia: The Creation of Nations*. New York: New York University Press, 2000.

Rubin, Barnett R. *The Fragmentation of Afghanistan*. New Haven: Yale University Press, 1995.

———. *The Search for Peace in Afghanistan*. New Haven: Yale University Press, 1995.

Ruffin, M. Holt, and Daniel Waugh. *Civil Society in Central Asia*. Seattle: University of Washington Press, 1999.

Sampson, Anthony. *The Seven Sisters: The Great Oil Companies and the World They Shaped*. New York: Viking, 1975.

Schaeffer, Robert. *Warpaths: The Politics of Partition*. New York: Hill & Wang, 1990.

Schlesinger, Arthur M., Jr. *The Cycles of American History*. Boston: Houghton Mifflin, 1980.

Sciolino, Elaine. *Persian Mirrors*. New York: Free Press, 2000.

Szulc, Tad. *Twilight of the Tyrants*. New York: Holt, 1959.

Service, Robert. *Lenin: A Biography*. Cambridge: Harvard University Press, 2000.

Shah, Idries. *The Sufis*. New York: Doubleday, 1964.

Shah, Sirdar Ikbal Ali. *Afghanistan of the Afghans.* London: Octagon, 1982.

Shawcross, William. *The Shah's Last Ride: The Fate of an Ally.* New York: Simon & Schuster, 1988.

Shuster, W. Morgan. *The Strangling of Persia.* New York: Century, 1912.

Sick, Gary. *All Fall Down.* New York: Penguin, 1985.

Smith, Graham, ed. *The Nationalities Question in Post-Soviet States.* London: Longman, 1996.

Smith, Tony. *The Pattern of Imperialism: The United States, Great Britain and the Late-Industrializing World Since 1815.* Cambridge: Cambridge University Press, 1981.

Soucek, Svat. *A History of Inner Asia.* Cambridge: Cambridge University Press, 2000.

Spain, James W. *The Way of the Pathans.* Karachi: Oxford University Press, 1972.

Steel, Ronald. *Pax Americana.* New York: Viking, 1967.

Stewart, Rhea Talley. *Fire in Afghanistan, 1914–1929: Faith, Hope and the British Empire.* New York: Doubleday, 1973.

U.S. Senate. Subcommittee on Monopoly. *The International Petroleum Cartel.* Washington, D.C.: Government Printing Office, 1952.

Suny, Ronald Grigor. *The Making of the Georgian Nation.* Bloomington: Indiana University Press, 1994.

———. *The Revenge of the Past: Nationalism, Revolution and the Collapse of the Soviet Union.* Palo Alto: Stanford University Press, 1993.

Swietochowski, Tadeusz. *Russia and Azerbaijan: A Borderland in Transition.* New York: Columbia University Press, 1995.

Sykes, Sir Percy. *A History of Persia.* 2 vols. London: Macmillan, 1951.

Tharoor, Shashi. *India: From Midnight to the Millennium.* New York: Arcade, 1997.

Thomas, Hugh. *Cuba: The Pursuit of Freedom.* New York: Harper & Row, 1971.

Thompson, Ewa M. *Imperial Knowledge: Russian Literature and Colonialism.* Westport, Conn.: Greenwood, 2000.

Trenin, Dmitri. *The End of Eurasia: Russia on the Border Between Geopolitics and Globalization.* Washington, D.C.: Carnegie Endowment for International Peace, 2002.

Ullman, Richard H. *Britain and the Russian Civil War, 1918–1920.* Princeton: Princeton University Press, 1968.

Walker, Christopher. *Armenia: The Survival of a Nation.* New York: St. Martin's, 1980.

Walker, Martin. *The Cold War: A History.* New York: Henry Holt, 1993.

Waller, John H. *Beyond the Khyber Pass.* New York: Random House, 1990.

Warburton, Robert, Colonel Sir. *Eighteen Years in the Khyber, 1879–1898.* London: John Murray, 1900.

Weaver, Mary Anne. *Pakistan: In the Shadow of Jihad and Afghanistan.* New York: Farrar, Straus & Giroux, 2002.

———. *A Portrait of Egypt: A Journey Through the World of Militant Islam.* New York: Farrar, Straus & Giroux, 1999.

Wilber, Donald. *Adventures in the Middle East.* Princeton, N.J.: Darwin, 1986.

Williams, William Appleman. *The Roots of Modern American Empire.* New York: Random House, 1969.

Winks, Robin W., ed. *The Oxford History of the British Empire: Historiography.* Oxford: University Press, 1999.

Wittfogel, Karl A. *Oriental Despotism.* New York: Vintage, 1981.

Wolpert, Stanley. *Gandhi's Passion.* New York: Oxford University Press, 2001.

———. *Jinnah of Pakistan.* New York: Oxford University Press, 1984.

Wright, Sir Denis. *The English Amongst the Persians.* London: Heinemann, 1977.

Yergin, Daniel. *The Prize: The Epic Quest for Oil, Money and Power.* New York: Simon & Schuster, 1991.

Yousaf, Mohammad, and Mark Adkin. *The Bear Trap: Afghanistan's Untold Story.* London: Leo Cooper, 1992.

Ziegler, Philip. *Mountbatten.* New York: Knopf, 1985.

ACKNOWLEDGMENTS

FRIENDS, STRANGERS AND scholars have been partners in the long voyage that preceded publication of this volume. It is gratifying to list some of the many who helped, though the author alone bears responsibility for factual lapses and misguided judgments. My first partner was Richard C. Leone, president of The Century Foundation, whom I approached in 1994 with the idea of writing a policy monograph as a pendant to a book dealing with Central Asia's past as an imperial battleground. By the time *Tournament of Shadows*, written with my wife Shareen Brysac, was published in 1999, the project goal had expanded, as had the region's strategic importance to the United States. The Century Foundation made possible travels to Turkey, the South Caucasus, Russia and Central Asia, before and after 9/11. This timing understandably affected the scope, the tone and the substance of *The Dust of Empire*. It needs to be added that my wife, though not formally coauthor, has otherwise been the indispensable coproducer as editor, critic, travel manager and computer expert.

My thanks first of all to Richard Leone, to his unfailingly helpful deputy, Carol Starmack, and to The Century Foundation staff for moral and material assistance. Thanks next to my former *Washington Post* colleague, Peter Osnos of PublicAffairs, and to his proficient team, most especially my editor, Paul Golob (so conscientious that he scoured Tudor genealogy to spare me from error); to the production editor, Melanie Peirson Johnstone; and to the house's all-around expediter, David Patterson. The flexibility of all concerned was especially welcome since my travels and writing had to fit around the quarterly deadline of the *World Policy Journal*, of which I became editor in summer 2000. Now twenty years old, the journal is published by the World Policy Institute at the New School University. To managing editor Linda Wrigley, to associate editor Ben

Pauker, and to our tireless intern, Tom Westerman, I am indebted for the editorial equivalent of system support. This applies as well to the institute's director, Stephen Schlesinger; to the chairman of its advisory board, Walter Eberstadt; and to its senior fellows, notably Nina Khrushcheva, Ian Bremmer, Mustapha Tlili and William Hartung. While writing these chapters I also benefited from feedback from alert undergraduates at Bard College's new international affairs program in New York, where I was assisted by the program director, James Chace, and his deputy James Miller.

Throughout I doubly profited from a long association with *The New York Times,* first from my tutelage in commenting on foreign affairs under three editorial page editors, Max Frankel, Jack Rosenthal and Howell Raines. Second, as an alumnus, I was courteously assisted by old and new friends on the staff, most especially Barbara Crossette, Stephen Kinzer, Pat Tyler, Michael Wines, Douglas Frantz, Elaine Sciolino, Sabrina Tavernise, Marion Greene, Maureen Muenster and Rosemary Shields. Other journalists who gave of time and advice include Susan B. Glasser (*Washington Post*); Steve LeVine (*Wall Street Journal*); Ahmed Rashid (*Far Eastern Economic Review*); Brigit Brauer (*Economist*); David Stern (*Financial Times*); and a discord of freelancers, among them Thomas de Waal, Anatol Lieven and Tatyana Malkina.

People who took time to read portions of this manuscript include Seymour Becker, Ian Bremmer, Robert Kaiser, Husain Haqqani, Perdita Burlingame, Tadeusz Swietochowski and Nicholas X. Rizopoulos. I benefited in London from counsel by William Hale (School of Oriental Studies), Dr. Roy Allison (Royal Institute of International Affairs) and our forbearing hosts, Michael and Gillian Darley Horowitz. The Soros Foundation and its country directors were invariable sources of help, notably Murat Auezov (Almaty); Medet Tulegenov (Bishkek); S. K. Rondeli in Tbilisi; and Anthony Richter in New York. Special thanks is owed to Andrew Rearick of Golden Eagle Service in Almaty, and to Folke von Knobloch of Central Asian Tourism. As members of a scholarly troupe led by Alexander Leskov, an outstanding authority on ancient Scythia, Shareen and I visited Kiev, Odessa and the Crimea, along with Renata and Oleg Holod, Victor Mair, Elfride (Kezia) Regina and Nico Knauer, Holly Pittman, Charles Williams, Nancy Boutides and Michael Frachetti, among others. At Stanford University, I am obliged to Adele Lee and Roger Olesen of the Silk Road Foundation, and at Berkeley, to David Stronach. In Baku, among many who took time out, I am especially indebted to the poet and parliamentarian Bakhtiyar Vahabzadeh, to Leila Aliyeva and to Hikmety Hadjy-Zadeh. In Tbilisi, those generous with their time included David Usupashili and Zaza Gachechiladze. In Moscow, I owe special thanks to Dmitri V. Trenin, deputy director of the Carnegie Moscow Center; to Sergei Rogov, director of the American and Canadian Studies Institute; to Gregory Feifer, of the Institute for Current World Affairs; to Svetlana Prudnirova and to the organizers of the Australian Arts Tour who on a moment's notice let us hitchhike on their circuit of the Golden Ring cities. My sister Susan E. Meyer and her partner Marsha Melnik of Roundtable Press provided (as before) vital technical advice. Also as before, I benefited en route from the assistance of the Pequot Library and its director, Mary Freedman, and Danielle Carriera and Sean Smith; and the New York Society Library and its director, Mark Piel. To Peter Sinnott of the School of International Affairs at Columbia University, I owe specialized information, amplified by attendance on successive years at SIPA's annual conferences on nationalities and nationalism. To these and many others, unnamed but not forgotten, I owe safe harbor on a voyage that I wish had lasted longer.

KARL E. MEYER

PERMISSIONS

INDEX

PublicAffairs is a publishing house founded in 1997. It is a tribute to the standards, values, and flair of three persons who have served as mentors to countless reporters, writers, editors, and book people of all kinds, including me.

I. F. Stone, proprietor of *I. F. Stone's Weekly,* combined a commitment to the First Amendment with entrepreneurial zeal and reporting skill and became one of the great independent journalists in American history. At the age of eighty, Izzy published *The Trial of Socrates,* which was a national bestseller. He wrote the book after he taught himself ancient Greek.

Benjamin C. Bradlee was for nearly thirty years the charismatic editorial leader of *The Washington Post.* It was Ben who gave the *Post* the range and courage to pursue such historic issues as Watergate. He supported his reporters with a tenacity that made them fearless, and it is no accident that so many became authors of influential, best-selling books.

Robert L. Bernstein, the chief executive of Random House for more than a quarter century, guided one of the nation's premier publishing houses. Bob was personally responsible for many books of political dissent and argument that challenged tyranny around the globe. He is also the founder and was the longtime chair of Human Rights Watch, one of the most respected human rights organizations in the world.

·   ·   ·

For fifty years, the banner of Public Affairs Press was carried by its owner Morris B. Schnapper, who published Gandhi, Nasser, Toynbee, Truman, and about 1,500 other authors. In 1983 Schnapper was described by *The Washington Post* as "a redoubtable gadfly." His legacy will endure in the books to come.

Peter Osnos, *Publisher*

SENESCENCE - THE STATE OR PROCESS OF BECOMING OLD

N

ESTONIA
St. Petersburg
Baltic Sea
LATVIA
LITHU-
ANIA
POLAND
Yaroslavl
R U S S I A N
BELARUS
⊙ Moscow
Borodino
Kazan
Kiev ⊙
Dnieper R.
Volga R.
UKRAINE
Don R.
ROMANIA
Odessa
MOLDOVA
Kherson
Volgograd
K A Z A K H S T A N
Sea of Azov
BULGARIA
CRIMEA
Bakhchiserai
Yalta
Sevastapol
Aral Sea
Syr Darya
Istanbul
Black Sea
CAUCASUS
Caspian Sea
Dardanelles
GEORGIA
U Z B E K I S T A N
⊙ Ankara
ARMENIA
AZERBAIJAN
KYZLKUM DESERT
T U R K E Y
See Inset Below
Khiva
Amu Darya (Oxus)
T U R K M E N I S T A N
Bokhar
LEBANON
Ashkabad ⊙
Mediterranean Sea
S Y R I A   I R A Q
ZAGROS MOUNTAINS
⊙ Tehran
Masshad
Qum
Herat
I R A N
Bushehr
Persian Gulf

Georgian Military Highway
CAUCASUS
INGUSHETIA
CHECHNYA
DAGHESTAN
Caspian Sea
ABKHAZIA
NORTH OSSETIA
Grozny
Black Sea
SOUTH OSSETIA
Mt. Kazbek
Pankisi Gorge
GEORGIA ⊙
Tbilisi
AZERBAIJAN
TURKEY
ARMENIA
NAGORNO-KARABAKH
Lachin Corridor
Baku
Yerevan
Miles
100
0
100
Kms.
NAKHICHEVAN (AZ.)
I R A N
Tabriz

©A. Karl/J. Kemp, 2003